CW00422177

Blackstone's

Police Q&A

General Police Duties 2012

Blackstone's
Police Q&A

General Police Duties 2012

Tenth edition

Huw Smart and John Watson

OXFORD
UNIVERSITY PRESS

OXFORD
UNIVERSITY PRESS

Great Clarendon Street, Oxford OX2 6DP

Oxford University Press is a department of the University of Oxford.
It furthers the University's objective of excellence in research, scholarship,
and education by publishing worldwide in

Oxford New York

Auckland Cape Town Dar es Salaam Hong Kong Karachi
Kuala Lumpur Madrid Melbourne Mexico City Mumbai Nairobi
New Delhi Shanghai Taipei Tokyo Toronto

With offices in

Argentina Austria Brazil Chile Czech Republic France Greece
Guatemala Hungary Italy Japan Poland Portugal Singapore
South Korea Switzerland Thailand Turkey Ukraine Vietnam

Oxford is a registered trademark of Oxford University Press
in the UK and in certain other countries

Published in the United States
by Oxford University Press Inc., New York

British Library Cataloguing in Publication Data
Data available

Library of Congress Cataloging in Publication Data
Data available

Typeset by Glyph International, Bangalore, India
Printed in Great Britain
on acid-free paper by
CPI Antony Rowe, Chippenham, Wiltshire

ISBN 978–0–19–969619–2

10 9 8 7 6 5 4 3 2 1

Contents

Contents

Introduction

Before you get into the detail of this book, there are two myths about multiple-choice questions (MCQs) that we need to get out of the way right at the start:

1. that they are easy to answer;
2. that they are easy to write.

Take one look at a professionally designed and properly developed exam paper such as those used by the Police Promotion Examinations Board or the National Board of Medical Examiners in the US and the first myth collapses straight away. Contrary to what some people believe, MCQs are not an easy solution for examiners and not a 'multiple-guess' soft option for examinees.

That is not to say that *all* MCQs are taxing, or even testing—in the psychometric sense. If MCQs are to have any real value at all, they need to be carefully designed and follow some agreed basic rules.

And this leads us to myth number 2.

It is widely assumed by many people and educational organisations that anyone with the knowledge of a subject can write MCQs. You need only look at how few MCQ writing courses are offered by training providers in the UK to see just how far this myth is believed. Similarly, you need only to have a go at a few badly designed MCQs to realise that it is a myth nonetheless. Writing bad MCQs is easy; writing good ones is no easier than answering them!

As with many things, the design of MCQs benefits considerably from time, training and experience. Many MCQ writers fall easily and often unwittingly into the trap of making their questions too hard, too easy or too obscure, or completely different from the type of question that you will eventually encounter in your own particular exam. Others seem to use the MCQ as a way to catch people out or to show how smart they, the authors, are (or think they are).

There are several purposes for which MCQs are very useful. The first is in producing a reliable, valid and fair test of knowledge and understanding across a wide range of subject matter. Another is an aid to study, preparation and revision for such examinations and tests. The differences in objective mean that there are slight differences in the rules that the MCQ writers follow. Whereas the design of fully validated MCQs to be used in high stakes examinations which will effectively determine who passes and who fails has very strict guidelines as to construction, content and style, less stringent rules apply to MCQs that are being used for teaching and revision. For that reason, there may be types of MCQ that are appropriate in the latter setting which would not be used in the former. However, in developing the MCQs for this book, the authors have tried to follow the fundamental rules of MCQ design but they would not claim to have replicated the level of psychometric rigour that is—and has to be—adopted by the type of examining bodies referred to above.

These MCQs are designed to reinforce your knowledge and understanding, to highlight any gaps or weaknesses in that knowledge and understanding and to help focus your revision of the relevant topics.

I hope that we have achieved that aim.

Good luck!

Blackstone's Police Q&As—Special Features

References to Blackstone's Police Manuals

Every answer is followed by a paragraph reference to Blackstone's Police Manuals. This means that once you have attempted a question and looked at an answer, the Manual can immediately be referred to for help and clarification.

Unique numbers for each question

Each question and answer has the same unique number. This should ensure that there is no confusion as to which question is linked to which answer. For example, Question 2.1 is linked to Answer 2.1.

Checklists

The checklists are designed to help you keep track of your progress when answering the multiple-choice questions. If you fill in the checklist after attempting a question, you will be able to check how many you got right on the first attempt and will know immediately which questions need to be revisited a second time. Please visit www.blackstonespolicemanuals.com and click through to the Blackstone's Police Q&As 2012 page. You will then find electronic versions of the checklists to download and print out. Email any queries or comments on the book to: police.uk@oup.com.

Acknowledgements

This book has been written as an accompaniment to Blackstone's Police Manuals, and will test the knowledge you have accrued through reading that series. It is of the essence that full study of the relevant chapters in each Police Manual is completed prior to attempting the Questions and Answers. As qualified police trainers we recognise that students tend to answer questions incorrectly either because they don't read the question properly, or because one of the 'distracters' has done its work. The distracter is one of the three incorrect answers in a multiple-choice question (MCQ), and is designed to distract you from the correct answer and in this way discriminate between candidates: the better-prepared candidate not being 'distracted'.

So particular attention should be paid to the *Answers* sections, and students should ask themselves 'Why did I get that question wrong?' and, just as importantly, 'Why did I get that question right?' Combining the information gained in the *Answers* section together with re-reading the chapter in the Police Manuals should lead to greater understanding of the subject matter.

The authors wish to thank all the staff at Oxford University Press who have helped put this publication together. We would particularly like to dedicate these books to Alistair MacQueen who sadly passed away in 2008. It was his vision and support that got this project off the ground. Without his help neither Huw nor John would have been able to make these Q&As the success they are. We would also like to show appreciation to Fraser Sampson, consultant editor of Blackstone's Police Manuals, whose influence on these Q&As is appreciated.

Huw would like to thank Caroline for her constant love, support and understanding over the past year—and her ability to withstand the pressures of being the partner to a workaholic! Special thanks to Lawrence and Maddie—two perfect young adults. Last but not least, love and special affection to Haf and Nia, two beautiful young girls.

John would like to thank Sue, David, Catherine and Andrew for their continued support, and understanding that 'deadline' means 'deadline'.

1 | Police

QUESTIONS

Question 1.1

Constable KERSLAKE is an undercover officer working for the drug squad. Constable KERSLAKE has recently been working on a case which involved working closely with the Serious Organised Crime Agency (SOCA). The officer enjoyed working with

SOCA and is wondering whether police officers can be seconded to work with the agency on attachment.

Considering that members of SOCA are not police officers, in respect of second-ments, which of the following statements is correct?

A A police officer cannot be seconded; they would have to permanently resign from the police service and apply for a post in SOCA.

B A police officer can be seconded; they would have to resign temporarily as a constable and would be re-appointed on their return to the police service.

C A police officer can be seconded; they would not have to resign and would be treated as having been suspended until they return to the police service.

D A police officer can be seconded; they would remain a constable until they return to the police service.

Question 1.2

Special Constable PATTERSON is an officer with Northshire Constabulary. Special Constable PATTERSON's home force has a Football League Club in its own area and Special Constable PATTERSON works regularly with the police spotters' team, identi-fying football hooligans. Special Constable PATTERSON has developed an expertise in this area and has been asked to attend away matches to assist regular police offi-cers with preventing crowd trouble.

Would Special Constable PATTERSON enjoy the powers and privileges of a special constable, when working in other police areas?

A Yes, Special Constable PATTERSON would enjoy the powers and privileges of a special constable when working in any police area.

B No, Special Constable PATTERSON would only enjoy the powers and privileges of a special constable when working in an adjoining area, on mutual aid.

C Yes, but Special Constable PATTERSON would only enjoy the powers and privileges of a special constable when working in an adjoining area.

D No, Special Constable PATTERSON would only enjoy the powers and privileges of a special constable when working on mutual aid, but this may be in any police area.

Question 1.3

Her Majesty's Inspector of Constabulary (HMIC) has submitted an inspection report to the Secretary of State in respect of Westshire Constabulary's efficiency and

effectiveness. The report is severely critical of the force's public protection procedures, highlighting recent national press attention relating to a series of undetected
murders in children's homes. The inspection uncovered systematic failures in partnership working and a number of investigative opportunities that were missed by
the force, which may have prevented some deaths.

Which of the following statements is correct in respect of directions that may be
given to Westshire Constabulary, under s. 40 of the Police Act 1996?

A Directions may be given to the Police Authority immediately to take remedial
measures to improve public protection procedures.

B Directions may be given to the Police Authority to take remedial measures to
improve public protection procedures, but only after the force has been given
an opportunity to respond to the report.

C Directions may be given to the Chief Constable to take remedial measures to
improve public protection procedures, but only after the force has been given
an opportunity to respond to the report.

D Directions may not be given in these circumstances, because the report only
highlights a part of the force which is considered to be inefficient or ineffective.

Question 1.4

MANGLEY has recently been promoted to the rank of chief inspector. MANGLEY has
a child under the age of 5 and is considering asking for flexible hours, to work part-
time, due to family commitments.

Would the Police Regulations 2003 allow MANGLEY to work part-time as a chief
inspector?

A Yes, any officer below the rank of superintendent may work part-time.

B No, only officers below the rank of inspector may work part-time.

C Yes, officers of any rank may work part-time.

D No, only officers of the rank of inspector or below may work part-time.

Question 1.5

Sergeant GUNNEY has been a part-time worker for two years. Due to a change in
personal circumstances, Sergeant GUNNEY has submitted a report asking to return
to full-time working within two weeks as a matter of urgency.

Would the Police Regulations 2003 allow Sergeant GUNNEY to return to full-time working within this time period?

A Yes, if it is considered reasonably practicable to do so.

B No, Sergeant GUNNEY should return to full-time working within one month.

C No, Sergeant GUNNEY should return to full-time working within three months.

D Yes, an officer can return to full-time duties at any time provided a request is made in writing.

Question 1.6

SAGNER works in the administration department of an international haulage company based in the United Kingdom. SAGNER has discovered that some of the drivers working for the company are engaged in people trafficking whilst driving on the continent. SAGNER has no evidence that any of the people are being trafficked into, or out of, the United Kingdom, but believes they engage in this activity between other European countries. SAGNER has considered reporting this to the company's management, but believes they may be aware of the activity and would turn a blind eye. SAGNER is considering disclosing this information to someone else.

Which of the following information is correct, in relation to 'protected disclosures', under the Public Interest Disclosure Act 1998?

A A 'protected disclosure' must be made to an employer, as the Act emphasises disclosures of an internal nature.

B A 'protected disclosure' must be made to an employer, or some other body nominated by the Secretary of State.

C This information would not amount to a 'protected disclosure', because it relates to possible criminal activity outside the United Kingdom.

D A 'protected disclosure' should be made to an employer, or some other body nominated by the Secretary of State, but in some cases may be made to another person.

Question 1.7

Constable CHEKAI has been in dispute with her sergeant because she was not supported for promotion. The officer discovered that her sergeant has taken a job outside work because of financial difficulties and has not applied for a business interest. Constable CHEKAI is considering reporting her sergeant to the Professional Standards Department, but is concerned that this will seriously affect her future promotion prospects.

If Constable CHEKAI were to disclose this information to the Professional Standards Department, would this amount to a 'protected disclosure' under the Public Interest Disclosure Act 1998?

A No, the Act only applies to disclosures for serious criminal offences.

B No, the Act only applies to disclosures for criminal offences.

C No, although such disclosures are not restricted to criminal offences, the disclosure of this information would not amount to a 'protected disclosure'.

D Yes, the Act applies to disclosures of any criminal or discipline offence.

ANSWERS

Answer 1.1

Answer **C** — Members of the Serious Organised Crime Agency (SOCA) are not police officers (although they may be endowed with the powers of a constable). A constable may be seconded to SOCA without resigning from the police service (answers A and B are incorrect). Where a constable is seconded to SOCA, s. 43(6) of the Serious Organised Crime and Police Act 2005 states that if the constable does not resign from the police service, they will be treated as having been suspended from that office until they return to the police service. Answer D is therefore incorrect.

General Police Duties, para. 4.1.2.3

Answer 1.2

Answer **A** — The terms under which special constables may be appointed and deployed are set out in s. 30 of the Police Act 1996. Previously, special constables would only have powers and privileges in their own areas or adjoining police areas, unless they were used in mutual aid schemes, when they would enjoy the powers of a special constable in the area in which they were providing mutual aid.

However, the Police and Justice Act 2006 introduced significant amendments: para. 21 of sch. 2 allows special constables to use their constabulary powers in forces throughout England and Wales, regardless of the duties they are performing. Answers B, C and D are therefore incorrect.

General Police Duties, para. 4.1.2.8

Answer 1.3

Answer **B** — Section 40 of the Police Act 1996 empowers the Secretary of State to give directions to a police authority where an inspection report by Her Majesty's Inspector of Constabulary (HMIC) is of the opinion that *all or part* of the force inspected is not efficient or effective, or will cease to be efficient or effective unless remedial measures are taken. Answer C is incorrect because the directions are made to the police authority and answer D is incorrect because the report may highlight inefficiencies in either the whole or part of the force.

In the event of any such report being received from the HMIC, the Secretary of State may direct the police authority to take 'remedial measures'. Any direction to this effect must be made by the Secretary of State in a report laid before Parliament but *only* after the police authority and the chief officer have been given sufficient information about the report and an opportunity to make representations and proposals for any remedial measures that would make a direction unnecessary. The Secretary of State must consider all representations and proposals before he/she has the power to direct any remedial measure to be taken. Answer A is incorrect.

General Police Duties, para. 4.1.3

Answer 1.4

Answer **C** — Regulation 5 of the Police Regulations 2003 allows a chief constable, after consultation with local representatives of the staff associations, to appoint an officer to perform part-time service *in any rank*. Answers A, B and D are therefore incorrect.

General Police Duties, para. 4.1.6.1

Answer 1.5

Answer **A** — The Police Regulations 2003 set out the required notice period for part-time workers who wish to return to full-time duties. Part-time officers may give notice in writing of their intention to be re-appointed as a full-time member and will be appointed within:

- one month of the date the notice is received by the police authority, where the authority has a suitable vacancy, or
- when three months have elapsed since the day the notice was received, or
- from an earlier date if reasonably practicable.

Therefore, the normal time period would be one month; if there is no suitable vacancy, this may be extended to three months. However, the police authority may allow such a change in duties from an earlier date if it is considered reasonably practicable to do so. Answers B, C and D are therefore incorrect.

General Police Duties, para. 4.1.6.1

Answer 1.6

Answer **D** — The Public Interest Disclosure Act 1998 refers to 'protected disclosures', which are generally disclosures made in accordance with the Act of information which, in the reasonable belief of the maker, generally tend to show criminal conduct, or environmental or health and safety breaches.

Because the Act is intended to protect disclosures of an internal nature, the person would normally be expected to report information to an employer. However, in some areas of employment, the Secretary of State has made regulations prescribing those people and bodies to whom some disclosures *can* be made where appropriate (e.g. the Independent Police Complaints Commission (IPCC) or the Inland Revenue).

The Act does not state that it is mandatory to make disclosures to an employer or a body nominated by the Secretary of State; in fact disclosures may be made to other persons, if:

- the employee reasonably believes that he/she will be subjected to a detriment by the employer if the disclosure is made; or
- there is no relevant or prescribed person and the employee reasonably believes that it is likely that evidence relating to the failure will be concealed or destroyed if a disclosure is made; or
- the employee has previously made a disclosure of substantially the same information to the employer or prescribed person.

Answers A and B are therefore incorrect.

Finally, it is immaterial that the relevant behaviour reported occurs or would occur outside the United Kingdom. Answer C is therefore incorrect.

General Police Duties, paras 4.1.7, 4.1.7.1

Answer 1.7

Answer **C** — The Public Interest Disclosure Act 1998 refers to 'protected disclosures', which are generally disclosures made in accordance with the Act of information which, in the reasonable belief of the maker, tends to show *one or more* of the following:

- a criminal offence has been committed, is being committed or is likely to be committed;
- a person has failed, is failing or is likely to fail to comply with any legal obligation to which he is subject;
- a miscarriage of justice has occurred, is occurring or is likely to occur;
- the health or safety of any individual has been, is being or is likely to be endangered;

- the environment has been, is being or is likely to be damaged;
- information tending to show any matter falling within any one of the preceding paragraphs has been, is being or is likely to be deliberately concealed.

Therefore, 'protected disclosures' are not specifically restricted to criminal offences (serious or otherwise)—answers A and B are incorrect.

However, the Act does not generally apply to disclosures of discipline offences (unless of course that disciplinary offence would tend to show one or more of the above). Answer D is therefore incorrect.

General Police Duties, para. 4.1.7.1

2 | Complaints and Misconduct

STUDY PREPARATION

Although the concept of police misconduct may seem an unpalatable subject at the start of your course of study, the maintenance of proper professional standards is paramount to all police officers, supervisors and managers—and the communities they serve.

The Police (Conduct) Regulations 2008 (SI 2008/2864) came about as a result of the Taylor Review, published in 2005, which recommended a complete overhaul of the existing procedures for dealing with police misconduct. The Taylor Review emphasises more involvement by line managers, less bureaucracy and simpler disciplinary hearings. They provide the Standards of Professional Behaviour—which provide the yardstick by which the conduct of police officers is to be judged.

The chapter guides you through the misconduct procedures, including the effect on individual officers and line managers, and misconduct meetings, tribunals, appeals and suspension from duties.

The Independent Police Complaints Commission (IPCC) has an oversight role in complaints against police officers, whether by supervising, managing or independently investigating a matter.

QUESTIONS

Question 2.1

Assistant Chief Constable MOREL was on suspension from duty, having been accused of a criminal offence under s. 2 of the Computer Misuse Act 1990. The officer was being investigated for accessing and using confidential information from a police computer system. Whilst on suspension, Assistant Chief Constable MOREL gave an interview to a national newspaper, claiming to be innocent and that he was being harassed by the force investigating the incident.

Could Assistant Chief Constable MOREL have breached the Standards of Professional Behaviour, under the Police (Conduct) Regulations 2008 (Discreditable Conduct), by giving the interview to the press?

A No, the Regulations only apply to police officers up to and including the rank of Chief Superintendent.

B Yes, the Regulations apply to all police officers, up to and including the rank of Assistant Chief Constable.

C No, the Regulations do not apply to police officers who are suspended, regardless of their rank.

D Yes, the Regulations apply to all police officers, whether they are suspended or not.

Question 2.2

Constable LEMON has been absent from work through illness three times in the past two months. Constable LEMON's sergeant has asked the officer to attend a meeting to discuss the absences. Constable LEMON is concerned about the meeting and has spoken to the sergeant about having a police 'friend' present.

Which of the following statements is correct, in relation to whether a police officer is entitled to have a police 'friend' present at a meeting under the Police (Performance) Regulations 2008?

A Police officers are entitled to have a police 'friend' present at a meeting to discuss performance or attendance matters.

B A police 'friend' may only be present at a conduct hearing; they may not be present at a meeting to discuss performance or attendance matters.

C A police 'friend' may only be present at a conduct meeting or hearing; they may not be present at a meeting to discuss performance or attendance matters.

D A police 'friend' may be present at a conduct meeting or hearing, or a meeting to discuss performance matters, but not a meeting to discuss attendance.

Question 2.3

Constable GOULDING is in police detention for providing a positive breath test, having been involved in a fail to stop road traffic collision whilst off duty. The officer in the case intends interviewing Constable GOULDING, who is represented by the duty solicitor.

Is Constable GOULDING also entitled to have a police 'friend' present at the interview, in these circumstances?

A No, a police 'friend' may not be present at an interview in connection with a criminal offence, which was committed off duty.

B Yes, Constable GOULDING would be entitled to have a police 'friend' present at the interview, as well as the solicitor.

C No, a police 'friend' may not be present at an interview in connection with a criminal offence.

D No, a police 'friend' may not be present at an interview in connection with a criminal offence, committed whilst off duty, when the offence is not connected to the person's role as a police officer.

Question 2.4

Constable KEMP has been charged with causing the death of a pedestrian by dangerous driving—the officer was pursuing a stolen vehicle at the time of the incident and was not trained to do so. The Independent Police Complaints Commission (IPCC) has decided to independently investigate the incident. Constable KEMP's force (the appropriate authority) is considering whether or not the officer should be suspended from duty.

Which of the following statements is correct, as to the role the IPPC should play in the decision as to whether Constable KEMP should be suspended?

A If the IPCC is independently investigating a matter, it has decision-making powers as to whether police officers should be suspended.

B If it is independently investigating a matter, the appropriate authority should consult with the IPCC, but the decision rests with the force.

C If it is supervising, managing or independently investigating a matter, the appropriate authority should consult with the IPCC, but the decision rests with the force.

D If the IPCC is supervising, managing or independently investigating a matter, it has decision-making powers as to whether police officers should be suspended.

Question 2.5

Constable WARE is being investigated for a misconduct offence. The complaint has been referred to the Independent Police Complaints Commission (IPCC) and has been returned to the force for a managed investigation. Detective Inspector SMALLING works in the Professional Standards Department and has been appointed to investigate the complaint.

Which of the following statements is correct, in respect of serving a written notification on Constable WARE?

A The responsibility for ensuring that the notice is served rests with Detective Inspector SMALLING, or the appropriate authority.

B The responsibility for ensuring that the notice is served always rests with the appropriate authority.

C The responsibility for ensuring that the notice is served rests with Detective Inspector SMALLING.

D Because this is a managed investigation, the responsibility for ensuring that the notice is served rests with the IPCC.

Question 2.6

Constable GILLING has been given a final written warning, as a result of a finding at a misconduct hearing.

What should Constable GILLING be told in respect of how long the warning will remain 'live'?

A Any further misconduct in the next 12 months may result in dismissal, without exception.

B Any further misconduct in the next 12 months may result in dismissal; in exceptional circumstances, this may be extended for a further 12 months.

C Any further misconduct in the next 18 months may result in dismissal, without exception.

D Any further misconduct in the next 18 months may result in dismissal; in exceptional circumstances, this may be extended for a further 18 months.

Question 2.7

Constable DAWSON is attending a misconduct meeting, having been accused of being abusive towards the complainant, FROST, during a routine road traffic check.

2. Complaints and Misconduct

FROST has been asked by the officer conducting the meeting to attend to give evidence of Constable DAWSON's behaviour.

Which of the following statements is correct in respect of FROST's attendance at the meeting?

A FROST must leave the meeting immediately after giving evidence.

B Because this is a misconduct meeting and not a hearing, FROST may remain for the entire proceedings.

C FROST must leave the meeting once the officer conducting it has made a finding.

D FROST may remain at the meeting after giving evidence, but must leave after any character reference/mitigation is given, before the outcome is decided.

Question 2.8

Sergeant GREEN attended a misconduct meeting and was given management advice as a result of a decision made by the officer conducting the meeting, Inspector BRAGA. Sergeant GREEN has submitted a written objection, appealing against the decision, which is being considered today by the superintendent.

If the superintendent determines today that Sergeant GREEN has arguable grounds of appeal, which of the following statements is correct?

A The appeal should normally be heard within five days from today.

B The appeal should normally be heard within five working days from today.

C The appeal should normally be heard within five working days from tomorrow.

D The appeal *must* be heard within five working days from today, without exception.

Question 2.9

Constable FARRELL has been found guilty of theft and has been sentenced by the court to six months' imprisonment. Constable FARRELL has appealed against the conviction and sentence and has informed the police service of this fact.

Are the circumstances sufficient for the appropriate authority to certify that this is a 'special case' and fast track misconduct procedures against Constable FARRELL?

A No, they should wait for the outcome of Constable FARRELL's appeal before making this decision.

B Yes, if there is sufficient documentary evidence available to prove the case, and it is in the public interest to dismiss Constable FARRELL.

C Yes, they can proceed with the procedure simply because Constable FARRELL has been convicted of a criminal offence.

D Yes, if there is sufficient oral evidence available to prove the case, and it is in the public interest to dismiss Constable FARRELL.

Question 2.10

Sergeant CORNISH was issued with a written warning at a misconduct meeting, conducted by the officer's inspector. Sergeant CORNISH was very upset about receiving the written warning and spoke to the Federation Representative about the possibility of appealing to a Police Appeals Tribunal.

Is Sergeant CORNISH entitled to make such an appeal in these circumstances?

A No, only police officers of the rank of assistant chief constable and above may appeal to a Police Appeals Tribunal, against the finding of a misconduct meeting.

B Yes, all officers regardless of their rank may appeal to a Police Appeals Tribunal, against the finding of a misconduct meeting.

C No, only police officers of the rank of chief superintendent and above may appeal to a Police Appeals Tribunal, against the finding of a misconduct meeting.

D No, police officers may only make an appeal to a Police Appeals Tribunal, against the finding of a misconduct hearing.

ANSWERS

Answer 2.1

Answer **D** — The Police (Conduct) Regulations 2008 replaced the Police (Conduct) Regulations 2004 and are supported by a code of ethics—the Standards of Professional Behaviour. The Standards apply to police officers of *all* ranks from chief constable to constable (including special constables). Answers A and B are incorrect. (If you answered A to this question, you may have been confused by the Police (Performance) Regulations 2008, which only apply to police officers (including special constables) up to and including the rank of chief superintendent.)

The Standards of Professional Behaviour do apply to police officers who are subject to suspension; therefore, answer C is incorrect.

General Police Duties, para. 4.2.2

Answer 2.2

Answer **A** — A police officer has a right to be accompanied by a police 'friend' at all stages of any misconduct proceedings (under the Police (Conduct) Regulations 2008). This includes interviews (unless the officer has been arrested or is being interviewed in connection with a criminal offence committed whilst off duty that has no connection with his or her role as a serving police officer), misconduct meetings and hearings. Answer B is incorrect.

A police officer also has a right to be accompanied by a police 'friend' at all stages of any performance or attendance proceedings (under the Police (Performance) Regulations 2008). Answers B, C and D are incorrect for this reason.

General Police Duties, para. 4.2.3

Answer 2.3

Answer **D** — A police officer has a right to be accompanied by a police 'friend' at all stages of any misconduct proceedings (under the Police (Conduct) Regulations 2008). This includes interviews, misconduct meetings and hearings.

A police officer is also entitled, in certain circumstances, to be accompanied by a police 'friend' at an interview in connection with a criminal offence. Answer C is incorrect.

However, the circumstances in which a police officer is entitled to be accompanied by a police 'friend' at an interview in connection with a criminal offence are very narrow. If the officer is arrested or interviewed in connection with a criminal offence committed whilst off duty *that has no connection with his or her role as a serving police officer*, then the police 'friend' has no right to attend the criminal interview of that police officer. Answers A and B are incorrect for this reason.

General Police Duties, para. 4.2.3

Answer 2.4

Answer **C** — In cases where the IPCC is supervising, managing or independently investigating a matter, the appropriate authority will consult with the IPCC before making a decision whether to suspend or not. Answer B is incorrect, as this requirement applies whether the IPCC is supervising, managing or independently investigating a matter.

However, whatever the role the IPCC plays in the investigation, it is the appropriate authority's decision whether to suspend a police officer or not. Answers A and D are incorrect.

Note that the appropriate authority must also consult the IPCC before making the decision to allow a police officer to resume his or her duties following suspension (unless the suspension ends because there will be no misconduct or special case proceedings or because these have concluded) in cases where the IPCC are supervising, managing or independently investigating a case involving that police officer.

General Police Duties, para. 4.2.5.1

Answer 2.5

Answer **C** — The responsibility for ensuring that the notice is served rests with the investigator or the appropriate authority. In both cases it is the investigator who must cause the officer concerned to be given the written notice. Therefore while the appropriate authority may do it, the responsibility for ensuring that the notice is served rests with the investigator.

However, where the IPCC is conducting an independent or managed investigation the responsibility for ensuring that the police officer is provided with the written notification (as soon as practicable) *rests with the investigator appointed or designated to conduct that investigation*. Since this is a managed investigation, it will have been returned to the force and the responsibility lies with the Inspector, and answers A, B and D are incorrect.

General Police Duties, para. 4.2.5.3

Answer 2.6

Answer **D** — When issued with a final written warning, the police officer will be told the reason for the warning, that any future misconduct may result in dismissal, that he or she has a right to appeal and the name of the person to whom the appeal should be sent, and that the final written warning will be put on their personal file and remain live for *18 months* from the date the warning is given. Answers A and B are incorrect.

Only in exceptional circumstances will further misconduct (that justifies more than management advice) not result in dismissal. In exceptional circumstances, the final written warning may be extended for a further 18 months on one occasion only. Answer C is therefore incorrect.

General Police Duties, para. 4.2.6.10

Answer 2.7

Answer **C** — A complainant and any person accompanying the complainant will be permitted to remain in the meeting/hearing up to and including any finding by the persons conducting the meeting/hearing, after having given evidence (if appropriate). Answers A and B are incorrect.

However, the complainant and any person accompanying the complainant will *not* be permitted to remain in the meeting/hearing while character references or mitigation are being given or the decision of the panel as to the outcome is being given. Answer D is incorrect, as the person must leave *before* the character reference or mitigation is given (which will also be before the outcome is given).

Note that the appropriate authority will have a duty to inform the complainant of the outcome of any misconduct meeting/hearing whether the complainant attends or not.

General Police Duties, para. 4.2.6.14

Answer 2.8

Answer **C** — A police officer has a right of appeal against the finding and/or the outcome imposed at a misconduct meeting. Where an officer determines that a police officer has arguable grounds of appeal, the appeal itself will normally be heard within five *working days beginning with the working day after* the determination that the officer concerned has arguable grounds of appeal. This effectively means that the appeal should be heard within five working days of tomorrow and answers A and B are incorrect.

The Regulations outline that the appeal should 'normally' be heard within the above timescales; however, if the police officer concerned or his or her police 'friend' is not available at the date or time specified by the person conducting the appeal, the police officer may propose an alternative time (provided that the alternative time is reasonable and falls within a period of five working days beginning with the first working day after that proposed by the person conducting the appeal). The appeal must then be postponed to that time. Answer D is therefore incorrect.

General Police Duties, para. 4.2.7.1

Answer 2.9

Answer **B** — The operation of the fast track misconduct procedures, referred to as 'special cases', are set out in Pt 5 of the Conduct Regulations. The special case procedures can only be used if the appropriate authority certifies the case as a special case, having determined that the 'special conditions' are satisfied or if the IPCC has given a direction under para. 20H(7) of sch. 3 to the Police Reform Act 2002.

The 'special conditions' are that there is sufficient evidence, in the form of written statements or other documents, *without the need for further evidence*, whether written or oral, to establish on the balance of probabilities, that the conduct of the police officer concerned constitutes gross misconduct, and it is in the public interest for the police officer concerned to cease to be a police officer without delay. Answer D is incorrect, as the hearing may proceed without oral evidence—in fact, the only oral evidence given at such a hearing will be from the police officer concerned (and the hearing may be heard in the officer's absence if necessary).

There is no requirement to wait for the outcome of the officer's appeal. The panel will merely need to decide, on the balance of probabilities, if it is in the public interest to dismiss the officer. Answer A is incorrect.

A person's conviction for a criminal offence will not automatically provide sufficient grounds for the appropriate authority to certify that this is a 'special case' and fast track misconduct procedures. However, such evidence would certainly be relevant. Answer C is incorrect.

General Police Duties, para. 4.2.8

Answer 2.10

Answer **A** — A police officer has a right of appeal to a Police Appeals Tribunal against any disciplinary finding and/or disciplinary outcome imposed at a misconduct hearing or special case hearing held under the Police (Conduct) Regulations 2008. *Senior* police officers (i.e. assistant chief constable and above), in addition, have the right to appeal to a Police Appeals Tribunal against any disciplinary finding and/or outcome imposed at a misconduct meeting.

For all other officers, an appeal against the finding and/or the outcome of a misconduct meeting will be heard by a member of the police service of a higher rank or a police staff manager who is considered to be of a higher grade, than the person who conducted the misconduct meeting.

Answers B, C and D are therefore incorrect.

General Police Duties, para. 4.2.9

3 | Unsatisfactory Performance and Attendance

STUDY PREPARATION

The previous chapter dealt with the impact of the Taylor Review on the Police (Conduct) Regulations 2008. In this chapter, we examine the Police (Performance) Regulations 2008 (SI 2008/2862), which were introduced at the same time.

These Regulations cover both performance and absence management and the chapter guides you through the procedures for dealing with both aspects of the regulations.

Again, the Taylor Review aimed to simplify processes, with the emphasis on *improving* poor performance and attendance, instead of punishing individuals. As a line manager, you will find that the aspects of misconduct and performance are closely related.

The final part of this chapter deals with the offences that can be committed by people in public offices, including police officers, who abuse their powers.

QUESTIONS

Question 3.1

Constable DALE has been asked to attend a second stage unsatisfactory performance (UPP) meeting, for continued poor performance. Constable DALE is disputing the evidence of poor performance and has expressed a wish to be legally represented at the meeting.

Is Constable DALE entitled to legal representation at this meeting?

A   Yes, police officers are entitled to legal representation at all stages of the misconduct and performance procedures.

B   No, legal representation is restricted to misconduct meetings and hearings.

C   No, but the officer will be entitled to legal representation if the matter progresses to the third stage.

D   No, in relation to performance, legal representation is restricted to cases of gross incompetence, at the third stage.

Question 3.2

Sergeant GANT has arranged a first stage meeting with Constable RUSH to discuss the officer's poor attendance record. Sergeant GANT intends issuing the officer with an improvement notice, seeking an improvement in the officer's attendance at work. Sergeant GANT is newly promoted and wishes to seek advice on how to conduct the meeting and the possible outcomes.

Which of the following statements is correct, in relation to the advice Sergeant GANT may seek?

A   Sergeant GANT may ask a Human Resources (HR) professional to be present, or a police officer with relevant experience, who is independent of the line management chain.

B   Sergeant GANT may seek advice from a HR professional, or a police officer with relevant experience, before the meeting, but they may not be present.

C   Because the meeting is to do with attendance and not performance, Sergeant GANT must have a HR professional present.

D   Sergeant GANT may ask a HR professional to be present, or a police officer who is part of the line management chain, provided the officer is not the second line manager.

Question 3.3

Constable HARDING has attended a second stage meeting for poor attendance. The officer has been issued with a written improvement notice and an action plan to improve attendance.

Which of the following statements is correct in relation to the length of the 'specified period', during which Constable HARDING is required to improve attendance?

A Because this is a second stage meeting, the period must not exceed three months.

B The period should not normally exceed three months, but it may be a longer period, not exceeding 12 months.

C The period should not normally exceed three months, but it may be a longer period, not exceeding six months.

D Because the meeting related to attendance matters, the period must not exceed three months.

Question 3.4

Inspector GREEGAN was due to hold a second stage unsatisfactory performance (UPP) meeting with Constable O'NEIL, regarding the continued submission of poor paperwork. An hour before the meeting, Inspector GREEGAN read a report from Constable O'NEIL's line manager outlining the officer's poor timekeeping. Constable O'NEIL had been warned several times recently for arriving at work late. A request was made that Inspector GREEGAN discuss the additional matter at the second stage meeting, alongside the original unsatisfactory performance matters.

Which of the following statements is correct, in relation to the request made by Constable O'NEIL's line manager?

A The planned meeting should continue and a separate first stage meeting should be arranged to discuss the additional matter. Unconnected UPP matters must always be dealt with separately.

B Due to the timing of the line manager's report, Inspector GREEGAN may adjourn the planned meeting and arrange a second stage meeting at a later date to discuss both matters.

C Inspector GREEGAN may discuss both matters at the planned meeting, because new information has come to light about Constable O'NEIL's performance during the specified period.

D The planned meeting should continue and a separate first stage meeting should be arranged to discuss the additional matter. Both matters may be consolidated if Constable O'NEIL reaches stage three of the procedures.

Question 3.5

Constable RICE has attended a second stage meeting, having failed to meet an action plan relating to poor attendance. Constable RICE has been given a written improvement notice and the second line manager has decided that the officer should be given a six-month action plan to improve attendance. Constable RICE has now approached a Police Federation representative to inquire whether there are grounds to appeal against the length of the period specified for improvement.

Which of the following statements is correct, according to the Police (Performance) Regulations 2008?

A An appeal may be made against the length of the period specified for improvement if it is unreasonable.

B An appeal may only be made if there was a breach of the procedures set out in the Regulations or some other unfairness relating to the meeting.

C An appeal may only be made against the actual finding that an officer's performance or attendance was unsatisfactory.

D An appeal may only be made against the length of the period specified for improvement if the matter relates to poor performance and not poor attendance.

Question 3.6

Sergeant OVERBY has been given written notification to attend a third stage meeting relating to poor attendance, having failed to meet action plans at the first and second stages. Sergeant OVERBY has sought legal advice, concerned that a reduction in rank may be one possible outcome of the meeting.

Is Sergeant OVERBY right to be concerned about being reduced in rank in these circumstances?

A Yes, a reduction in rank is one possible outcome of the meeting.

B No, reduction in rank is only applicable in cases of gross incompetence.

C No, reduction in rank is only applicable in cases of poor performance.

D Yes, a reduction in rank is a possible outcome of the meeting, but this must be sanctioned by the chief officer of police.

Question 3.7

COLLINS is the senior Special Constable in Westshire Constabulary and has been asked to attend a third stage unsatisfactory performance (UPP) meeting in relation to Special Constable WATKINS, regarding the continued submission of poor work.

In relation to COLLINS's presence at the meeting, which of the following statements is correct?

A COLLINS will be a member of the panel and will have a role in determining whether or not Special Constable WATKINS's performance is unsatisfactory.

B COLLINS must attend the meeting to advise the panel, but will not have a role in determining whether or not Special Constable WATKINS's performance is unsatisfactory.

C COLLINS must attend to advise the panel beforehand, but must not be present at the meeting with Special Constable WATKINS.

D COLLINS must attend the meeting to advise the panel, and will have a role later in determining whether or not Special Constable WATKINS's performance is unsatisfactory.

Question 3.8

FENTON is a member of the British National Party (BNP), although she does not actively take part in politics herself. She is considering joining the police force, but is unsure as to the regulations in relation to the political party she is affiliated to.

In relation to sch. 1 to the Police Regulations 2003 (SI 2003/527) (restrictions on the private lives of officers) could FENTON be a member of the BNP, as a police officer?

A Yes, she may be a member of this political party, provided she does not take an active part in politics.

B No, she may not be a member of any political party under this schedule.

C No, she may not be a member of this particular party.

D Yes, she may be a member of any political party, provided she does not take an active part in politics.

Question 3.9

Constable PURSEY creates a false piece of intelligence as a joke relating to a male believed to be in possession of a firearm. As a result of this a member of the public is stopped by the local Armed Response Vehicle and challenged with live police firearms. The member of the public is not happy and wishes to take action against the police for misconduct in a public office.

Which of the following is correct?

A The officer's actions amount to a tort (civil wrong) only and action in the High Court should be commenced.

B The officer's actions amount to a criminal offence only and criminal proceedings should be started.

C The officer's actions amount to a tort (civil wrong) and a criminal offence and both criminal and civil proceedings can be started.

D The officer's actions amount to a tort (civil wrong) and a criminal offence; however only civil *or* criminal proceedings can be started, not both.

Question 3.10

The police had attended several calls during the week relating to a domestic disagreement between FRENCH and HOLLOWAY. On each occasion, the incidents had been classified as 'verbal arguments' and no action was taken. Both FRENCH and HOLLOWAY were usually very drunk. One evening, Constable NAPIER was contacted by the control room and told that FRENCH had telephoned to say that HOLLOWAY had threatened to kill him and asked for the police to attend urgently. Constable NAPIER refused to attend the call on the grounds that previous calls to the address had been a waste of the police's time. Approximately an hour later, the police received a call that HOLLOWAY had actually killed FRENCH.

Could Constable NAPIER be guilty of the common law offence of misconduct in public office, in these circumstances?

A No, this offence cannot be committed because of a failure to do something; it relates to the actions a person actually took.

B Yes, but only if it can be shown Constable NAPIER was aware of the duty to take particular action, and failed to do so.

C Yes, if it can be shown Constable NAPIER was aware of the duty to take particular action, and failed to do so, or was reckless as to the existence of the duty.

D No, this could not amount to a criminal offence; however, Constable NAPIER could be guilty of gross incompetence or misconduct.

Question 3.11

FARR is aware that special constables are entitled to free travel on the local buses. FARR makes a false warrant card with the term 'Special Constable' on it and a picture of himself. Every day he travels on the bus and produces this card to obtain free rides. He never states he is a special constable; he merely shows the bus driver his card.

Has FARR committed an offence of impersonating a police officer contrary to s. 90(1) of the Police Act 1996?

A No, as he did not say he was a special constable.
B No, as the legislation does not apply to impersonating special constables.
C Yes, provided his intention was to deceive.
D Yes, provided his intention was to obtain an advantage.

ANSWERS

Answer 3.1

Answer **D** — In relation to unsatisfactory performance (UPP), a police officer may seek legal advice at any time. However, legal representation for UPP matters is confined to third stage meetings where the procedure has been initiated at that stage. In other words, the officer is accused of gross incompetence and has by-passed the normal step-by-step process and has been fast tracked to a hearing. Answer A is incorrect. This also means that if the officer arrives at level three having passed through the other stages, he or she is not entitled to legal representation at the level three meeting. Answer C is incorrect.

Answer B is incorrect, because a police officer *can* have legal representation in relation to performance matters, albeit in limited circumstances.

General Police Duties, para. 4.3.2

Answer 3.2

Answer **A** — The formal procedures to deal with unsatisfactory performance and attendance are set out in the Police (Performance) Regulations 2008 and are referred to as 'UPPs'. There are potentially three stages to the UPP process, each of which involves a different meeting composition and possible outcomes. However, the process is the same whether the officer is being asked to account for their poor performance or their attendance. Answer C is therefore incorrect.

A line manager may ask a HR professional or police officer (who should have experience of UPPs) to attend a UPP meeting to advise him or her on the proceedings at the first stage meeting. Answer B is incorrect. The line manager may also seek such advice before the meeting and answer C is also incorrect in this respect, because attendance at the meeting is optional and not mandatory.

If the experienced police officer is to attend the meeting, he or she must be independent of the line management chain (and not part of it at any level). Answer D is therefore incorrect.

General Police Duties, para. 4.3.8

Answer 3.3

Answer **B** — Under the Police (Performance) Regulations 2008, the 'specified period' of an improvement notice is a period specified by the manager conducting the meeting (having considered any representations made by or on behalf of the police officer) within which the police officer must improve his/her performance or attendance.

It is expected that the specified period for improvement would not normally exceed three months. However, depending on the nature and circumstances of the matter, it may be appropriate to specify a longer or shorter period for improvement (but which should not exceed 12 months). Answer C is incorrect.

The specified period is the same whether the officer is attending a first stage or second stage meeting and no additional provisions are made for officers attending meetings for attendance matters. Answers A and D are therefore incorrect.

General Police Duties, para. 4.3.8

Answer 3.4

Answer **B** — Generally, a police officer can only move to a later stage of the UPPs in relation to unsatisfactory performance or attendance that is similar to, or connected with, the performance or attendance referred to in any previous written improvement notice. Where failings relate to different forms of unsatisfactory performance or attendance it will be necessary to commence each UPP at the first stage (unless the failing constitutes gross incompetence). If more than one UPP is commenced, then, given that the procedures will relate to different failings and will have been identified at different times, the finding and outcome of each should be without prejudice to the others.

However, there may be circumstances where procedures have been initiated for a particular failing and an additional failing comes to light prior to the first or second stage meeting. In such circumstances it is possible to consolidate the two issues at the planned meeting provided that there is sufficient time prior to the meeting to comply with the notification requirements. Answer A is incorrect.

If there is insufficient time to comply with the notification requirements (as was the case in this scenario), either the meeting should be rearranged to a date which allows the requirements to be met or a separate first stage meeting should be held in relation to the additional matter.

Therefore, Inspector GREEGAN would have the option to adjourn the second stage meeting to discuss both matters at the same meeting, but should not discuss the additional matter at the planned meeting. There would be no requirement to wait until the officer reaches stage three of the UPPs to consolidate the unsatisfactory performance matters. Answers C and D are incorrect.

General Police Duties, para. 4.3.8.2

Answer 3.5

Answer **A** — According to the Police (Performance) Regulations 2008, a police officer has a right of appeal against the finding and the terms of the improvement notice imposed at stage two of the UPPs and against the decision to require him/her to attend the meeting. Any appeal should be made in writing and must clearly set out the grounds and evidence for the appeal.

One ground for an appeal is that there was a breach of the procedures set out in the Regulations or some other unfairness which could have materially affected the finding of unsatisfactory performance or attendance or the terms of the written improvement notice. Amongst the other grounds are that the finding of unsatisfactory performance or attendance is unreasonable, or any of the terms of the improvement notice are unreasonable. This would include an appeal against the length of the period specified for improvement. Answers B and C are incorrect.

An appeal may be made against the length of the period specified for improvement if the matter relates to poor performance *or* poor attendance. Answer D is therefore incorrect.

General Police Duties, para. 4.3.10.3

Answer 3.6

Answer **C** — According to the Police (Performance) Regulations 2008, a reduction in rank is one of the possible outcomes where a police officer has reached a stage three meeting, following stages one and two. Answer B is incorrect.

However, this outcome only applies to stage three meetings which relate to performance matters. Answers A and D are therefore incorrect.

Note that a third stage meeting for gross incompetence will only take place where there are concerns about a police officer's performance, not their attendance.

General Police Duties, paras 4.3.11, 4.3.11.1

Answer 3.7

Answer **B** — In cases where the police officer is a special constable, the force will appoint a member of the special constabulary of sufficient seniority and experience to attend the meeting to advise the panel (this is for the purpose of fairness). Since this person will be present at the meeting, answer C is incorrect.

However, the special constable adviser will not form part of the panel (answer A is incorrect), nor will he or she have a role in determining whether or not the officer's performance or attendance is unsatisfactory. Answer D is incorrect.

General Police Duties, para. 4.3.11.3

Answer 3.8

Answer **C** — Schedule 1 provides that a member of a police force:

- shall at all times abstain from any activity which is likely to interfere with the impartial discharge of his/her duties or which is likely to give rise to the impression amongst members of the public that it may so interfere;
- shall in particular—
  (a) not take any active part in politics;
  (b) not belong to any organisation specified or described in a determination of the Secretary of State.

For this purpose, the Secretary of State has determined that no member of the police force may be a member of the British National Party (BNP), Combat 18 or the National Front. Answers A and D are therefore incorrect. The wording of sch. 1 does not actually prohibit police officers from being members of other political parties; they are merely prevented from taking an active part in politics, which means that a police officer *could* be a member of any other party, and answer B is incorrect.

General Police Duties, para. 4.3.17.1

Answer 3.9

Answer **C** — Misconduct in a public office is defined by common law as follows:

It is a misdemeanour at common law for the holder of a public office to do anything that amounts to a malfeasance or a 'culpable' misfeasance

(*R* v *Wyatt* (1705) 1 Salk 380)

This primordial common law idiosyncrasy is both a tort and a criminal offence, which could give rise to litigation in both the criminal and civil courts. Answers A, B and D are therefore incorrect.

Misfeasance can cover many misdemeanours committed by police officers from deliberately mistreating prisoners to improper use of the National Intelligence Model.

General Police Duties, para. 4.3.18.1

Answer 3.10

Answer **C** — It is a misdemeanour at common law for the holder of a public office to do anything that amounts to a malfeasance or a 'culpable' misfeasance (*R* v *Wyatt* (1705) 1 Salk 380). The conduct can be separated into occasions of *mal* feasance and *mis* feasance. The first requires some degree of wrongful motive or intention on the part of the officer while the second is more likely to apply where there has been some form of wilful neglect of duty: both are notoriously difficult to prove, but either could constitute an offence. Answers A and D are therefore incorrect.

A death in police custody has led to a clarification as to the nature of the criminal common law offence of misconduct in public office (see *Attorney General's Reference (No. 3 of 2003)* [2004] EWCA Crim 868). The elements of the offence were summarised by the Court of Appeal (Criminal Division) as follows:

A public officer acting as such [who]:

- wilfully neglects to perform his duty and/or wilfully misconducts himself,
- to such a degree as to amount to an abuse of the public's trust in the office holder,
- without reasonable excuse or justification [may be guilty of the criminal offence.]

Since the offence requires 'an awareness of the duty to act or a subjective reckless ness as to the existence of the duty', answer B is incorrect.

General Police Duties, para. 4.3.18.1

Answer 3.11

Answer **C** — Impersonating a police officer is defined in the Police Act 1996. Section 90(1) states:

Any person who with intent to deceive impersonates a member of a police force or special constable, or makes any statement or does any act calculated falsely to suggest that he is such a member or constable shall be guilty of an offence ...

As can be seen from the definition, the legislation applies to special constables, and therefore answer B is incorrect. The offence includes not only statements but also acts that suggest the person is a special constable. Such acts would include producing a false warrant card, and therefore answer A is incorrect. This is a crime of 'specific' intent and intention to deceive must be proved, not just an intention to gain an advantage, and therefore answer D is incorrect.

General Police Duties, para. 4.3.18.2

4 | Extending the Policing Family

QUESTIONS

Question 4.1

Under Pt 4 of the Police Reform Act 2002, chief officers of police are given the authority to confer policing powers on non-police officers (such as Police Community Support Officers).

What flexibility, if any, does a chief officer of police have when it comes to conferring policing powers on an individual who has been designated for such a role?

A A chief officer must confer some powers on an individual, but has flexibility to choose which ones.

B A chief officer may confer limited powers on an individual, following consultation with the Secretary of State.

C A chief officer does not have to confer any powers whatsoever on an individual and has the flexibility to decide for him or herself.

D A chief officer may confer limited powers on an individual, following consultation with the Association of Chief Police Officers (ACPO).

Question 4.2

McCARTNEY and COLE have started work for Westshire Police on the same day. McCARTNEY is to work as a police community support officer (PCSO) and COLE is to work as an investigating officer.

Which of the following statements is correct, in relation to whether either McCARTNEY or COLE should be employed by Westshire Police, in order to perform their roles?

A Both McCARTNEY and COLE must be employed by Westshire Police before they can perform their roles.

B As an investigating officer, only COLE must be employed by Westshire Police.

C As a PCSO, only McCARTNEY must be employed by Westshire Police.

D Neither person needs to be employed by Westshire Police in order to perform their roles.

Question 4.3

JANEWAY is a self-employed security guard who works in an out-of-town shopping centre. A number of shops have formed a Business Crime Reduction Partnership and JANEWAY's wages are paid by the Partnership. The estate has been suffering anti-social behaviour by local youths and is considering whether JANEWAY could be 'accredited' with powers under a statutory Community Safety Accreditation Scheme to deal with the anti-social behaviour.

Would the Partnership be entitled to accredit JANEWAY in this way?

A Yes, provided JANEWAY enters into a contract with the local police authority and the relevant local authority.

B No, a self-employed person cannot be accredited under this scheme.

C Yes, provided JANEWAY enters into a contract with the local police authority.

D Yes, provided JANEWAY enters into a contract with the local police authority and the Business Crime Reduction Partnership.

Question 4.4

FLETCHER is employed by Westshire Police as an investigating officer and has been 'designated' by the chief constable to perform this role. A complaint has been made that FLETCHER committed a serious assault on a suspect during an interview and the matter is being investigated by the Professional Standards Department. The officer in charge of the case is considering making a referral to the Independent Police Complaints Commission (IPCC).

Could the IPCC have jurisdiction over a complaint made against a designated employee, such as FLETCHER?

A No, because FLETCHER is not a police officer and is not covered by the Police (Conduct) Regulations 2008.

B Yes, but only if a joint allegation is made against a police officer and a designated employee.

C Yes, but only because a criminal allegation has been made against FLETCHER.

D Yes, regardless of whether the allegation is of a criminal nature, or whether a police officer was involved.

Question 4.5

Whilst on patrol in a local park, PCSO HILLIER spoke to BARTON, who was responsible for a dog which had fouled in a children's play area. PCSO HILLIER was designated to issue a fixed penalty notice for this offence. BARTON demanded to know what authority PCSO HILLIER had to issue such a notice.

Is PCSO HILLIER obliged to produce any documentary evidence of his authority, in these circumstances?

A No, provided PCSO HILLIER was in uniform.

B Yes, PCSO HILLIER must produce evidence of his designation as a PCSO.

C Yes, PCSO HILLIER must produce details of all the standard and non-standard powers he has as a PCSO.

D Yes, PCSO HILLIER must produce evidence of his designation as a PCSO and any non-standard power he has.

Question 4.6

BECK is employed as a Detention Officer in a custody office on the same shift as Sergeant DELGADO. BECK is one of a number of people from a private security company contracted by the force to perform custody detention duties. Sergeant DELGADO has had to warn BECK several times of a failure to conduct visits and update custody records in a timely manner.

Which of the following statements is correct, in relation to whether Sergeant DELGADO can deal with BECK, either under the Police (Performance) Regulations 2008, or the Police (Conduct) Regulations 2008?

A BECK may only be dealt with under the Performance Regulations in these circumstances.

B BECK may only be dealt with under the Conduct Regulations in these circumstances.

C Neither of the Regulations applies in these circumstances, but BECK may be dealt with under police staff Regulations relating to poor performance.

D BECK is not an employee and may not be dealt with under any police officer or police staff Regulations in these circumstances.

Question 4.7

VAUGHAN has been appointed as an accredited employee who works on a large housing estate, which has suffered significant anti-social behaviour problems. A Community Safety Accreditation Scheme (CSAS) has been agreed between the police, the local authority and VAUGHAN's employers, a housing association company. A complaint has been made about VAUGHAN's behaviour, alleging that she is aggressive towards residents.

Which organisation has responsibility for dealing with a complaint made about VAUGHAN's behaviour?

A Any of the three organisations could deal with the complaint.

B The complaint should be dealt with by the police.

C The complaint should be dealt with by VAUGHAN's employer.

D The complaint could be dealt with by the police or VAUGHAN's employer.

Question 4.8

WALTERS is an accredited employee who works closely with the Neighbourhood Policing Team in an out-of-town shopping centre. WALTERS is employed by one of the larger stores in the centre, as part of a CSAS agreed between the police, the local authority and WALTERS' employers. Sergeant POWELL has received a complaint from a store manager, that WALTERS has regularly been seen socialising with people suspected of committing a number of shoplifting offences in the centre. Sergeant POWELL has submitted a report asking for WALTERS' accreditation to be withdrawn.

What process must take place before WALTERS' accreditation may be withdrawn in these circumstances?

A The chief officer of police may withdraw the accreditation, simply by issuing a written notice to WALTERS.

B A meeting must be held between the police and WALTERS' employers and a joint decision must be reached to withdraw the accreditation.

C A meeting must be held between the police and WALTERS' employers, but the final decision to withdraw the accreditation rests with the police.

D A meeting must be held between the police, WALTERS' employers and the local authority, but the final decision to withdraw the accreditation rests with the police.

Question 4.9

HANSEN is an accredited employee in her local policing area. ADEDEYO is considering making a civil claim as a result of an incident involving HANSEN. ADEDEYO claims that HANSEN unlawfully detained him while acting in her capacity as an accredited employee.

If ADEDEYO were to make a civil claim for unlawful detention, against whom should the claim be made?

A Either the police authority, or HANSEN or HANSEN's employer.

B Both the police authority and HANSEN.

C Both the police authority and HANSEN's employer.

D The police authority, HANSEN and HANSEN's employer.

Question 4.10

MOHAMMED and BEVAN are retired police officers, having both been experienced detectives before their retirement. They are now employed by a police force as designated investigating officers, and are currently attached to an inquiry team investigating a murder. The team have arrested a suspect for the offence, and MOHAMMED and BEVAN have been sent to his home address to conduct a search, under s. 18(1) of the Police and Criminal Evidence Act 1984, for material relevant to the murder.

If necessary, would MOHAMMED and BEVAN be entitled to use force to enter the suspect's home in these circumstances?

A Yes, but only if they are accompanied by, and under the supervision of, a police officer.

B Yes, they have the power to use force on their own in these circumstances.

C No, they have no power to use force in any circumstances.

D No, they may use force in order to enter premises only to save life or limb, or to prevent serious damage to property.

ANSWERS

Answer 4.1

Answer **C** — Under Pt 4 of the Police Reform Act 2002, chief officers of police are given the authority to confer policing powers on non-police officers, such as police community support officers, investigating officers, detention officers and escort officers. Part 4 allows the relevant chief officer to confer certain powers on different groups of people by designating or accrediting them.

The chief officer does *not have* to confer any powers on any such groups and he or she can decide to confer only a reduced number of powers or to place further limitations on those powers: the Act simply gives the chief officer the freedom and flexibility to do so. Answers A, B and D are therefore incorrect.

General Police Duties, para. 4.4.2

Answer 4.2

Answer **A** — Some roles created under the Police Reform Act 2002 (such as police community support officers and investigating officers) can *only* be carried out by police employees; if you do not work directly for the police, you cannot have these powers or perform these roles. In other roles (detention officers and escort officers), the person does not necessarily have to be employed by the police.

Answers B, C and D are therefore incorrect.

General Police Duties, para. 4.4.2.1

Answer 4.3

Answer **B** — The Police Reform Act 2002 allows people to be 'accredited' with powers that can only come from their accreditation under a statutory Community Safety Accreditation Scheme. If the person is not employed by the force, then their employer must have a contract with the relevant police authority. These people will have their powers contained in a 'designation' from the relevant chief officer. Since the contract must be with the police authority, answers A and D are incorrect.

In order to perform *any* of the roles and exercise *any* of the powers under Pt 4 of the Act, an individual must be employed by somebody because it is through the person's employer that the chief officer or the relevant police authority can exercise a degree of control over those auxiliary staff who are not directly employed by the police. Therefore, the legislation will not allow a person who is unemployed or self-employed to have the powers or to carry out any of the relevant functions. Answers A, C and D are incorrect for this reason also.

General Police Duties, para. 4.4.2.1

Answer 4.4

Answer **D** — Where designated staff are employees of the relevant force, the chief officer is responsible for dealing with reports of misconduct and complaints against them in the normal way.

The Independent Police Complaints Commission (IPCC) *also* has jurisdiction over any allegations or complaints made against designated staff who are employees of the relevant force. Answer A is incorrect.

This is regardless of whether the allegation is of a criminal nature, or refers purely to a misconduct matter and there is no requirement for the allegation to be made jointly against a police officer. Answers B and C are incorrect.

General Police Duties, para. 4.4.3

Answer 4.5

Answer **D** — Section 9 of the Police and Justice Act 2006 introduces sch. 5 which makes various amendments to provisions in the Police Reform Act 2002. Paragraph 3 of the schedule amends s. 42 of the 2002 Act so that PCSOs, when exercising powers or duties, must produce on demand evidence of their designation as a community support officer and of any non-standard power which they exercise that has been conferred on them by their chief officer under s. 38. Answer A is incorrect as evidence must be produced. Answer B is incorrect as the evidence must include any non-standard powers the PCSO has.

PCSOs will not have to carry with them details of *all* the standard powers which have been conferred upon them by an order under s. 38A. The requirement to produce evidence of a designation could be satisfied by production of the designation itself, but could also be satisfied by something less, such as some form of document or card. Answer C is therefore incorrect.

General Police Duties, para. 4.4.3.1

Answer 4.6

Answer **D** — Under s. 39 of the Police Reform Act 2002, a police authority may enter into a contract with a private company for the provision of services relating to the detention or escorting of people in custody. This allows the chief officer to designate employees of the contractor as either Detention Officers or Escort Officers or both.

Although their employee status is the source of control over these employees' activities and performance, the first thing to note is that they are *not* employed by the police force. These contracted-out personnel cannot be given the powers of PCSOs and investigating officers as they are not police employees, but they are given the same powers as police officers to conduct certain functions, such as searching and fingerprinting and photographing.

Because they are neither police officers, nor members of police staff, designated employees are not covered by the Police (Performance) Regulations 2008, the Police (Conduct) Regulations 2008 or any other performance regulations relating to police staff employees. Answers A, B and C are therefore incorrect.

Although s. 39 of the Act allows the Secretary of State to make regulations regarding the handling of complaints and misconduct issues arising out of the functions of designated employees, the practical answer to this question is that the police force involved may withdraw BECK's designation by giving the employee notice and asking for his or her services to be withdrawn (s. 42(3)). This power of revocation or amendment is absolute and there is no requirement for any misconduct or poor performance on the part of the employee.

General Police Duties, paras 4.4.4, 4.4.4.3

Answer 4.7

Answer **C** — Under s. 40(9) of the Police Reform Act 2002, it will be the duty of a chief officer of police who establishes and maintains a CSAS to ensure that the employers of the persons on whom powers are conferred by the grant of accreditations under s. 41 have established and maintain satisfactory arrangements for handling complaints relating to the carrying out by those persons of the functions for the purposes of which the powers are conferred.

Therefore, the chief officer of police has responsibility to ensure that VAUGHAN's *employers* have satisfactory arrangements for handling complaints. This implies that the employers actually have responsibility for dealing with the complaint.

Answers A, B and D are therefore incorrect.

General Police Duties, para. 4.4.4.2

Answer 4.8

Answer **A** — Section 42(3) allows an accredited employee's designation or accreditation to be withdrawn at any time by a chief officer of police.

There is no requirement to consult with the local authority, the police authority or the person's employer; therefore, answers B, C and D are incorrect.

General Police Duties, para. 4.4.4.3

Answer 4.9

Answer **D** — Under s. 42 of the Police Reform Act 2002, any liability for civil wrongs arising out of conduct in the course of an employee's accreditation or designation will be apportioned jointly between the police authority, the employer and the individual (therefore answers B and C are incorrect). Answer A is incorrect, as the claim should be made against all three.

General Police Duties, para. 4.4.4.3

Answer 4.10

Answer **A** — Under s. 38(6) of the Police Reform Act 2002, a designated employee is able to exercise the same powers as a constable to use reasonable force, if a constable were entitled to use force in the circumstances. Answer C is therefore incorrect. Section 117 of the Police and Criminal Evidence Act 1984 would allow a constable to enter premises in these circumstances, using force if necessary; therefore the designated investigating officers in the question are also entitled to do so.

However, s. 38(9) of the 2002 Act allows designated employees to use force to enter premises only either if they are in the company and under the supervision of a constable, or to save life or limb, or to prevent serious damage to property. Answer D is incorrect, as the power may be used in both these circumstances. Since there is no suggestion that there is a danger to any person or their property, the investigating officers would be able to enter the premises only when accompanied by a constable, so answer B is incorrect.

General Police Duties, para. 4.4.5

5 | **Human Rights**

QUESTIONS

Question 5.1

HART works as a prison officer in a private prison. On several occasions GRANGER, a prisoner, had been rude to her. In order to teach GRANGER a lesson, HART made GRANGER stand in the shower for a whole hour while she looked on.

Have GRANGER's rights been breached under Art. 3 of the European Convention on Human Rights (right to freedom from torture)?

A No, because HART does not work for a public authority.

B Yes, because HART's employer performs a public function.

C No, because HART does not work for a government authority.

D Yes, regardless of the employer that HART works for.

Question 5.2

The police are conducting observations near a lay-by, which is a meeting place for gay men. They are seeking to detect offences of homosexual activity in public, under the Sexual Offences Act 1956. DANE regularly frequents the area, and is also a member of a gay and lesbian group. He has sought legal advice in order to challenge police action under the Human Rights Act 1998.

In relation to whether DANE may use the Act to challenge the police activity, which statement is correct?

A He may do so as an individual only, whether he has been arrested or not.

B He may do so as part of a group, but only if he has been arrested for an offence.

C He may do so as part of a group, or as an individual, whether he has been arrested or not.

D He may do so as an individual only if he has been proceeded against for an offence.

Question 5.3

FRIAR appeared in Crown Court, having been charged with supplying Class A drugs. The court heard that FRIAR had been the subject of a directed surveillance operation by plain clothes police officers. During the hearing, it was revealed that the officers had omitted to obtain the correct authorisation under the Regulation of

Investigatory Powers Act 2000 and the judge ordered the case to be dismissed. FRIAR intends bringing proceedings against the police for infringing Art. 8 of the European Convention on Human Rights (the right to private life).

Section 7(5)(a) of the Human Rights Act 1998 provides a limited time period during which a victim must bring proceedings against a public authority. In FRIAR's case, when did that time period begin?

A When the infringement of FRIAR's human rights actually took place.

B When FRIAR realised an infringement of human rights had taken place.

C When the court dismissed the case.

D When FRIAR notifies the court of an intention to institute proceedings under this section.

Question 5.4

Constable ANDERSON is an authorised firearms officer who was responsible for the fatal shooting of a suspect whilst on duty and was called to give evidence in the Coroner's Court. Constable ANDERSON applied to give evidence anonymously on the grounds that she was a member of the local community and if her identity were revealed, it would represent a risk of serious harm to herself and her family. The court rejected the application by the officer.

Would there be any restriction on Constable ANDERSON bringing proceedings against the Coroner's Court (a public authority) for infringing Art. 2 of the European Convention on Human Rights (the right to life) in these circumstances?

A Yes, Constable ANDERSON was acting in the execution of her duty, which makes this an employment matter.

B No, this is not an employment matter and Constable ANDERSON may bring proceedings.

C No, there are no restrictions on police officers relying on the Convention rights.

D No, the only restriction on police officers relying on the Convention rights is in relation to recruitment proceedings.

Question 5.5

LAWTON was the father of an 8-year-old boy who was murdered by his neighbour, PEARSON, a convicted sex offender. Prior to the murder, LAWTON had made several complaints to the police that PEARSON had been seen pestering his child. Following PEARSON's conviction, LAWTON brought an action against the police under Art. 2

of the European Convention on Human Rights, alleging that the police had failed to prevent his son's death.

What must LAWTON prove to the court in order to convince it that the police failed to prevent the death of his son?

A Nothing—the police have an absolute obligation to protect life under Art. 2.

B That the police actually foresaw the risk to life, and that they failed to act upon it.

C That the police failed to see a risk to life which would have been obvious to a reasonable person.

D That the police did not do all that was expected of them to avoid a real and immediate risk to life.

Question 5.6

ANDERSON was found guilty of raping and murdering a 5-year-old girl after confessing during an interview. ANDERSON is now appealing against his conviction by using Art. 3 of the European Convention on Human Rights (right to freedom from torture). ANDERSON claims that police officers showed him several pictures of the mutilated body of the young girl prior to the interview and that this caused him severe mental anguish. ANDERSON claims that he was not guilty of the offence and his conviction was unsafe on the grounds that he was psychologically affected by the photographs, because his own daughter was murdered two years previously, and he would not have admitted the offence had he not been shown them.

Which of the following statements is correct, in respect of whether ANDERSON's confession should be admitted in evidence?

A The evidence should not be admitted if the court finds, on the balance of probabilities, it was obtained by torture.

B The evidence should be admitted because mental anguish does not constitute torture.

C The evidence should not be admitted if the court finds beyond reasonable doubt that the evidence was obtained by torture.

D All evidence should be admitted and heard by the court and there should be no exceptions.

Question 5.7

Constable WILSON was called to an incident in a local supermarket. The manager was complaining about SHEPPARD, who was homeless. SHEPPARD had entered the store and told the manager that he had scabies and a severe lice infection, both of which were highly contagious and needed treatment. The manager feared that customers and staff would be infected by disease and requested that the officer remove SHEPPARD from the store.

> What power does Art. 5 of the European Convention on Human Rights (the right to liberty and security) provide in relation to an arrest in these circumstances?
>
> **A** SHEPPARD can be arrested, provided he is taken to a medical centre.
> **B** SHEPPARD can be arrested and taken to a place of safety.
> **C** SHEPPARD cannot be arrested under the Convention; the officer would need to seek powers from elsewhere.
> **D** SHEPPARD can be arrested and brought before a competent legal authority.

Question 5.8

ZILICH is suspected of entering the country illegally and is wanted for murder in Kosovo. ZILICH has been held in a detention centre for over three years while the immigration authorities attempt to organise extradition procedures. ZILICH is fighting the extradition procedure by using Art. 5 of the European Convention on Human Rights (right to liberty and security), citing that his detention is unjust and oppressive because of the three-year delay.

> What obligation, if any, do the authorities have to demonstrate that ZILICH's detention is not unjust and oppressive?
>
> **A** They need only show that the detention was necessary—there is no requirement to justify the delay in ZILICH's extradition.
> **B** There is no requirement to show either that the detention was necessary, or to justify the delay in ZILICH's extradition.
> **C** They must show that the detention was necessary and that the delay in ZILICH's extradition was justified, otherwise the detention may be unlawful.
> **D** ZILICH has been 'detained' for deportation; this does not constitute an 'arrest' and therefore Art. 5 does not apply.

Question 5.9

FOX was arrested for an offence under s. 4 of the Road Traffic Act 1988 (unfit to drive through drink or drugs). FOX was taken to a police station where subsequent blood tests proved negative. FOX is now considering bringing a case of unlawful arrest against the police, under Art. 5 of the European Convention on Human Rights (the right to liberty and security). The basis of FOX's case is that the arresting officer had formed a suspicion that she was drunk based on evidence provided by a member of the public. FOX claims that this suspicion was not 'reasonable' and, consequently, the arrest was unlawful.

In considering FOX's case, how should the court assess the officer's 'reasonable suspicion' that an arrest was necessary?

A Whether the officer was satisfied that the information received about FOX prior to the arrest amounted to a 'reasonable suspicion' that she was drunk.

B Whether an ordinary person would be satisfied that the information received about FOX prior to the arrest amounted to a 'reasonable suspicion' that she was drunk.

C Whether an objective observer would be satisfied that the information received about FOX prior to the arrest amounted to a 'reasonable suspicion' that she was drunk.

D Whether the witness in the case had formed a 'reasonable suspicion' that she was drunk.

Question 5.10

Article 6 of the European Convention on Human Rights states that everyone is entitled to a fair and public hearing within a reasonable time by an independent and impartial tribunal established by law.

Which of the following statements is correct, regarding the presumption that the hearing must be in public?

A In some circumstances, cases in civil courts may be held in private; however, all cases in criminal courts must be held in public.

B Cases in either court may be held in private, and the court may determine that the judgment may also be pronounced privately.

C Cases in either court may be held in private, but the judgment must always be pronounced publicly.

D Cases in either court may be held in private, but only when, in the opinion of the court, that publicity would prejudice the interests of justice, or affect national security.

Question 5.11

MORTON is a well-known public figure and is taking legal advice about bringing a case against the police, under Art. 8 of the European Convention on Human Rights (respect for private and family life). The circumstances were that MORTON reported to the police her suspicion that someone was trying to hack into her emails. MORTON alleges that the police failed to act and as a result, the hacker subsequently managed to download several photographs of her with no clothes on, from emails sent by a friend. The photographs were displayed on the Internet and MORTON claims this was potentially ruinous to her career.

Which of the following statements is correct, in relation to MORTON's potential claim?

A The aim of Art. 8 is to protect a person's life from interference by 'public authorities': it therefore does not apply in these circumstances.

B The State has a positive obligation to prevent others from interfering with an individual's right to private life; therefore, Art. 8 may apply in these circumstances.

C The State has a positive obligation to prevent others from interfering with an individual's right to private life, but this does not extend to a person's correspondence; therefore, Art. 8 would not apply in these circumstances.

D The State has a positive obligation to prevent others from interfering with an individual's right to private life, but this duty only extends to maintaining public safety; therefore, Art. 8 would not apply in these circumstances.

Question 5.12

CLAYTON is appearing in the Crown Court, having been charged with an offence of stirring up racial hatred under s. 18 of the Public Order Act 1986. He had displayed a picture in his shop window, indicating that he would not serve refugees. He is pleading not guilty, claiming that his human rights have been interfered with, as he is entitled to express his opinions freely.

Would CLAYTON be able to use Art. 10 of the European Convention on Human Rights (freedom of expression) as a defence in these circumstances?

A No, as his actions are probably not proportionate to the crime committed.

B Yes, every person has a right to express themselves freely.

C No, but he could use Art. 9 (freedom of thought) as a defence.

D Yes, provided he held a genuine belief that his rights had been interfered with.

Question 5.13

The Westford anti-hunt lobby arranged a demonstration outside a farm where a fox hunt was being organised. The organisers of the hunt arranged for marshals to be present and the local police were also in attendance. Demonstrators protested peacefully in the road nearby but, on the instructions of the hunt organisers, the marshals attempted to move the protestors away from the scene. The demonstrators felt intimidated by the marshals, but the police did nothing.

In these circumstances, do the police officers at the scene appear to have infringed Art. 11 of the European Convention on Human Rights (freedom of assembly and association)?

A No, as they have not interfered with the rights of the protestors or the members of the hunt.

B Yes, they should have stopped the protest; it breached the rights of the hunters and the farm owner.

C Yes, they had a duty to prevent the unlawful interference with the rights of the protestors by the marshals.

D No, they would have a duty to act only if public order offences were imminent.

Question 5.14

PUGACH returned from working abroad to find that people were squatting in his flat. PUGACH obtained documentation from the court proving that he was a protected intending occupier, but used all his money doing so. PUGACH contacted the police, asking for assistance to remove the trespassers, but was told this was a civil matter and the police would not get involved. PUGACH tried several times over a six-month period, explaining that he had no money to go to court, but the police did not help. PUGACH eventually contacted a solicitor, who advised him that the police may have breached his human rights and that he should sue them.

Given that PUGACH was a protected intending occupier and the police *could* have used their powers under s. 7 of the Criminal Law Act 1977 to deal with the squatters, could they be in breach of Protocol 1, Art. 1 to the European Convention on Human Rights (right to enjoy possessions), in these circumstances?

A No, the police did not take possession of PUGACH's property at any time.

B Yes, the police could be liable in these circumstances.

C No, 'possessions' do not include land or premises for the purposes of this Protocol.

D No, the police cannot be held liable for a matter which is civil and not criminal.

ANSWERS

Answer 5.1

Answer **B** — Under Art. 3 of the European Convention on Human Rights, a person must not be subjected to torture, inhuman or degrading treatment or punishment. Therefore, the actions of the guard would amount to a breach.

Under s. 6 of the Human Rights Act 1998, it is unlawful for a public authority to act in a way that is incompatible with a Convention right. An individual working for an authority is included in the definition.

'Public authorities' are divided into 'pure public authorities' (such as the police and courts, etc.) and 'quasi-public authorities'. There has been no test as yet as to who might fall into the second category, but they do include authorities who have a duty to discharge some public duties (such as security companies running private prisons and government contractors). Therefore, answer A is incorrect.

Answer C is incorrect because 'government authorities' are not mentioned; and answer D is incorrect as regard must be given to the type of authority a person works for.

General Police Duties, para. 4.5.3.3

Answer 5.2

Answer **A** — Under s. 7(1) of the Human Rights Act 1998, a person who claims that a public authority has acted (or proposed to act) in a way that is incompatible with his or her human rights (s. 6(1)) may bring proceedings against the authority in the appropriate court or tribunal.

In order to rely on s. 7, however, a person must first be a 'victim', and must show that he or she is either directly affected or at risk of being directly affected. Section 7 will not enable public interest groups to institute proceedings, only individuals. Therefore, answers B and C are incorrect.

Answer A is correct because DANE is an individual who is at risk of being directly affected. The circumstances are similar to the case of *Dudgeon* v *United Kingdom* (1983) 5 EHRR 573, where the petitioner was able to challenge the law proscribing consensual homosexual activity even though he had not been prosecuted under the legislation himself. A person may institute proceedings under s. 7 regardless of whether or not he or she has been convicted of an offence. This is known as using the European Convention on Human Rights as a 'sword' against a public authority. Answer D is therefore incorrect.

Of course, whether the police should have been engaged in such surveillance, bearing in mind the Regulation of Investigatory Powers Act 2000, is another issue!

General Police Duties, para. 4.5.3.6

Answer 5.3

Answer **A** — Section 7(5)(a) of the Human Rights Act 1998 states that proceedings under s. 7(1)(a) must generally be brought before the end of one year beginning with *the date on which the act complained of took place*, or such longer period as the court or tribunal considers equitable having regard to all the circumstances. Answers B, C and D are therefore incorrect.

General Police Duties, para. 4.5.3.6

Answer 5.4

Answer **B** — There are restrictions on police officers relying on the Convention rights in the context of recruitment *and* disciplinary procedures. Answers C and D are incorrect.

The European Court of Justice regards police officers in Member States as being government servants and as such they cannot generally rely on their Convention rights against the employer (see *Pellegrin* v *France* (2001) 31 EHRR 26). Since the officer was not seeking to bring proceedings in an employment context, answer A is incorrect.

There are certain circumstances where police officers *may* be able to rely on their Convention rights, for example in *R (on the application of A and B)* v *HM Coroner for Inner South District of Greater London* [2004] EWCA Civ 1439, where the coroner refused to allow police officers to give evidence anonymously in a fatal shooting case. The Divisional Court held the risk of serious harm to the officers and their families was sufficient to engage Art. 2 and the coroner ought to have protected their anonymity.

General Police Duties, paras 4.5.3.6, 4.5.5

Answer 5.5

Answer **D** — The circumstances are similar to those in the case of *Osman* v *United Kingdom* (2000) 29 EHRR 245, where a man had been killed by a person who had become fixated with him. Although there the European Court of Human Rights dismissed the case, it examined the positive obligation of the State to protect life under Art. 2.

First, the positive obligation on the State to protect life is not an absolute one (and answer A is incorrect). Other factors should be taken into consideration, such as the source and degree of danger and the means available to combat it. The court said in *Osman* that it will be enough for the applicant to show that the authorities did not do all that could reasonably be expected of them to avoid a real and immediate risk to life of which they have or ought to have knowledge. Answer B is incorrect, as there is no need to show that the State actually saw the risk and failed to act upon it. Answer C is incorrect, as the 'reasonable person' test is not mentioned in this ruling.

General Police Duties, para. 4.5.5.2

Answer 5.6

Answer **A** — Under Art. 3 of the European Convention on Human Rights (right to freedom from torture), no person shall be subjected to torture or to inhuman or degrading treatment or punishment. The prohibition contained in Art. 3 of the European Convention on Human Rights is absolute and the treatment goes far beyond the traditional image of 'torture'. Included in this treatment are the following broad categories:

* torture—deliberate treatment leading to serious or cruel suffering;
* inhuman treatment—treatment resulting in intense suffering, both physical and mental;
* degrading treatment—treatment giving rise to fear and anguish in the victim, causing feelings of inferiority and humiliation.

It has been held by the European Commission of Human Rights that causing mental anguish without any physical assault could be a violation of Art. 3 (see *Denmark* v *Greece* [1969] 12 YB Eur Conv HR special vol.). Answer B is incorrect.

In *A & Others* v *Secretary of State for Home Department* [2005] 3 WLR 1249, it was held that, if on the balance of probabilities, it was concluded that any evidence had been obtained by torture then it should not be admitted. Answers C and D are therefore incorrect.

General Police Duties, para. 4.5.6

Answer 5.7

Answer **C** — Under Art. 5 of the European Convention on Human Rights, every person has the right to liberty and security of person. This is a qualified right, and exceptions are provided in Art. 5(1), allowing the lawful arrest in certain cases, where the procedure is prescribed by law.

Article 5(1)(e) provides that a person may be detained without his or her human rights being infringed where his or her detention is necessary 'for the prevention of the spreading of infectious diseases, of persons of unsound mind, alcoholics or drug addicts or vagrants'. However, the Convention itself does not provide a specific power of arrest for the above offences, and arresting officers would have to rely on existing legislation to detain a person (which is why answer C is correct and answers A, B and D are incorrect).

Article 5(1) merely sets out the conditions under which the State may remove a person's liberty. (In real terms, it is hard to imagine that the legislators intended to provide a power to arrest all people with infectious diseases, drug addicts, alcoholics and vagrants!)

General Police Duties, paras 4.5.7, 4.5.7.6

Answer 5.8

Answer **B** — Under Art. 5 of the European Convention on Human Rights, every person has the right to liberty and security of person. When it comes to unauthorised entry into the country and deportation/extradition matters, a detainee is *still* afforded protection by virtue of Art. 5(1)(f). Answer D is therefore incorrect.

However, the House of Lords has ruled that unlike Art. 5(1)(c), Art. 5(1)(f) does not require the detention to be necessary to be justified (see *R (on the application of Saadi and others)* v *Secretary of State for the Home Department* [2002] UKHL 41).

In that case it was held that the temporary detention of asylum seekers pending their application to remain in the United Kingdom was not unlawful simply by reason of it not being necessary. Answers A and C are therefore incorrect.

In *Owalabi* v *Court Number Four at the High Court of Justice in Spain* [2005] EWHC 2849 (Admin), it was held that where a person was being extradited to Spain, the hearing was entitled to conclude that the delay of over five years between the individual's arrest and their extradition did not render the extradition unjust or oppressive. Answer C is also incorrect for this reason.

General Police Duties, paras 4.5.7, 4.5.7.7, 4.5.7.8.

Answer 5.9

Answer **C** — 'Reasonable suspicion' will be assessed objectively and the court will look for 'the existence of facts or information which would satisfy an *objective observer* that the person may have committed the offence' (see *Fox* v *United Kingdom* (1991) 13 EHRR 157).

Answers A, B and D are therefore incorrect.

General Police Duties, para. 4.5.7.4

Answer 5.10

Answer **C** — Article 6(1) of the European Convention on Human Rights states that:

In the determination of his civil rights and obligations or of any criminal charge against him, everyone is entitled to a fair and public hearing within a reasonable time by an independent and impartial tribunal established by law.

Judgment shall be pronounced publicly but the press and public may be excluded from all or part of the trial in the interest of morals, public order or national security in a democratic society, where the interests of juveniles or the protection of the private life of the parties so require, or to the extent strictly necessary in the opinion of the court in special circumstances where publicity would prejudice the interests of justice.

Since there are several reasons for determining whether a case can be heard in private, answer D is incorrect.

Even where the press and/or the public have been excluded from all or part of the trial, the judgment must always be pronounced publicly (answer B is incorrect).

Finally, Art. 6(1) does not distinguish between civil and criminal cases; therefore, answer A is incorrect.

General Police Duties, para. 4.5.8

Answer 5.11

Answer **B** — Article 8 of the European Convention on Human Rights states:

1. Everyone has the right to respect for his private and family life, his home and his correspondence.
2. There shall be no interference by a public authority with the exercise of this right except such as is in accordance with the law and is necessary in a democratic society in the interests of national security, public safety or the economic wellbeing of the country, for the prevention of disorder or crime, for the protection of health or morals, or for the protection of the rights and freedoms of others.

The provisions of Art. 8 extend a right to respect for a person's correspondence (as well as their private life, family life and home). Answer C is incorrect.

Whilst the main aim of the Article is to protect these features of a person's life from arbitrary interference by 'public authorities', the State *does* have a positive obligation to prevent others from interfering with an individual's right to private life (see *Stjerna* v *Finland* (1994) 24 EHRR 194) and this duty extends beyond simply maintaining public safety. Answers A and D are therefore incorrect.

General Police Duties, para. 4.5.10

Answer 5.12

Answer **A** — Under Art. 10 of the European Convention on Human Rights, everyone has a right to freedom of expression. However, as with all aspects of human rights, this has to be balanced against other social needs. In the case of *Hutchinson* v *DPP*, The Independent, 20 November 2000, a conviction for criminal damage was upheld when it was decided that there were other ways in which the defendant could have expressed her opinions without committing a crime. Answer B is incorrect for this reason.

Because his actions were probably not proportionate, CLAYTON would not be able to use Art. 9 as a 'shield' for the same reasons as above (making answer C incorrect).

A person's belief, no matter how genuine, that his or her rights had been interfered with, will not provide an automatic defence to a criminal offence if that belief is not proportionate to the crime committed. Answer D is therefore incorrect.

General Police Duties, para. 4.5.11

Answer 5.13

Answer **C** — Under Art. 11 of the European Convention on Human Rights, everyone has the right to freedom of peaceful assembly. Therefore, the protestors had the right to protest, provided they were going about it peacefully. They do not appear to have interfered with the rights of the members of the hunt or the farm owner on these facts. Answer B is incorrect for this reason.

The State (or public authority) has two main obligations in these circumstances. In the first instance, it must not interfere with the protestors' rights to peaceful assembly. However, equally as important, it has a positive duty to prevent others from interfering with that right (which is why answer C is correct).

Therefore, even though the officers at the scene did not actively prevent the protest, arguably they should have acted to stop the marshals from doing so (which is why answers A and D are incorrect).

General Police Duties, para. 4.5.12

Answer 5.14

Answer **B** — First of all, we need to examine whether PUGACH had a right of occupation of the premises. The Criminal Law Act 1977, s. 7(1), states that:

> subject to the following provisions of this section and to section 12A(9) below, any person who is on any premises as a trespasser after having entered as such is guilty of an offence if he fails to leave those premises on being required to do so by or on behalf of—
>
> (a)   a displaced residential occupier of the premises; or
>
> (b)   an individual who is a protected intending occupier of the premises.

By obtaining written evidence that PUGACH was a protected intending occupier of the premises, the police could certainly have dealt with the squatters for a criminal offence.

However, the question mainly deals with the question of whether PUGACH's human rights were violated by the police's failure to take action on his behalf. Protocol 1, Art. 1 to the Convention states that every natural or legal person is entitled to the peaceful enjoyment of his possessions.

An example of how this right might be used against a public authority can be seen in *AO* v *Italy* (2001) 29 EHRR CD 92. In that case the Italian police were held to have violated the applicant's right to peaceful enjoyment of his property when they continually failed to send any officers to his flat, which he was trying to repossess from squatters. The above case shows that this right can be violated even in circumstances where the police have no direct contact with an individual's property (and answer A is incorrect).

Although the action for repossession in *AO* v *Italy* had been going on for over four years, the case also illustrates one way in which private law matters can become issues of liability for public authorities such as police services. Answer D is therefore incorrect.

Finally, this Protocol *does* cover premises and the term 'possessions' can be interpreted very widely and, under European case law, has extended to land, contractual rights and intellectual property. Answer C is therefore incorrect.

General Police Duties, paras 4.5.15, 4.16.9.5

6 | Powers of Arrest (including Code G Codes of Practice) and Other Policing Powers

STUDY PREPARATION

The areas covered in this chapter could hardly be more important. In practical terms, this chapter contains the police officer's tool kit—and if it is relevant in practice, it is highly relevant in preparing for an examination or course of study.

In deciding what to do in any given situation, it is vital that you know what you are *empowered* to do. Following on from the previous chapter, it is also important to realise that each police power equals a reduction of, or interference with, someone's human rights. As holders of such powers, police officers are under a duty to exercise them properly—lawfully, proportionately and fairly.

The Serious Organised Crime and Police Act 2005 introduced extensive changes to policing powers, in respect of arrest and detention, with particular emphasis on the 'necessity' test to be applied before arrests are made, and the abolition of 'arrestable offences'.

QUESTIONS

Question 6.1

PERRY entered a large retail clothing shop and whilst being watched by IQBAL, a store detective, PERRY hid a pair of jeans in her carrier bag. PERRY left the store without paying and was stopped outside by IQBAL. IQBAL decided that it was necessary to arrest PERRY for theft.

Does IQBAL have to inform PERRY of the grounds for the arrest, under s. 28 of the Police and Criminal Evidence Act 1984?

A Yes, unless it is made impracticable by her escaping arrest before the information could be given.

B No, IQBAL would only have to inform PERRY of the fact that she was under arrest.

C No, s. 28 applies to police officers only.

D Yes, unless it is impracticable due to her condition or behaviour.

Question 6.2

Section 24 of the Police and Criminal Evidence Act 1984 describes circumstances in which a constable may arrest a person where it is necessary to do so.

In which of the following circumstances might it be necessary for a constable to arrest a person who has provided his or her name?

A Where the constable has reasonable grounds for suspecting that the person has not given his or her real name.

B Where the constable knows that the person has not given his or her real name.

C Where the constable has reasonable grounds for believing that the person has not given his or her real name.

D Where the constable has reasonable grounds for doubting that the person has given his or her real name.

Question 6.3

Constable POTTER was called to a domestic disturbance at the home of HENDERSON and LeBOW. On the officer's arrival, HENDERSON was shouting loudly at LeBOW and making threats. Constable POTTER arrested HENDERSON for a breach of the peace and HENDERSON began struggling violently. Constable POTTER later recorded the facts in a pocket notebook, noting that HENDERSON had not been cautioned at the time of the arrest because of the violent struggle.

Which of the following statements is correct in relation to the requirement to caution a person, according to Code C, para. 10.4 of the PACE Codes of Practice?

A There was no requirement for Constable POTTER to caution HENDERSON at the time of arrest, because of her behaviour.

B There was no requirement for Constable POTTER to caution HENDERSON at the time of arrest, because she was not being arrested for an offence.

C Constable POTTER was required to caution HENDERSON at the time of arrest, because she was not in the process of escaping from the officer.

D There was no requirement for Constable POTTER to caution HENDERSON at the time of arrest, because of her behaviour; however, the officer was required to caution her as soon as practicable afterwards.

Question 6.4

POINTER entered an off-licence with another man and they stood near the wine display. The two left without buying anything. However, the owner, STROUD, noticed that three bottles of wine were missing. STROUD checked the CCTV, which showed POINTER and the other man removing the bottles of wine, but they had their backs to the camera and it was unclear which of the two had actually taken the wine. STROUD had placed the bottles on display before the men had entered the shop and no other customers had been in since that time, and the bottles were now missing. STROUD saw POINTER alone in the street the next day; he was just around the corner from the local police station at the time he saw him.

Does STROUD have a power to arrest POINTER for theft in these circumstances?

A No, POINTER was not actually in the act of committing an indictable offence.

B No, as it is reasonably practicable for a police officer to make the arrest if necessary.

C Yes, as an indictable offence had been committed and STROUD has reasonable grounds for suspecting that POINTER is guilty.

D Yes, as an indictable offence had been committed and STROUD has reasonable grounds to believe that POINTER is guilty.

Question 6.5

Constable FRENCH, an officer from Dumfries and Galloway Constabulary, was pursuing a vehicle which was stolen from the Dumfries and Galloway Constabulary area. The vehicle crossed the Scottish border into Cumbria Constabulary's area, in England, where it eventually stopped. Before officers from Cumbria Constabulary arrived at the scene, Constable FRENCH arrested the driver, KELLEY.

What action should now be taken, in respect of KELLEY?

A KELLEY must be taken to the nearest designated station in Scotland, where the original offence took place.

B KELLEY must be taken to the nearest designated station in England, where the arrest took place.

C KELLEY must be taken to the nearest designated station in Scotland or to the nearest designated police station in England.

D KELLEY should be further arrested by an officer from Cumbria Constabulary and be taken to the nearest designated station in England.

Question 6.6

DC SHARPE was interviewing HUNTER for a burglary. The officer suspected that HUNTER had committed more than one burglary, but only had reasonable grounds to arrest him for the one offence. In the interview, HUNTER provided DC SHARPE with reasonable grounds to suspect he should be arrested for two other offences. At that time, the officer made a decision that HUNTER would be further arrested for those offences, but not until after the interview. HUNTER was actually arrested for the further offences two hours after the interview concluded.

Considering s. 31 of the Police and Criminal Evidence Act 1984, which of the following statements is correct in relation to the timing of HUNTER's arrest?

A HUNTER should have been arrested when DC SHARPE had reasonable grounds to suspect him of further offences; the officer has acted unlawfully.

B HUNTER should have been arrested when DC SHARPE made the decision to arrest him for the further offences; the officer has acted unlawfully.

C HUNTER should have been arrested before the end of the interview; the officer has acted unlawfully.

D DC SHARPE has acted lawfully; there was no requirement to arrest HUNTER before the officer did so.

Question 6.7

Constable SHAW was searching in the vicinity of a recent burglary, when she saw CARSON, who matched the description of the suspect. The officer arrested CARSON and radioed for transport. While they were waiting, CARSON told Constable SHAW that he could not have committed the burglary, as he was at home at the time. The transport was being driven by SANTOS, a designated Escort Officer. Constable SHAW asked SANTOS to take CARSON to his home address, while she attended there in her own vehicle, to check out his alibi. There was no reply at the address and SANTOS then took CARSON to the station.

Which of the following statements is correct in relation to s. 30(10) of the Police and Criminal Evidence Act 1984 (delay in taking an arrested person to a police station)?

A The delay in taking CARSON to the station was unlawful; SANTOS only has the authority to convey a person directly to a police station.

B The delay in taking CARSON to the station was lawful, provided the investigation into his alibi was conducted immediately.

C The delay in taking CARSON to the station was lawful, provided the investigation into his alibi was conducted as soon as reasonably practicable.

D The delay in taking CARSON to the station was unlawful; checking out an alibi would not amount to an 'investigation' as permitted under s. 30.

Question 6.8

Inspector TORRES is working a night shift and has been informed that the custody officer has reported sick. Inspector TORRES has made inquiries with neighbouring areas but no other sergeants are available to act as custody officer. There are five detainees in the cells. Inspector TORRES has asked Constable AVERY to return to the station urgently to act as custody officer. Constable AVERY is an experienced officer and is qualified to the rank of sergeant.

Has Inspector TORRES acted correctly by requiring Constable AVERY to act as the custody officer?

A Yes, as no other custody officer is available.

B No, Inspector TORRES should contact a superintendent, who may authorise Constable AVERY to act as custody officer.

C No, the custody office should be closed down and the detainees transferred to another custody office, as no other sergeant is available.

D Yes, provided no superintendent is available to make the decision and a custody officer is required urgently.

Question 6.9

SPEARS is aged 14 and has been issued with a disorder penalty notice under s. 2 of the Criminal Justice and Police Act 2001 for throwing fireworks on a main road.

Who would be liable for paying the fine attached to such a notice, should SPEARS accept liability for this offence?

A SPEARS only, as the person responsible for the offence.
B SPEARS' parent or guardian, because of her age.
C Either SPEARS or her parent or guardian.
D Neither SPEARS nor her parent or guardian; she should not have been issued with a notice because of her age.

Question 6.10

ADAMS has been removed from a shopping centre under s. 136(1) of the Mental Health Act 1983 and brought to a police station. As a result of a phone call, the custody officer has discovered that no one is available to attend the custody office to examine ADAMS for at least four hours. The custody officer is considering whether or not ADAMS should be taken to a nearby hospital, which has appropriately trained staff to assess people with mental health problems.

What options are available to the custody officer in these circumstances?
A ADAMS must be detained at the custody office, the point where she first arrived at a place of safety.
B ADAMS may be removed to the hospital and detained for up to 72 hours from the time she arrives there.
C ADAMS may be removed to the hospital and detained for up to 72 hours from the time of her removal from a public place.
D ADAMS may be removed to the hospital and detained for up to 72 hours from the time she arrived at the police station.

Question 6.11

Magistrates have issued a warrant under s. 135(1) of the Mental Health Act 1985 in relation to SHORT, whose family has been concerned that his mental health has deteriorated significantly recently. The warrant authorises SHORT to be removed to a place of safety.

Which of the following statements is correct, in relation to the execution of the warrant issued by the court?
A The warrant must be executed by a constable, who must be accompanied either by a mental health professional or a registered medical practitioner.
B The warrant must be executed either by a mental health professional or a registered medical practitioner, who may ask for a constable to be present if there is reason to believe SHORT may become violent.

C The warrant may be executed either by a constable or a mental health professional, who must be accompanied by a registered medical practitioner.

D The warrant must be executed by a constable, who must be accompanied by a mental health professional and a registered medical practitioner.

Question 6.12

Constable McHENRY was on patrol and came across an elderly man who had fallen and possibly broken an ankle, being cared for by HAMILTON, a paramedic. The person appeared confused and didn't know where he was. HAMILTON wanted to take him to hospital but he refused to go, stating he wanted to go home. Constable McHENRY and HAMILTON discussed the possibility of forcibly taking the person to hospital to prevent him from coming to further harm.

Considering the Mental Capacity Act 2005, which of the following statements is correct?

A Only Constable McHENRY could make this decision, provided she reasonably believed it was in the person's best interests and that he lacked the capacity to make the decision himself.

B Only HAMILTON could make this decision, provided she reasonably believed it was in the person's best interests.

C Either Constable McHENRY or HAMILTON could make this decision, provided they reasonably believed it was in the person's best interests.

D Either Constable McHENRY or HAMILTON could make this decision, provided they reasonably believed it was in the person's best interests and that he lacked the capacity to make the decision himself.

Question 6.13

Constable ROBERTS attended a large retail store, where the occupants of a green 4×4 vehicle had been captured on closed circuit television (CCTV) as they entered the store and stole two bottles of wine from within. The vehicle was seen to make off immediately prior to Constable ROBERTS's arrival. Constable ROBERTS contacted the control room and asked the duty sergeant to authorise an urgent road check, under s. 4 of the Police and Criminal Evidence Act 1984, for the vehicle and its occupants.

Can the officer's request be granted in these circumstances?

A Yes, but Constable ROBERTS could have authorised the road check himself.

B Yes, provided the sergeant authorises it.

C No, only an inspector may authorise a road check in urgent circumstances.

D No, only a superintendent may authorise a road check in any circumstances.

Question 6.14

Superintendent HAYES has provided written authorisation for a road check to take place. Officers in Superintendent HAYES' area are investigating a case of causing death by dangerous driving and the suspect was believed to have driven away from the scene without stopping in a red Nissan motor vehicle. The superintendent has authorised that all red vehicles of a similar size and colour are to be stopped at the location of the incident, at the approximate time of day, for the next seven days. No useful information was gleaned during the initial period of seven days and the officer in the case has asked Superintendent HAYES to extend the period.

If Superintendent HAYES agrees to extend this period, what would be the maximum period that may be granted beyond the initial seven days?

A One further period of seven days.

B Two further periods of seven days.

C Three further periods of seven days, to a maximum period of 28 days.

D Unlimited period, provided the authorisations are for seven days at a time.

Question 6.15

Detective Constables COPE and FRIEDEL received information from NEWMAN, a security guard at a private flying club based in a small airport, who suspected the importation of drugs was taking place. NEWMAN stated that every Saturday morning, a car attended the club and met a light aircraft and people loaded packages into the car. They tasked NEWMAN to keep an eye out and one Saturday, NEWMAN called them, reporting the car was at the airport. On their arrival, they saw WILLARD standing near the suspected car.

What powers, if any, did the officers have to search WILLARD or the car, in these circumstances, utilising powers under s. 24B of the Aviation Security Act 1982?

A None, they were not in uniform.

B None, the power relates to searching aircraft only.

C They may search WILLARD and the vehicle.

D None, this Act relates to commercial airports, not private ones.

ANSWERS

Answer 6.1

Answer **A** — Section 28(1) of the Police and Criminal Evidence Act 1984 states that subject to subs. (5) below, where a person is arrested, otherwise than by being informed that he or she is under arrest, the arrest is not lawful unless the person arrested is informed that he or she is under arrest as soon as is practicable after his or her arrest.

Under s. 28(3), subject to subs. (5) below, no arrest is lawful unless the person arrested is informed of the ground for the arrest at the time of, or as soon as is practicable after, the arrest. This subsection applies to arrests made by members of the public as well as police officers; therefore, answers B and C are incorrect.

Section 28(5) states that nothing in this section is to be taken to require a person to be informed—

(a) that he or she is under arrest; or

(b) of the ground for the arrest,

if it was not reasonably practicable for him or her to be so informed by reason of his or her having escaped from arrest before the information could be given.

Answer D is therefore incorrect.

General Police Duties, para. 4.6.2.1

Answer 6.2

Answer **D** — Under s. 24(5) of the Police and Criminal Evidence Act 1984 the officer must have 'reasonable grounds for doubting' that the name furnished by the relevant person is his or her real name. This would appear to be a very wide expression, and is not limited to suspecting that the name given is false, and therefore answers A, B and C are incorrect. However the officer is required to show that he/she has reasonable grounds for believing that the details given are in doubt. These must be objective grounds and not just simple opinion on the part of the officer.

General Police Duties, para. 4.6.4.4

Answer 6.3

Answer **A** — Code C, para. 10.4 of the PACE Codes of Practice requires that a person must be cautioned on arrest or further arrest. However, there is no longer a requirement that the arrest be for an 'offence'. Answer B is incorrect, because a person must be cautioned whether they are being arrested for an offence or not (such as for a breach of the peace).

There are exceptions to the requirement to administer the caution and these are:

- where it is impracticable to do so by reason of the person's condition or behaviour at the time; or
- where he/she has already been cautioned immediately before the arrest in accordance with Code C, para. 10.1 (requirement to caution where there are grounds to suspect commission of an offence).

Section 28(5) of PACE allows that a person need not be informed of the reason or grounds for their arrest if it was not reasonably practicable by reason of his/her having escaped from arrest before the information could be given. However, this exception is not listed in Code C, para. 10.4, which relates to cautions. Answer C is incorrect.

There is nothing in Code C requiring a person to be cautioned as soon as practicable after their arrest, if they were not cautioned at the time and answer D is incorrect.

General Police Duties, para. 4.6.5

Answer 6.4

Answer **B** — Under s. 24A of the Police and Criminal Evidence Act 1984 certain powers of arrest are provided for any person. Section 24A states:

(1) A person other than a constable may arrest without a warrant—
   (a) anyone who is in the act of committing an indictable offence;
   (b) anyone whom he has reasonable grounds for suspecting to be committing an indictable offence.

(2) Where an indictable offence has been committed, a person other than a constable may arrest without a warrant—
   (a) anyone who is guilty of the offence;
   (b) anyone whom he has reasonable grounds for suspecting to be guilty of it.

(3) But the power of summary arrest conferred by subsection (1) or (2) is exercisable only if—

    (a) the person making the arrest has reasonable grounds for believing that for any of the reasons mentioned in subsection (4) it is necessary to arrest the person in question; and

    (b) it appears to the person making the arrest that it is not reasonably practicable for a constable to make it instead.

(4) The reasons are to prevent the person in question—

    (a) causing physical injury to himself or any other person;

    (b) suffering physical injury;

    (c) causing loss of or damage to property; or

    (d) making off before a constable can assume responsibility for him.

The power is not limited to the time an indictable offence is actually being committed (answer A is therefore incorrect), but extends to where an indictable offence has been committed and there are reasonable grounds to 'suspect' (not the higher test of 'believe') a person of that offence; answer D is therefore incorrect.

However, note the element in s. 24A(3)(b) on the practicality of a constable making the arrest; being just round the corner from the police station it is unlikely that STROUD could say it was not reasonably practicable. This means it would be wrong for him to use his powers under s. 24A; answer C is therefore incorrect.

However were an officer to be called to arrest, they would have to ensure that the 'necessity test' was passed (as outlined in s. 24(5) of the 1984 Act) prior to their making such an arrest.

General Police Duties, paras 4.6.7

Answer 6.5

Answer **C** — The Criminal Justice and Public Order Act 1994 (ss. 136 to 140) makes provision for officers from one part of the United Kingdom to go into another part of the United Kingdom to arrest someone there in connection with an offence committed within their jurisdiction, and gives them powers to search on arrest.

A Scottish officer may arrest someone suspected of committing an offence in Scotland who is found in England, Wales or Northern Ireland if it would have been lawful to arrest that person had he or she been found in Scotland. Since this power is granted to Constable FRENCH, there is no requirement for an officer from an English police force to further arrest KELLEY and answer D is incorrect.

Where a Scottish officer has arrested someone suspected of committing an offence in Scotland, who is found in England, the officer must take the person to the nearest convenient designated police station in Scotland *or* to the nearest convenient designated police station in England or Wales (see s. 137(7)).

Section 137(7) goes on to say that the person must be taken to the police station as soon as reasonably practicable. This would suggest that the arrested person should be taken to the nearest police station if the distance to one or another is too great. Since the arresting officer has a choice of police stations, answers A and B are incorrect.

General Police Duties, para. 4.6.8.5

Answer 6.6

Answer **D** — Section 31 of the Police and Criminal Evidence Act 1984 states that where:

(a) a person—
    (i) has been arrested for an offence; and
    (ii) is at a police station in consequence of that arrest; and
(b) it appears to a constable that, if he were released from that arrest, he would be liable to arrest for some other offence,

he shall be arrested for that other offence.

In *R v Samuel* (1988) 87 Cr App R 232, the Court of Appeal said that the purpose of the s. 31 requirement was to prevent the release and immediate re-arrest of an offender—therefore, the court noted, s. 31 did not prevent any further arrest from being delayed until the release of the prisoner for the initial arrest was imminent.

Therefore, there was no requirement to arrest HUNTER at any time before he was actually arrested. The only obligation under s. 31 is that the person should not be released from police detention and then re-arrested, when there were sufficient grounds to arrest him/her before he or she was released. Answers A, B and C are therefore incorrect.

General Police Duties, para. 4.6.10

Answer 6.7

Answer **B** — Section 30(10) of the Police and Criminal Evidence Act 1984 allows a police officer to delay taking an arrested person to a police station where his/her presence elsewhere is necessary in order to carry out such investigations as it is reasonable to carry out *immediately*. This was confirmed in the case of *R v Kerawalla* [1991] Crim LR 451, when it was decided that the delay permitted under s. 30(10) will only apply if the matter requires *immediate* investigation; if it can wait, the exception will not apply and the person must be taken straight to a police station. Answer C is incorrect.

The provisions allowing a delay in taking the prisoner to a police station (s. 30(10)) will also apply to any exercise of the powers by a designated Escort Officer (see the Police Reform Act 2002, sch. 4, pt 4). Answer A is incorrect.

Taking an arrested person to check out an alibi before going to a police station may be justified in some circumstances (see *Dallison* v *Caffery* [1965] 1 QB 348). Answer D is incorrect.

Note that where there is such a delay, the reasons for it must be recorded when the person first arrives at the police station (s. 30(11)).

General Police Duties, para. 4.6.11

Answer 6.8

Answer **A** — Under s. 36(3) of the Police and Criminal Evidence Act 1984, custody officers must be appointed and be of at least the rank of sergeant.

However, under s. 36(4), an officer of any rank may perform the functions of a custody officer at a designated police station if a custody officer is not readily available to perform them. The case of *Vince* v *Chief Constable of Dorset Police* [1993] 1 WLR 415, made it clear that this should only be an exception. Answer C is incorrect.

There is nothing in s. 36(4) stating that a person performing the function in these circumstances must be authorised (whether by an inspector or a superintendent). Answers B and D are incorrect.

General Police Duties, para. 4.6.13

Answer 6.9

Answer **B** — Under s. 2 of the Act, a disorder penalty notice may be issued to a person who is 10 years or over, where there is reason to believe the person has committed a s. 1 offence (previously the age limit was 16 years). Answer D is therefore incorrect.

Where the recipient of a notice is under 16, the relevant chief officer of police must notify such parent or guardian as he/she sees fit (see Penalties for Disorderly Behaviour (Amendment of Minimum Age) Order 2004 (SI 2004/3166)). Where a parent or guardian of a young penalty recipient is notified in this way, then they are liable to pay the penalty under the original notice (see art. 5). Answers A and C are therefore incorrect.

General Police Duties, paras 4.6.14, 4.6.14.2

Answer 6.10

Answer **D** — Under s. 136(1) of the Mental Health Act 1983, if a constable finds in a place to which the public have access a person who appears to him to be suffering from mental disorder and to be in immediate need of care or control, the constable may, if he or she thinks it necessary to do so in the interests of that person or for the protection of other persons, remove that person to a place of safety. Places of safety are defined under s. 135(6) and generally include hospitals and other medical premises. Police stations are also included; however, Home Office Circular 07/2008 states that police stations should only be used as a place of safety in exceptional circumstances, for example where the person's behaviour would pose an unmanageably high risk to other patients, staff or users of a health care setting.

Under s. 136(2) of the Act, a person removed to a place of safety under this section may be detained there for a period not exceeding 72 hours for the purpose of enabling him/her to be examined by a registered medical practitioner and to be interviewed by an approved social worker and of making any necessary arrangements for his treatment or care. The 72 hours is calculated from the time of the person's arrival at a place of safety. Answer C is incorrect.

The Mental Health Act 2007 amended the 1983 Act, so that a person may be transferred from one place of safety to another (see s. 136(3) and (4)) and answer A is incorrect. However, their detention is subject to an overall time limit of 72 hours. When a person is transferred in these circumstances, the time will be calculated from the time they arrived at the first place of safety, and answer B is incorrect.

General Police Duties, para. 4.6.15.1

Answer 6.11

Answer **D** — Under s. 135(1) of the Mental Health Act 1985, where there is reasonable cause to suspect that a person believed to be suffering from a mental disorder—

(a) has been, or is being ill-treated or neglected, or

(b) is unable to care for himself/herself and is living alone,

a warrant may be issued by a magistrate authorising a *constable* to enter any premises specified and to remove the person to a place of safety. Answers B and C are incorrect.

In doing so, the officer *must* be accompanied by an approved mental health professional and a registered medical practitioner. Answer A is incorrect.

General Police Duties, para. 4.6.15.2

Answer 6.12

Answer **D** — Section 5 of the Mental Capacity Act 2005, states:

(1) If a person (D) does an act in connection with the care or treatment of another person (P), the act is one to which this section applies if—

    (a) before doing the act, D takes reasonable steps to establish whether P lacks capacity in relation to the matter in question, and

    (b) when doing the act, D reasonably believes—

        (i) that P lacks clarity in relation to the matter and

        (ii) that it will be in P's best interests for the act to be done.

(2) D does not incur any liability in relation to the act that he would not have incurred if P—

    (a) had had capacity to consent in relation to the matter, and

    (b) had consented to D's doing the act.

The Act was brought into force to provide a statutory framework to empower and protect vulnerable people who are not able to make their own decisions. It covers a wide range of decisions in all areas of life and provides protection from legal liability for acts done in connection with care and treatment if done in a person's best interests and in keeping with the Act. Importantly, it can provide police officers with a power to act in a person's best interests, effectively as if they had the person's consent, although the power is not just given to police officers, but anyone acting in the person's best interest; answers A and B are therefore incorrect.

Section 5(1)(b) is clear that before making a decision to remove such a person, he or she must reasonably believe that the person lacks clarity in relation to the matter *and* that it will be in their best interests for the act to be done. Since both tests must apply, answers B and C are incorrect.

Note that s. 6 of the Act places a further responsibility on the person acting under s. 5 to apply a necessity test to the removal (s. 6(2)), to consider whether such a response is proportionate to the likelihood of them suffering harm (s. 6(3)(a)) and the seriousness of that harm (s. 6(3)(b)).

General Police Duties, para. 4.6.15.5

Answer 6.13

Answer **A** — Section 4 of the Police and Criminal Evidence Act 1984 states that a road check may be authorised only where the officer has reasonable grounds for believing that the offence committed is an indictable offence. Therefore, as the offence is one of shoplifting, which is indictable, a road check can be authorised. Generally speaking an officer of at least the rank of superintendent must authorise a road check.

In urgent cases the authorising officer may be any rank below the rank of superintendent, and in this case Constable ROBERTS could have authorised the check provided a written record is made and a superintendent informed as soon as possible; answers B, C and D are therefore incorrect as the officer could have authorised the road check himself.

General Police Duties, para. 4.6.16

Answer 6.14

Answer **D** — Section 4 of the Police and Criminal Evidence Act 1984 states that a road check may be authorised only where the officer has reasonable grounds for believing that the offence committed is an indictable offence. Generally the authorisation will be given by a superintendent; however, an officer of any rank may authorise the road check in urgent circumstances.

Section 4(11)(a) states that the authorising officer must specify a period, not exceeding seven days, during which the road check may continue. This period may be either continuous, or conducted at specified times during that period. If it appears to a superintendent that the road check ought to continue beyond the initial seven days, he/she may authorise a further period of seven days during which it may continue. There is no limit as to how many road checks may be authorised, provided each period does not exceed seven days. Answers A, B and C are therefore incorrect.

General Police Duties, para. 4.6.16.1

Answer 6.15

Answer **C** — Under s. 24B of the Aviation Security Act 1982 (policing of airports or aerodromes), a police constable may stop and search, without warrant, any person, vehicle or aircraft in any area of an airport (excluding a dwelling house). Answer B is therefore incorrect.

6. Powers of Arrest and Other Policing Powers

The search may be conducted if the constable has reasonable grounds to suspect that he or she will find stolen or prohibited articles. There is no mention of the constable having to be in uniform; therefore, answer A is incorrect.

The term aerodrome, as defined by s. 38(1) of the 1982 Act, is used rather than airport, as it has a wider meaning and covers major airports as well as airfields used only by private flying clubs. Answer D is incorrect.

General Police Duties, para. 4.6.17

7 | Stop and Search

STUDY PREPARATION

One of the main functions of the police service is to prevent and detect crime. A key power given to police officers is the ability to stop and search individuals, or the vehicles they are in, to establish whether they are in possession of articles which are either stolen, or which may be used to commit crimes.

The police service has for years struggled to strike a balance between a pro-active approach to the use of these powers for the above reasons, and a proportionate response to the needs of our diverse communities.

The Police and Criminal Evidence Act 1984 (PACE) and the accompanying Codes of Practice provide the main legislative basis for police officers' use of stop and search powers; it is for line managers to ensure that they are used proportionately and in a non-discriminatory manner.

This chapter also covers the extended search powers available under the Aviation Security Act 1982, the Criminal Justice and Public Order Act 1994 and the Terrorism Act 2000.

QUESTIONS

Question 7.1

Constable MULLER was on patrol one evening when he saw KELLS, aged 15. Constable MULLER was aware that KELLS was a divisional target suspected of committing several burglaries, none of which could be proved. Constable MULLER intended stopping and searching KELLS; however, he had no particular reason to suspect that he might be in possession of stolen or prohibited articles. Constable MULLER stopped KELLS and spoke to him, eventually obtaining his consent to submit to a search. The search proved negative.

Were the officer's actions legal in these circumstances?

A No, because of KELLS' age.

B Yes, provided Constable MULLER submits a search form.

C No, regardless of KELLS' age.

D Yes, and a search form need not be submitted.

Question 7.2

Constable AMIR was on patrol looking for a person who had committed theft from a vehicle. Witnesses had given a description of the person responsible, who they said was carrying a screwdriver. Constable AMIR discovered JACKSON, who matched the description, in the front garden of a house. JACKSON lived some three miles away from the house.

Would Constable AMIR have the power to search JACKSON for the screwdriver in these circumstances?

A No, as JACKSON was in the garden of a dwelling.

B Yes, as JACKSON was not inside a dwelling.

C No, as JACKSON was not in a public place.

D Yes, as JACKSON was not in his own garden.

Question 7.3

Constable TALLAC was on patrol when he heard a message on his radio describing a male person who had broken into a car. The description had been given by an anonymous caller to the control room. Constable TALLAC saw PEARSON walking along the street and realised that his clothing was similar to that of the person described in the radio message. Constable TALLAC intended stopping PEARSON in order to search him for prohibited articles.

Would Constable TALLAC be entitled to search PEARSON, based on the information from the radio message alone?

A No, anonymous information would not provide reasonable grounds for suspicion to conduct the search.

B Yes, provided a reasonable person would think that there were reasonable grounds for suspicion to conduct the search.

C No, the anonymous information would amount to hearsay, which would not provide reasonable grounds for suspicion to conduct the search.

D Yes, regardless of whether a reasonable person would think that there were reasonable grounds for suspicion to conduct the search.

Question 7.4

A football match is due to take place in Inspector CARTER's area, and she is the officer in charge of a support unit positioned outside the train station. Intelligence has suggested that approximately 200 away supporters will be arriving, and staff on the train have reported seeing several weapons being carried by fans. Inspector CARTER is considering searching all supporters before they leave the train station.

In relation to the powers to authorise searches under s. 60 of the Criminal Justice and Public Order Act 1994, which statement is correct?

A The inspector may authorise the searches, but only if she suspects there will be incidents involving serious violence.

B The inspector may authorise the searches, but only of those suspected of carrying weapons.

C The inspector may authorise the search of any of the fans, in these circumstances alone.

D The inspector may not authorise the searches; this power is restricted to superintendents.

Question 7.5

A disturbance occurred in the Horse and Groom public house on a Friday evening, when rival bikers from the nearby Swan public house attended to confront bikers from the Horse and Groom. Two bikers from the Horse and Groom were attacked with a sword, sustaining serious injuries. The incident was not reported to the police; however, a call was received from the hospital the next morning reporting that the two bikers were in a critical condition. Information was received that the bikers from the Swan were gathering at their pub that afternoon, intending to return to the Horse and Groom that night. Superintendent GRADY, the on-call senior officer for the area, was approached by Inspector BRUNMAN to discuss a planned operation to attend the Swan to search any persons there for the weapon.

Would Superintendent GRADY be able to authorise searches at the Swan public house, under s. 60(1) of the Criminal Justice and Public Order Act 1994, in these circumstances?

A Yes, but only if it is believed further incidents of serious violence will take place in the locality.

B No, as this is a preventative power, Superintendent GRADY could only authorise s. 60 powers to search anyone approaching the Horse and Groom.

C Yes, provided it is intended that the searches will take place within 24 hours of the original incident.

D Yes, provided the Horse and Groom and the Swan public houses are in the locality covered by Superintendent GRADY.

Question 7.6

Constable WILLIS was on patrol in uniform in the early hours of the morning in an area where there had recently been outbreaks of serious public disorder between two gangs, who were known to carry weapons. An order was in force, under s. 60 of the Criminal Justice and Public Order Act 1994, to stop and search persons in the locality. Constable WILLIS saw MOORE walking in the street wearing a ski mask, which was concealing his face.

In what circumstances could Constable WILLIS ask MOORE to remove his mask?

A If he reasonably believed that MOORE was likely to be involved in violence.

B No further circumstances are required, as an order is in force under s. 60.

C If he reasonably believed that MOORE was attempting to conceal his identity.

D If he reasonably believed that MOORE was carrying a dangerous instrument or an offensive weapon.

Question 7.7

Section 44 of the Terrorism Act 2000 provides a power for the police to authorise stop and search operations, in order to prevent acts of terrorism. In certain circumstances, police community support officers (PCSOs) may be utilised to assist in such operations.

What restrictions, if any, are placed on PCSOs, when exercising their powers under s. 44?

A They must be accompanied by a police officer; they have the power to stop and search pedestrians or vehicles.

B They may stop and search both pedestrians and vehicles, while on their own, or while accompanied by a police officer.

C They must be accompanied by a police officer; they have no power to stop persons or vehicles, but may assist officers to conduct searches.

D They must be accompanied and supervised by a police officer; they have the power to stop and search pedestrians or vehicles.

Question 7.8

Constable SAXTON stopped and searched KELLY, using powers under s. 1 of the Police and Criminal Evidence Act 1984, whilst on foot patrol in the early hours of the morning. It was the middle of winter at the time of the stop and it was pouring with rain. KELLY had been stopped previously by the police and requested that Constable SAXTON make a record of the search there and then and asked for a copy.

What does Code A, para. 3 of the Codes of Practice state, about making a written record of the search?

A Constable SAXTON must make a record at the time, if it is reasonably practicable to do so.

B Constable SAXTON must make a record at the time, unless it is wholly impracticable to do so.

C Constable SAXTON must make a record at the time; there are no exceptions.

D Constable SAXTON must make a record at the time, unless KELLY is drunk, violent or likely to become violent.

Question 7.9

Constable NORTON has arrested BLOOM for possession of Class A drugs, following a successful stop and search. BLOOM has now been taken to a designated police station and is being booked in by the custody officer.

Which of the following statements is correct, in respect of the details which must be recorded on BLOOM's custody record?

A Constable NORTON must complete a search form and make sure the details of the search are noted on BLOOM's custody record.

B Constable NORTON must complete a search form and the custody officer must make sure the details of the search are noted on BLOOM's custody record.

C Constable NORTON must make sure that the search record forms part of BLOOM's custody record; there is no requirement to complete a separate form.

D Either Constable NORTON or the custody officer may ensure that the search record forms part of BLOOM's custody record; there is no requirement to complete a separate form.

Question 7.10

Constable LIPINSKI conducted a stop and search of GRANTHAM, who was driving a motor vehicle on a road, and the vehicle itself. The officer correctly provided GRANTHAM with a copy of the stop/search form. GRANTHAM was not the owner of the vehicle and indicated that MORLING, the actual owner, would probably wish to have a copy at some stage.

Which of the following statements is correct, in relation to MORLING being allowed a copy of the stop/search record?

A If MORLING requests a copy, one should be provided within three months of the date of the search.

B MORLING is not entitled to a copy; Constable LIPINSKI has correctly supplied GRANTHAM with one as the driver of the vehicle and the person searched.

C MORLING must be provided with a copy within three months of the date of the search.

D If MORLING requests a copy, one should be provided within 12 months of the date of the search.

Question 7.11

Constable BAIRD attended a suspicious incident reported by POOLE, a closed circuit television (CCTV) operator. POOLE saw two men acting suspiciously near a four-wheel-drive vehicle, and saw one of the men hand the other a bag of white powder. He believed the bag was placed inside the cover of the spare wheel attached to the rear door of the vehicle. As a result of this information, Constable BAIRD searched the spare wheel, but found nothing inside.

Is Constable BAIRD required to supply a notice of this search, under s. 2 of the Police and Criminal Evidence Act 1984?

A Yes, it should be placed on the vehicle, and a copy sent to the registered owner.

B No, a notice is not required as the inside of the vehicle was not searched.

C Yes, it should be placed inside the vehicle, which may be entered by force to do so.

D Yes, a notice must be placed somewhere on the vehicle.

ANSWERS

Answer 7.1

Answer **C** — The officer did not have the grounds to conduct a search in these circumstances. Code A, para. 1.5 provides that:

> An officer must not search a person, even with his or her consent, where no power to search is applicable. Even where a person is prepared to submit to a search voluntarily, the person must not be searched unless the necessary legal power exists, and the search must be in accordance with the relevant power and the provisions of this Code. The only exception, where an officer does not require a specific power, applies to searches of persons entering sports grounds or other premises carried out with their consent given as a condition of entry.

Answers B and D are incorrect, regardless of whether the officer submits a search form. Section 1 makes no mention of an age limit in relation to searches.

The search was unlawful because of the above reasons, and not the person's age, making answer A incorrect.

General Police Duties, para. 4.7.3

Answer 7.2

Answer **D** — Powers to stop, search and seize are essentially intended for use in public places, meaning places to which the public, or any section of the public, has access, on payment or otherwise, as of right or by virtue of express or implied permission, or any other place to which people have ready access at the time when it is proposed to exercise the powers but which is not a dwelling (s. 1(1)(a) and (b) of the Police and Criminal Evidence Act 1984).

However, although powers to stop and search may not be exercised in a dwelling house, they may be exercised in a garden or yard of a house (s. 1(4) and (5)), provided it is not the person's own garden, and the officer has reasonable grounds for believing that he or she does not have permission (express or implied) to be there.

Therefore, although the search could not take place under s. 1(1)(b), the officer may use powers available under s. 1(4) and (5) as JACKSON was not in his own garden. For these reasons answers A, B and C are incorrect.

General Police Duties, para. 4.7.4.2

Answer 7.3

Answer **B** — In order to conduct a search under s. 1 of the Police and Criminal Evidence Act 1984, a constable must have 'reasonable grounds for suspecting' that he or she will find the required articles as a result of the search. Suspicion has been described as 'a state of conjecture or surmise when proof is lacking' (*Shaabin Bin Hussein* v *Chong Fook Kam* [1970] AC 492). That suspicion can be based on any evidence, even if the evidence would be inadmissible in a trial (e.g. because of hearsay). Also, the courts have accepted that reasonable grounds for suspicion can arise from anonymous information (see *O'Hara* v *Chief Constable of the Royal Ulster Constabulary* [1997] 1 All ER 129). Answers A and C are therefore incorrect.

It must be shown that the grounds on which the officer acted would be enough to give rise to that suspicion in a 'reasonable person' (*Nakkuda Ali* v *Jayaratne* [1951] AC 66). This means that answer B is correct, and answer D is incorrect.

General Police Duties, para. 4.7.4.4

Answer 7.4

Answer **C** — Under s. 60 of the Criminal Justice and Public Order Act 1994, if an inspector reasonably believes that incidents of serious violence may take place in his or her area, or that people are carrying dangerous instruments or offensive weapons, he or she may give an authorisation to stop any pedestrian and search him or her for offensive weapons or dangerous instruments.

The power used to be restricted to superintendents, but may now be exercised by an inspector (which is why answer D is incorrect). However, when the power is exercised by an inspector, he or she must inform an officer of the rank of superintendent as soon as is reasonably practicable.

The authorisation may be given either for incidents of serious violence *or* to search for dangerous instruments or offensive weapons (making answer A incorrect). The power is to search any pedestrian, and is not restricted to those who may be carrying dangerous instruments or offensive weapons (which is why answer B is incorrect).

General Police Duties, para. 4.7.4.5

Answer 7.5

Answer **D** — Under s. 60(1) of the Criminal Justice and Public Order Act 1994, if an inspector reasonably believes:

(a) that incidents involving serious violence may take place in any locality in his/her police area, and that it is expedient to give an authorisation under this section to prevent their occurrence, or

(aa) that—
   (i)   an incident involving serious violence has taken place in England and Wales in his/her police area;
   (ii) a dangerous instrument or offensive weapon used in the incident is being carried in any locality in his/her police area by a person; and
   (iii) it is expedient to give an authorisation under this section to find the instrument or weapon; or

(b) that persons are carrying dangerous instruments or offensive weapons in any locality in his police area without good reason,

he may give an authorisation that the powers conferred by this section shall be exercisable at any place within that locality for a specified period not exceeding 24 hours.

The authorisation under s. 60(1)(aa) is provided specifically to enable the police to search for dangerous instruments or offensive weapons used in an incident which involved serious violence. Answer B is incorrect, because an authorisation may be given in relation to an incident that *has* occurred, as well one which may occur in the future.

There is no requirement for the authorising officer to reasonably believe that further incidents of serious violence will occur before making an authorisation under s. 60(1)(aa), therefore A is incorrect.

Although an authorisation is exercisable at any place within the locality for a specified period, which does not exceed 24 hours, s. 60(1)(aa) does not state that the searches must be conducted within 24 hours of the incident involving serious violence. Answer C is therefore incorrect.

General Police Duties, para. 4.7.4.5

Answer 7.6

Answer **C** — Under s. 60AA(1) of the Criminal Justice and Public Order Act 1994, where an authorisation under s. 60 is in force, a constable in uniform may require any person to remove any item which the constable reasonably believes that person is wearing wholly or mainly for the purpose of concealing his or her identity. The power is not absolute, as the constable has reasonably to believe that the person is wearing the item to conceal his or her identity (therefore answer B is incorrect). There is no need, however, for the constable reasonably to believe that the person is carrying a dangerous instrument or an offensive weapon, or that the person is likely to be involved in violence, in order to exercise the power under s. 60AA(1). Those matters would have been considered before the authorisation was granted under s. 60. Answers A and D are therefore incorrect.

General Police Duties, para. 4.7.4.9

Answer 7.7

Answer **D** — Under s. 44 of the Terrorism Act 2000, an assistant chief constable/ commander may authorise stop and search operations within his or her area, in order to prevent acts of terrorism. When an authorisation has been given, a police constable in uniform may stop and search vehicles and their passengers, or pedestrians, for articles in connection with terrorism. These same powers are also given to PCSOs by virtue of sch. 4, para. 15(2) to the Police Reform Act 2002 (answer C is incorrect). However, in order to exercise these powers, PCSOs must be in the company and under the supervision of a constable. Answers A and B are incorrect for this reason.

General Police Duties, para. 4.7.4.15

Answer 7.8

Answer **B** — Section 3(1) of the Police and Criminal Evidence Act 1984 states that a written record of a search under s. 1 need not be made at the time, when it is not practicable to do so. However, Code A, para. 4.1 of the Codes of Practice narrows this exception to those occasions where it is wholly impracticable to make the record. Answer B reflects the wording of Code A; therefore answers A and D are incorrect. If the officer does not record the search at the time, he or she must do so as soon as reasonably practicable after the search has been completed.

This exception will be met only if there is virtually no chance of the officer being able to make the written record (e.g., the officer has been called to an emergency immediately after the search). Since an exception does exist, answer C is incorrect.

Note that when an officer makes a record of the stop and search electronically and is able to provide a copy at the time, he or she must do so (e.g. if the officer has access to a portable printer) and a copy of the record must be provided.

General Police Duties, para. 4.7.6

Answer 7.9

Answer **C** — Under Code A, para. 4.2B, where a person is arrested as a result of a stop and search and taken to a police station, the constable who carried out the search must ensure that the search record forms part of the person's custody record (rather than completing a separate form). Answers A and B are incorrect.

In all other cases the constable must make the record of the search at the time it takes place or as soon as practicable after completion of the search.

The *custody officer* has responsibility for ensuring that the person is asked if they want a copy of the record and, if they do, that they are given a copy as soon as practicable. Answer D is therefore incorrect.

General Police Duties, para. 4.7.6

Answer 7.10

Answer **A** — Where a search record has been made, the person searched, the owner or the person who was in charge of any vehicle that was searched, will be entitled to a copy of the record. Answer B is incorrect.

The person must be supplied with a copy *if he/she requests one*. Answer C is incorrect, as this will be supplied on request.

The Crime and Security Act 2010 reduced the entitlement from 12 months to three months; therefore, answer D is incorrect.

General Police Duties, para. 4.7.6.2

Answer 7.11

Answer **D** — Section 2(6) of the Police and Criminal Evidence Act 1984 states that 'on completing the search of an unattended vehicle, or anything in or on such a vehicle, a constable shall leave a notice'. Therefore, even though the spare tyre was not actually in the vehicle, a notice must be left and answer B is incorrect.

There may be occasions when officers have to force entry into a vehicle in order to search it. On such an occasion, the officer must, if practicable, leave the vehicle secure (Code A, para. 4.10). However, where the vehicle has not been damaged during the search, s. 2(7) states that 'the constable shall leave the notice inside the vehicle unless it is not reasonably practicable to do so without damaging the vehicle'. Answer C is therefore incorrect.

There is no obligation on the officer to send a notice to the registered owner's address, and answer A is incorrect.

General Police Duties, para. 4.7.6.2

8 | Entry, Search and Seizure

STUDY PREPARATION

In the previous chapter, we examined the powers to search people and vehicles for evidence of an offence. This chapter deals with the powers to enter and search *premises* either to seize evidence of an offence, or to arrest a person. These powers generally fall into two categories:

1. search of premises under the authority of a warrant;
2. search of premises without the authority of a warrant.

Knowing and understanding these powers leads to confidence, not just as a student or exam candidate but as a police officer generally.

Changes were made to PACE procedures by the Serious Organised Crime and Police Act 2005, in respect of the application and execution of warrants and the extent to which some non-warranted police staff may enter and search premises to seize evidence of an offence.

Part 2 of the Criminal Justice and Police Act 2001 provides a power allowing officers searching premises to seize documents and sift through them at a different location.

QUESTIONS

Question 8.1

DC HALL is investigating an allegation that FRISK, who owns a building company, paid bribes to officers in a local authority planning department over a number of years, to push through planning applications. DC HALL has recovered evidence from a search of FRISK's offices and anticipates seizing numerous documents and computers at the local authority offices. DC HALL is seeking a multiple entry search warrant, but is uncertain how many visits will be required to complete the evidence-gathering process.

> Which of the following statements is correct, in relation to the type of warrant DC HALL is seeking?

A DC HALL must state the maximum number of entries desired in the application for the warrant.

B DC HALL may apply for a warrant authorising unlimited entries in these circumstances, because the maximum number is unknown.

C DC HALL is not required to specify the number of entries desired; the warrant will automatically authorise unlimited entries.

D DC HALL is not required to specify the number of entries desired; an inspector may authorise further entries if necessary.

Question 8.2

As a result of an investigation into child pornography, DC BEALE has attended a premises with a warrant to search for evidence. DC BEALE is accompanied by FROUD, a civilian investigator and a computer expert, who is there to assist the officer at the search.

> Which of the following statements is correct in relation to FROUD's powers at the premises?

A FROUD has the authority to search the premises and seize property, but would have no powers to search people inside the premises.

B FROUD has the authority to search the premises and people inside the premises, but would have no powers to seize property.

C FROUD has the same powers as DC BEALE whilst searching the premises.

D FROUD has the authority to enter the premises, for the purposes of identifying property; an authorised person has no additional powers.

Question 8.3

DC GRANT is investigating a case involving a series of frauds. The officer has obtained an all premises warrant which authorises the search of PEDERSON's office and home address. DC GRANT has recovered documents that suggest PEDERSON owns two other premises where evidence may be found.

Will the warrant in DC GRANT's possession authorise the search of the other two premises?

A Yes, provided entry to those premises is authorised by an inspector in writing.

B Yes, provided entry to those premises is authorised by a superintendent in writing.

C No, DC GRANT will have to apply to a magistrate for another all premises warrant to search those premises.

D Yes, provided entry to those premises is authorised by an inspector in writing, or if one is not readily available, the senior officer on duty.

Question 8.4

Constable MURRAY has made an application for a search warrant to a justice of the peace, in order to search FODEN's home address for stolen goods.

Which of the following must the justice of the peace be satisfied with, in order to grant such a warrant under s. 8 of the Police and Criminal Evidence Act 1984?

A That there is material on the premises which is likely to be of value to the investigation of the offence.

B That there is material on the premises which is likely to be of substantial value to the investigation of the offence.

C That there is material on the premises which is likely to be connected to the investigation of the offence, or may provide intelligence relating to the offence.

D That there is material on the premises which is likely to be connected to the investigation of the offence.

Question 8.5

Detective Constable PRICE is investigating a fraud case and has uncovered evidence that a number of solicitors from a local firm may be involved. The officer has applied to a justice of the peace for a warrant under s. 8 of the Police and Criminal Evidence Act 1984, to enter and search the solicitors' offices for evidence relating to the offence. Detective Constable PRICE has reasonable cause to believe that there may be communications between solicitors and clients referring to the fraud. The officer is aware that there may be a substantial amount of paper and computer records on the premises and is anticipating having to use powers under s. 50 of the Criminal Justice and Police Act 2001 to seize and sift evidence.

Which of the following statements is correct, in relation to items subject to legal privilege which may be on the premises?

A Any communication between solicitors and clients is subject to legal privilege and cannot be searched for or seized under the terms of a warrant.

B Any items found that relate to criminal offences are not subject to legal privilege and may be searched for or seized.

C A warrant cannot authorise a search for legally privileged material and if such material is inadvertently seized, it would render the search unlawful.

D The possession of a warrant under s. 8 authorises any material found on the premises to be seized and sifted.

Question 8.6

Constable ADDLINGTON is dealing with a burglary and has received reliable information that some of the property stolen is being stored in FEELAN's flat. The information suggests that FEELAN is preparing to move the property, therefore Constable ADDLINGTON is seeking authorisation for a search warrant. The officer has prepared the necessary paperwork, but unfortunately, the on-duty inspector is engaged with a firearms incident.

What does Code B, para. 3.4 state about who should sign the application for a search warrant?

A It must be an inspector in uniform, but if one is not readily available, the senior officer on duty may authorise the application.

B It must be an inspector, but if one is not readily available, the senior officer on duty may authorise the application.

C It must be an inspector; Constable ADDLINGTON will have to find another inspector to sign the application.

D It must be an inspector, but in urgent cases, if one is not readily available, the senior officer on duty may authorise the application.

Question 8.7

Detective Constable ULHAQ has been called to a house fire and is the first officer on scene; he is not in uniform. He is unsure if there are persons present in the building or not and is considering whether he has power to force entry, using s. 17 of the Police and Criminal Evidence Act 1984.

Which of the following is correct?

A The officer may enter immediately to save life and limb, whether he believes there are persons in there or not.

B The officer may enter immediately to save life and limb if he has reasonable cause to *suspect* there are persons in there.

C The officer may enter immediately to save life and limb if he has reasonable cause to *believe* there are persons in there.

D The officer may not enter using s. 17 as he is not in uniform.

Question 8.8

Constable WILSON attended a burglary in the early hours of the morning. A witness, COLE, had seen a man breaking into a shop and removing two video recorders. COLE saw the man enter a house next to the shop. A short while later COLE saw the same man emerge empty handed and walk up the street. Constable WILSON made a search of the area and arrested GREEN, who matched the description given, nearby within minutes.

Constable WILSON considered searching the house GREEN had been seen entering. What authority would she have to do so in these circumstances?

A She has no authority to search immediately and would have to seek permission under s. 18 of the Police and Criminal Evidence Act 1984.

B She would have authority to search any premises which GREEN was in at any time prior to his arrest under s. 32 of the Police and Criminal Evidence Act 1984.

C She would have authority to search any premises which GREEN was in immediately prior to his arrest under s. 32 of the Police and Criminal Evidence Act 1984.

D She would have authority to search any premises occupied or controlled by GREEN and which he was in immediately prior to his arrest under s. 32 of the Police and Criminal Evidence Act 1984.

Question 8.9

Constable AHMED has arrested GRANT for an offence of burglary. Constable AHMED has been advised to seek permission from the duty inspector to search GRANT's home address, under s. 18 of the Police and Criminal Evidence Act 1984.

In relation to where Constable AHMED may search, and what he may search for, which of the following statements is correct?

A Premises occupied or controlled by GRANT, for evidence related to the offence for which he is in custody, or another similar indictable offence.

B Premises suspected to be occupied or controlled by GRANT, for evidence related to the offence for which he is in custody, or other similar indictable offences.

C Premises occupied or controlled by GRANT, for evidence related to the offence for which he is in custody only.

D Premises occupied or controlled by GRANT, for evidence related to the offence for which he is in custody, or any other indictable offence.

Question 8.10

HUDSON was arrested by Constable BALL from the Stolen Vehicle Squad, following the execution of a warrant at HUDSON's garage, where several stolen vehicles were found. Constable BALL received intelligence that HUDSON had another vehicle, which was parked outside his house. Constable BALL suspected that this vehicle might also be stolen.

In relation to searching and seizing the vehicle or its contents under ss. 18 and 19 of the Police and Criminal Evidence Act 1984, what powers would be available to Constable BALL?

A The vehicle is 'premises', which cannot be seized; the officer may search it and seize any contents obtained as a consequence of the commission of an offence.

B The vehicle is not 'premises' and may not be searched under s. 18; the officer would have to use powers available under s. 1 of the Act.

C The vehicle may be searched and seized if it is suspected it was obtained as a consequence of the commission of an offence, or for intelligence purposes.

D The vehicle and its contents may be searched and seized if it is suspected they were obtained as a consequence of the commission of an offence.

ANSWERS

Answer 8.1

Answer **B** — Section 15(2)(iii) of the Police and Criminal Evidence Act 1984 states:

> if the application is for a warrant authorising entry and search on more than one occasion, the ground on which he applies for such a warrant, and whether he seeks a warrant authorising an unlimited number of entries, or (if not) the maximum number of entries desired;

Therefore, an officer will normally be required to specify the number of entries desired and the warrant will *not* automatically authorise unlimited entries. Answer C is therefore incorrect.

On the other hand, s. 15(2)(iii) above does provide some flexibility in case the number of entries is unknown (answer A is incorrect).

Section 16(3B) of the Act deals with the authority required from an inspector in relation to multiple entry warrants. Under this section, premises may not be entered or searched for the second or any subsequent time under a warrant which authorises multiple entries, unless a police officer of at least the rank of inspector has authorised that in writing. The section does not give an inspector the power to authorise multiple entries; on the contrary, it places a restriction on such warrants so that each entry must be authorised by an inspector, even when multiple entries have been authorised by a magistrate. Answer D is therefore incorrect.

General Police Duties, paras 4.8.3.1, 4.8.3.2

Answer 8.2

Answer **C** — Section 16(1) of the Police and Criminal Evidence Act 1984 states that a warrant to enter and search premises may be executed by any constable. Section 16(2) provides that such a warrant may authorise persons to accompany any constable who is executing it. The authorised person may only exercise those powers in the company, and under the supervision, of a constable (subs. (2B)).

Under subs. (2A), an authorised person has the same powers as the constable whom he or she accompanies in respect of the execution of the warrant and the seizure of anything to which the warrant relates.

Answers A, B and D are therefore incorrect.

General Police Duties, para. 4.8.3.2

Answer 8.3

Answer **A** — Section 16 of the Police and Criminal Evidence Act 1984 states:

(3A) If the warrant is an all premises warrant, no premises which are not specified in it may be entered or searched unless a police officer of at least the rank of inspector has in writing authorised them to be entered.

There is no provision under this section for a senior officer on duty to authorise entry to new premises if an inspector is not readily available and there is no requirement for a superintendent to sign the authorisation. Answers B and D are incorrect.

Also, there will be no requirement for the officer to apply to a magistrate for another all premises warrant to search those premises. Answer C is incorrect.

General Police Duties, para. 4.8.3.2

Answer 8.4

Answer **B** — Section 8(1) of the Police and Criminal Evidence Act 1984 states that if on an application made by a constable a justice of the peace is satisfied that there are reasonable grounds for believing—

(a) that an indictable offence has been committed; and

(b) that there is material on premises mentioned in subsection (1A) below which is likely to be of substantial value (whether by itself or together with other material) to the investigation of the offence; and

(c) that the material is likely to be relevant evidence; and

(d) that it does not consist of or include items subject to legal privilege, excluded material or special procedure material; and

(e) that any of the conditions specified in subsection (3) below applies in relation to each set of premises specified in the application

he may issue a warrant authorising a constable to enter and search the premises.

Therefore, the officer applying for a warrant under s. 8 must have reasonable grounds for believing that material which is *likely to be of substantial value to the investigation of the offence* is on the premises specified. Answers A and D are incorrect, because s. 8 is clear as to the standard placed on the value of the evidence believed to be on the premises.

Material which is solely of value for *intelligence* purposes may not be seized under a s. 8 warrant. Answer C is incorrect.

When executing such a warrant, the officer must be able to show that any material seized thereunder fell within that description (*R v Chief Constable of the Warwickshire Constabulary, ex parte Fitzpatrick* [1998] 1 All ER 65).

General Police Duties, para. 4.8.3.7

Answer 8.5

Answer **B** — Section 10(1) of the Police and Criminal Evidence Act 1984 states that subject to subsection (2), 'items subject to legal privilege' means—

(a) communications between a professional legal adviser and his client or any person representing his client made in connection with the giving of legal advice to the client;

(b) communications between a professional legal adviser and his client or any person representing his client or between such an adviser or his client or any such representative and any other person made in connection with or in contemplation of legal proceedings and for the purposes of such proceedings; and

(c) items enclosed with or referred to in such communications and made—
  (i) in connection with the giving of legal advice; or
  (ii) in connection with or in contemplation of legal proceedings and for the purposes of such proceedings,

when they are in the possession of a person who is entitled to possession of them.

Generally, material which falls within the definition in s. 10(1) above is subject to legal privilege which means that it cannot be searched for or seized. However, items held with the intention of furthering a criminal purpose are no longer subject to this privilege (s. 10(2)). Occasions where this will happen are very rare, but could include instances where a solicitor's firm is the subject of a criminal investigation (see *R v Leeds Crown Court, ex parte Switalski* [1991] Crim LR 559). Answer A is incorrect.

Although a warrant cannot authorise a search for legally privileged material, the fact that such material is inadvertently seized in the course of a search authorised by a proper warrant does not render the search unlawful (*HM Customs & Excise, ex parte Popely* [2000] Crim LR 388). Answer C is therefore incorrect.

Possession of a warrant under s. 8 does not authorise police officers to seize *all* material found on the relevant premises to be taken away and 'sifted' somewhere else (*R v Chesterfield Justices, ex parte Bramley* [2000] 2 WLR 409). Officers using seize and sift powers will have to be able to show that it was essential (rather than simply convenient or preferable) to do so. Answer D is incorrect.

General Police Duties, paras 4.8.3.7, 4.8.3.8, 4.8.8.7

Answer 8.6

Answer **D** — Applications for all search warrants must be made with the written authority of an officer of at least the rank of inspector (Code B, para. 3.4). There is no mention of the inspector having to be in uniform and answer A is incorrect.

Code B, para. 3.4 also states that *in cases of urgency* where no such officer is 'readily available', the senior officer on duty may authorise the application. Answers B and C are incorrect.

Note that 'readily available' is not defined. However, most forces are likely to have more than one inspector on duty, even if that person works in a neighbouring area, therefore, it would be unusual to have no one available of inspector rank to sign the application. The urgency of the situation may dictate whether or not the officer seeks out another available inspector, or obtains a signature from the senior officer on duty.

General Police Duties, para. 4.8.4

Answer 8.7

Answer **A** — Section 17 of the Police and Criminal Evidence Act 1984 provides authority for a constable to enter premises to arrest a person in several circumstances.

Under s. 17(1)(e), a constable may enter premises for the purposes of saving life or limb, or preventing serious damage to property. When entering premises, including dwellings, to search for a person, the constable must have reasonable grounds for believing that the person he is seeking is on the premises (s. 17(2)(a)). This expression is narrower than 'reasonable cause to suspect' and you must be able to justify that belief before using this power (although see *Kynaston v DPP* (1988) 87 Cr App R 200, where the court accepted reasonable cause to suspect). Note however that 'having reasonable cause to believe' does not extend to the power to enter to save life and limb; answers B and C are therefore incorrect.

Some parts of s. 17 require the officer to be in uniform; these relate to arresting a person for offences specified in s. 17, but again do not extend to entry to save life and limb; answer D is therefore incorrect.

No doubt persons trapped in buildings that are on fire will thank the legislator for such a commonsense approach to powers of entry.

General Police Duties, para. 4.8.5.1

Answer 8.8

Answer **C** — Authority is provided under s. 32(2)(b) of the Police and Criminal Evidence Act 1984 for a constable to enter and search any premises in which the person was when arrested or immediately before being arrested, if the constable has reasonable grounds for believing that there is evidence on the premises in consequence of the commission of an offence. As COLE had been in the premises immediately before his arrest, the officer could use s. 32; answer A is therefore incorrect. The search may be conducted for the purpose of finding evidence relating to the offence for which the person was arrested. As the defendant in the scenario was arrested within minutes of leaving the premises, this would be classed as 'immediately' (although the term 'immediately' is open to interpretation).

Answer B is incorrect as the search relates to premises the person was in immediately prior to arrest.

The Divisional Court has held that where a person had not been in the relevant premises (where he did not live) for over two hours preceding his arrest, the power under s. 32 may not be used (see *Hewitson* v *Chief Constable of Dorset Police* [2003] EWHC 3296).

Answer D is incorrect, as s. 32 does not state that the premises must be one which is occupied or controlled by the person arrested. (This requirement may be found in s. 18 of the Act.)

General Police Duties, para. 4.8.5.2

Answer 8.9

Answer **A** — Under s. 18 of the Police and Criminal Evidence Act 1984, a constable may enter and search any premises occupied or controlled by a person who is under arrest for an indictable offence, if there are reasonable grounds to suspect that there are items on the premises that relate to that offence, *or* to some other indictable offence which is connected with or similar to that offence.

Answer B is incorrect because the premises must be controlled or occupied by the person; it is not enough that the officer suspects or believes that they are.

Answers C and D are incorrect as the officer may search for evidence relating to either the offence for which the suspect has been arrested, or those which are similar.

General Police Duties, para. 4.8.5.3

Answer 8.10

Answer **D** — Under s. 18 of the Police and Criminal Evidence Act 1984, a constable may enter and search any premises occupied or controlled by a person who is under arrest for an indictable offence if there are reasonable grounds to suspect that there are items on the premises that relate to that offence, or to some other indictable offence which is connected with or similar to that offence. For the purposes of the section, a vehicle is 'premises'. (Therefore, answer B is incorrect.)

Under s. 19 of the 1984 Act, an officer may seize anything which is on premises, if he or she has reasonable grounds for believing that it has been obtained in consequence of the commission of an offence and that it is necessary to do so in order to prevent it from being concealed, lost, damaged, altered or destroyed. Section 19 does not allow the seizure of property for intelligence purposes, and answer C is incorrect for this reason.

Where the 'premises' searched is a vehicle (see s. 23), the vehicle can itself be seized (*Cowan* v *Commissioner of Police of the Metropolis* [2000] 1 WLR 254) (making answer A incorrect).

This power has now also been added to the PACE Codes of Practice, Code B, Note 7B.

General Police Duties, para. 4.8.8.1

9 | Harassment, Hostility and Anti-social Behaviour

STUDY PREPARATION

The focus on community safety within the whole criminal justice process has been sharply defined since the Crime and Disorder Act 1998. A range of statutory measures exist, giving the police (and other agencies) duties in relation to community safety and powers to help them take positive action and work together to deal with harassment and intimidation. The Anti-social Behaviour Act 2003 provided the police and statutory partners further tools in the tool kit to protect the community from fear, intimidation and anti-social behaviour.

The main legislation is supported by other enactments, such as the Fireworks Regulations 2004, the Noise Act 1996 and the Environmental Protection Act 1990 (litter). Taken together, these measures feature highly in regional and local policing strategies to tackle crime and the fear of crime. This makes them important, not only to police officers but also, as a result, to those training and examining police law.

Also covered in this chapter are the powers given to the police and the courts to deal with *personal* harassment, which are covered in various pieces of legislation such as the Protection from Harassment Act 1997 and the Public Order Act 1986.

QUESTIONS

Question 9.1

MEREDITH is a racist. One day he was at home with several friends who share his beliefs, when COWANS, who is black, knocked on his door collecting money on behalf of charity. MEREDITH invited COWANS into his house on the pretext of looking for money. When they were in the living room of the house, MEREDITH began racially abusing COWANS in front of his friends. His intention all along was to stir up racial hatred. When COWANS eventually left the house, he contacted the police to report the incident.

Considering offences under s. 18 of the Public Order Act 1986 (using words or behaviour or displaying written material stirring up racial hatred), does the fact that the incident took place in a dwelling affect whether or not the police can take any action?

A No, the offence may be committed anywhere.

B Yes, the offence may only be committed in a public place.

C No, the offence may be committed in a public or private place.

D Yes, the offence may not be committed when both persons are in a dwelling.

Question 9.2

HAWKINS was walking through a city centre after a lunchtime drink one afternoon. At the time, a religious Hindu festival was taking place, involving people in traditional dress, who were walking to a place of worship nearby. HAWKINS began shouting, 'If these people want to live in our country, they should adopt a proper religion' and 'Look at those stupid costumes they've got on, they're ridiculous'. HAWKINS' words were heard by pedestrians standing nearby, but not by the people in the procession. HAWKINS' intention was to insult the people taking part in the procession, because of their religious beliefs, and to stir up hatred amongst passers-by who did not share the same beliefs.

Would HAWKINS' behaviour amount to an offence under s. 29B of the Public Order Act 1986 (use of words or behaviour intended to stir up religious hatred)?

A Yes, as HAWKINS' intention was to stir up religious hatred.

B Yes, whether or not HAWKINS intended stirring up religious hatred.

C No, as HAWKINS' words were not threatening.

D No, as the people in the procession did not hear the comments.

Question 9.3

WADE lives in a small cul-de-sac and is openly homophobic. WADE became aware that two people of the same sex had bought a house in the street and the rumours amongst the neighbours were that the people were in a homosexual relationship. One day, neighbours noticed several posters in the front windows of WADE's house, on which were written, 'Sign my petition to get rid of sexual deviants from this street'. WADE's intention was to make the new neighbours uncomfortable about living in the area, so that they would move out.

Could WADE be guilty of an offence under s. 29AB of the Public Order Act 1986, of stirring up hatred against the neighbours, on the grounds of sexual orientation?

A No, WADE has not made threats to the neighbours, intending to stir up hatred on the grounds of their sexual orientation.

B Yes, WADE has used threatening, abusive or insulting words or behaviour, intending to stir up hatred on the grounds of their sexual orientation.

C No, this offence can only be committed where a person uses words or behaviour, and does not include the use of written materials.

D Yes, WADE has used threatening, abusive or insulting words or behaviour, intending to stir up hatred on the grounds of sexual orientation, or where hatred was likely to be stirred up.

Question 9.4

KNIGHT has been charged with an offence under the Protection from Harassment Act 1997 and is due to appear in court.

What must the prosecution show in relation to KNIGHT's state of mind (*mens rea*) in order to prove the offence of harassment?

A That KNIGHT knew the behaviour amounted to harassment.

B That KNIGHT ought to have known the behaviour amounted to harassment.

C That KNIGHT suspected or believed the behaviour amounted to harassment.

D That KNIGHT knew or ought to have known the behaviour amounted to harassment.

Question 9.5

BARON has sent two threatening letters to his probation officer. However, the second letter was not received until four-and-a-half months after the first.

Could BARON be guilty of harassment contrary to ss. 1 and 2 of the Protection from Harassment Act 1997?

A No, as probation officers are unlikely to be distressed.

B No, owing to the length of time between the letters.

C Yes, but only if the probation officer is likely to be alarmed and distressed.

D Yes, but only if actual distress is caused to the probation officer.

Question 9.6

CRUTCHER and BOYCE are members of an animal rights extremist group and were targeting two companies, which CRUTCHER and BOYCE believed were suppliers to a third company, which tested its products on animals. Following a discussion between the two, CRUTCHER sent a threatening letter to the chief executive of one company and BOYCE sent a threatening email to the chief executive of the other. Their intention was to persuade both companies to stop supplying the third company with their products.

Given that the recipients are likely to be caused alarm and distress by the communications, would CRUTCHER and BOYCE's actions amount to a 'course of conduct' in respect of an offence under s. 1(1A) of the Protection from Harassment Act 1997?

A Yes, their conduct would be sufficient to amount to a 'course of conduct' in these circumstances.

B No, each person would have to send communications to at least two people.

C No, each person would have to send communications to at least two people from each company.

D No, because the communication they sent to each person was in a different form.

Question 9.7

COHEN is appearing in Crown Court, having been charged with an offence of harassment, contrary to s. 2 of the Protection from Harassment Act 1997. COHEN's solicitor has submitted to the court that the defendant suffers from mental health problems and the criterion that a person 'ought to know' that conduct amounted to harassment could not be met because of this illness.

Section 1(2) of the Protection from Harassment Act 1997 outlines a 'reasonable person' test in dealing with whether or not a person 'ought to know' that conduct amounted to harassment. Which of the following statements is true when considering this test, and COHEN's illness?

A The nature of COHEN's illness would provide a defence to this charge.

B The jury must consider COHEN's personal circumstances when deciding whether or not the criterion is met.

C The jury need only consider whether a reasonable person would think that COHEN's conduct amounted to harassment.

D In these circumstances, the jury would have to consider whether COHEN knew that the conduct amounted to harassment.

Question 9.8

STOCKWIN is infatuated with a female colleague from work; however, she has rejected his attempts to go out with her. STOCKWIN was upset and telephoned his colleague, threatening to burn her house down, but she was not concerned by his threats. A week later, STOCKWIN again telephoned his colleague and threatened to do the same thing and on this occasion, she *was* put in fear that he would carry out the threat and contacted the police.

Would STOCKWIN be guilty of an offence under s. 4 of the Protection from Harassment Act 1997 in these circumstances?

A Yes, as the work colleague was put in fear of violence on at least two occasions.

B No, as the work colleague was not put in fear of violence on at least two occasions.

C Yes, provided that it can be shown that violence was intended by STOCKWIN.

D Yes, provided that it can be shown that STOCKWIN actually knew that the work colleague was in fear of violence.

Question 9.9

Following the break-up of a long-term relationship with FRAMPTON, CLARKSON moved away to live with friends in Scotland. Before leaving, CLARKSON was convicted of harassment against FRAMPTON, contrary to s. 2 of the Protection from Harassment Act 1997. FRAMPTON has heard that CLARKSON intends returning to live nearby and has also been told by friends that CLARKSON is still angry about the break-up and will try to resume contact. FRAMPTON intends seeking a County Court injunction against CLARKSON, to avoid being subjected to further harassment.

Could a County Court issue an injunction in such circumstances, when there has been no evidence that CLARKSON has actually committed a further offence contrary to the Protection from Harassment Act 1997?

A No, only the High Court may issue an injunction in respect of an apprehended breach of the 1997 Act.

B No, an injunction may not be issued in respect of an apprehended breach of the 1997 Act.

C No, an injunction could only be issued in these circumstances if CLARKSON had previously been convicted of an offence contrary to s. 4 of the 1997 Act.

D Yes, the County Court could issue an injunction even for an apprehended breach of the 1997 Act.

Question 9.10

Members of a gang were responsible for serious anti-social behaviour on an estate. The behaviour included throwing stones and rubbish and spitting from balconies, causing damage to windows, doors and motor vehicles, starting fires, defacing walls with graffiti, shouting and screaming, playing loud music, obstructing, abusing and threatening residents, and smoking drugs. The police and the council obtained anti-social behaviour orders (ASBOs) against seven members of the gang aged 15, 16 and 18. Following the magistrates' court hearing, the police and the council wish to publish a leaflet entitled 'Keeping Crime off the Streets' in which they hope to identify (by name, age and photograph) the gang members who are subject to the ASBOs and summarise what they have done and the restrictions that they are subject to.

Which of the following is correct?

A They can name the gang members, their ages and can publish their photographs.

B They can name the gang members and their ages but they can only publish the photographs of those aged at least 18 years.

C They can name the gang members and their ages but cannot publish photographs.

D They cannot advertise in this way at all as this is a direct violation of the youths' rights under Art. 8 of the European Convention on Human Rights.

Question 9.11

STEPHENS, aged 19, was convicted by the magistrates' court for using threatening behaviour contrary to s. 5 of the Public Order Act 1986, towards an elderly resident living on an estate near his own home. He received a conditional discharge for the offence. Prior to issuing his sentence, the court heard that he had previously received both a reprimand and a final warning for the same offence, towards other residents in the area, while he was a youth. Although no application was made by the CPS, the magistrates took the decision to issue an ASBO against STEPHENS, utilising the evidence provided during his hearing, preventing him from entering the housing estate where the offences took place.

In relation to the ASBO issued, has the court acted within its powers in these circumstances?

A No, the court should not have issued an ASBO of its own volition; it may only respond to an application by a relevant authority.

B No, but the actions of the court *would* have been permissible if STEPHENS had not been given a conditional discharge for the offence.

C No, the evidence heard during the prosecution's case should not have been re-used to support an ASBO.

D Yes, the court has acted properly in the circumstances, and the ASBO against STEPHENS will be lawful.

Question 9.12

GRIFFIN has been made subject of an ASBO by the Magistrates' Court. The court decided that because drug misuse had been a major cause of the behaviour that led to the ASBO being made, it would be appropriate for GRIFFIN to also receive an intervention order.

Over what period of time could GRIFFIN be made to comply with the intervention order?

A A minimum of three months.

B A minimum of six months.

C A maximum of six months.

D A maximum of 12 months.

Question 9.13

The police and local authority are holding a strategy meeting to discuss COLE, who is nine years of age. Numerous referrals have been made to the anti-social behaviour co-ordinator over several months, showing evidence that COLE has been acting in an anti-social manner towards CHECK, an elderly next-door neighbour who lives alone.

Given that COLE has acted in an anti-social manner against CHECK, could an ASBO be applied for in these circumstances?

A No, because only one other household has been affected by COLE's behaviour.

B No, although the behaviour amounts to anti-social behaviour, an ASBO cannot be applied for because of COLE's age.

C Yes, the behaviour amounts to anti-social behaviour, and COLE's age is not relevant.

D No, because only one person in another household has been affected by COLE's behaviour.

Question 9.14

PENGELLI is 15 years of age and has been convicted of a burglary, which occurred during the night. The court has heard that PENGELLI has one unrelated previous conviction, but has recently taken up friendship with a group of young people who were the source of encouragement for the burglary. The court is considering making a Youth Rehabilitation Order (YRO), and the Probation Report has indicated that a curfew might be suitable to prevent PENGELLI from getting into further trouble.

Which of the following statements is correct, in relation to the proposal to implement a curfew as part of the YRO?

A PENGELLI is over 13 and can therefore be made subject of a curfew as part of the YRO.

B PENGELLI can be made subject of a curfew, as there are no restrictions on a person's age in respect of this type of intervention.

C PENGELLI is under 16 and cannot therefore be made subject of a curfew as part of the YRO.

D PENGELLI can be made subject of a curfew, as there are no restrictions on a person's age in respect of any intervention required by the court.

Question 9.15

REGAN is the subject of an exclusion order under s. 205 of the Criminal Justice Act 2003, preventing her from entering a shopping centre on weekends, due to previous anti-social behaviour. Constable MALIK has been called to the centre by security staff who are aware of the order and have spotted REGAN in the centre on CCTV.

What potential powers are available to Constable MALIK, to deal with REGAN in these circumstances?

A   He may take REGAN's details and serve a written notice on her that she was in breach of the order. He may send a copy of the notice to the court.

B   He may direct REGAN to leave the premises verbally; if she fails, she may be prosecuted.

C   He may arrest her for breach of the exclusion order.

D   He may summons her for breach of the exclusion order, unless an arrest is necessary.

Question 9.16

A Part 1A closure order has been issued in respect of a house, which is owned by RAWLINGS. RAWLINGS rents it out to a tenant, who only uses it on weekends to hold all-night parties. The parties have been the source of numerous complaints by residents because of the significant disorder they attract. The closure order was applied for by the police and Sergeant MEDINA wishes to secure the premises and post notices before the next party. Sergeant MEDINA has been in discussion with the manager of the local authority housing department about the best way to secure the premises.

Who does the closure order authorise to enter the premises to secure them in these circumstances—the police or the local authority?

A   Only the police, because the premises are privately owned.

B   Either organisation, provided they have consulted with each other about the order.

C   Only the police, because the order was applied for by a police officer.

D   Either organisation, but if force is to be used, a member of the local authority must be accompanied by a police officer.

Question 9.17

Constable ELSOM is part of a Neighbourhood Policing Team and has been liaising with the local authority about premises that have been subject to a number of complaints at public meetings because of persistent anti-social behaviour problems. Constable ELSOM is considering whether a Part 1A closure notice should be applied for in respect of the premises.

Which of the following statements best describes the 'persistent' element, which must be apparent before a closure notice may be made in respect of the premises?

A The premises must have been associated with significant and persistent disorder in the past 24 hours, or persistent serious nuisance in the preceding two months.

B The premises must have been associated with significant and persistent disorder in the past month, or persistent serious nuisance in the preceding three months.

C The premises must have been associated with significant and persistent disorder or persistent serious nuisance in the preceding two months.

D The premises must have been associated with significant and persistent disorder or persistent serious nuisance in the preceding three months.

Question 9.18

WATTS was responsible for a house, which was in an extremely poor state and likely to fall down. The house was on a highway that was used by several people, including those going to a nearby school. Its ruinous state was endangering people using the highway, and a few have to cross the road every day to avoid it. WATTS has continually refused to do anything about the house.

Could WATTS be guilty of public nuisance?

A No, as the offence does not include omissions, only actions by the accused.

B No, as not everyone is affected, only a few had to cross the road.

C Yes, provided WATTS intended to cause a public nuisance.

D Yes, as people's material rights have been interfered with.

Question 9.19

MULLER owns a company which organises large firework displays, for which he is authorised. He has several employees working for him, who help in his warehouse, accepting delivery of fireworks from the manufacturer and loading them into his van prior to displays. One such person is PLATT, who is 17 years of age. PLATT does not accompany MULLER to the displays; however, on a daily basis in the warehouse he handles large fireworks, which are specified as category 4 fireworks under the Fireworks Regulations 2004.

Does PLATT commit an offence under reg. 4(1) of the Fireworks Regulations 2004, by being in possession of fireworks that fall under category 4?

A Yes, as he is under the age of 18.

B No, as he is handling the fireworks as part of his work.

C Yes, regardless of his age.

D No, as he is not in a public place.

Question 9.20

Regulation 7(2) of the Fireworks Regulations 2004 provides certain exemptions to the prohibition on the use of fireworks at night.

In which of the following cases will the person be exempt from the prohibition on using adult fireworks during night hours?

A WU who began using fireworks at 11.00 pm on the first day of the Chinese New Year and carried on until 12.30 am the following day.

B ANDREWS who is a professional firework company employee setting off fireworks at midnight at a local authority display.

C REELEY who is using fireworks at 12.15 am on 6 November.

D COYNE who is using fireworks at 1.30 am on 1 January.

Question 9.21

The Noise Act 1996 allows for the serving of warning notices in relation to 'excessive noise' emanating from one house which can be heard in another at night.

During what time is 'night'?

A 10.30 pm–6.30 am.

B 10.00 pm–6.00 am.

C 11.00 pm–7.00 am.

D 11.30 pm–7.30 am.

Question 9.22

Section 87(1) of the Environmental Protection Act 1990 creates an offence of depositing litter.

Which of the sentences below best describes where such an offence may take place?

A Any public place.

B Any place in the area of a local authority, in the open air.

C Any place in the open air.

D Any public place in the area of a local authority, in the open air.

Question 9.23

Constable WHEELER was called to a local shopping centre because of a person causing annoyance. On arrival, Constable WHEELER saw GRAY sitting in a shop doorway, playing a guitar, busking for money. There were coins on a blanket in front of GRAY. At the officer's request, GRAY packed away the guitar and moved away from the doorway. However, the officer then observed GRAY approach a pedestrian and ask them for money.

Would GRAY's behaviour, as observed by Constable WHEELER, amount to an offence of begging, contrary to s. 3 of the Vagrancy Act 1824?

A No, GRAY's behaviour would not amount to begging in these circumstances.

B Yes, but only when GRAY asked for money; busking would not amount to begging.

C Yes, GRAY committed offences both when asking for money and whilst busking.

D Yes, but only when GRAY was busking; approaching one person to ask for money would not amount to begging.

ANSWERS

Answer 9.1

Answer **D** — An offence is committed contrary to s. 18(1) of the Public Order Act 1986, where a person uses threatening, abusive or insulting words or behaviour, intending to stir up racial hatred (or where it is likely to be stirred up). Certainly, the behaviour of the person in the question would meet these criteria. However, s. 18(2) states that the offence may be committed in a public or private place, but not when the words or behaviour used are not heard by persons other than those in that or another dwelling. The requirement is similar to those under ss. 4 and 5 of the same Act, and since both persons were in the same dwelling, no offence is committed, whatever MEREDITH's intentions! Answers A, B and C are incorrect for this reason.

General Police Duties, para. 4.9.2.1

Answer 9.2

Answer **C** — Section 29B(1) of the Public Order Act 1986 states that:

> A person who uses threatening words or behaviour, or displays any written material which is threatening, is guilty of an offence if he/she intends thereby to stir up religious hatred or hatred on the grounds of sexual orientation.

This offence is similar to the one contained in s. 18 of the Act, where a person may be guilty of stirring up racial hatred by using threatening, abusive or insulting words or behaviour (or displays any written material) with intent to stir up racial hatred or where it is likely to be stirred up. One of the key differences between these offences is that under s. 29B, the words or behaviour must amount to some sort of threat. To reinforce this, s. 29J of the Act provides that the offences of stirring up religious hatred are not intended to limit or restrict discussion, criticism or expressions of antipathy, dislike, ridicule or insult or abuse of a particular religion or belief.

Therefore, even though HAWKINS' words were insulting and intended to stir up religious hatred, this particular offence would not be made out. (There may of course be a case to prosecute HAWKINS for an offence under s. 18 or even s. 4A of the Public Order Act 1986.) Answers A and B are incorrect.

Since it is the defendant's intent that is relevant under this section, it is immaterial whether or not religious hatred was actually stirred up, or whether the people who were subject of the behaviour were actually concerned by it. Answer D is therefore incorrect.

General Police Duties, para. 4.9.2.5

Answer 9.3

Answer **A** — Part 3A of the Public Order Act 1986 (hatred against persons on religious grounds) has been amended to include similar offences involving stirring up hatred on the grounds of sexual orientation.

Section 29AB of the 1986 Act defines 'hatred on the grounds of sexual orientation'. The definition covers hatred against a group of persons defined by reference to their sexual orientation, be they heterosexual, homosexual or bi-sexual. The new ss. 29B to 29G of the 1986 Act have extended the various religious hatred offences in those sections to cover hatred on the grounds of sexual orientation. The offence may involve the use of words or behaviour or *display of written material* (s. 29B). Therefore, answer C is incorrect.

However, the offences differ from the offences of stirring up racial hatred in two respects. First, the offences apply only to 'threatening' words or behaviour, rather than 'threatening, abusive or insulting' words or behaviour. Answers B and D are incorrect, because the behaviour exhibited, whilst being very insulting, did not contain threats. The second difference is that in this section, the offences apply only to words or behaviour if the accused 'intends' to stir up hatred on grounds of sexual orientation. They do not apply in circumstances which are 'likely' to stir up hatred and answer D is incorrect for this reason also.

General Police Duties, para. 4.9.3

Answer 9.4

Answer **D** — Section 1(1) of the Protection from Harassment Act 1997 states:

A person must not pursue a course of conduct—
(a) which amounts to harassment of another, and
(b) which he knows or ought to know amounts to harassment of the other.

Answers A, B and C are therefore incorrect.

General Police Duties, para. 4.9.4.1

Answer 9.5

Answer **D** — If an accused intends to cause alarm or distress and actually does so, that is likely to meet the requirements of s. 1 (*Baron* v *Crown Prosecution Service*, 13 June 2000, unreported), provided he follows a course of conduct. Course of conduct has been considered by the courts. In *Lau* v *DPP* [2000] 1 FLR 799, the Divisional Court held that although only two incidents are necessary, the fewer the number of incidents and the further apart they are, the less likely it is that there will be a finding of harassment. In *Baron*, the court accepted that the more spread out and limited in number the incidents and the more indirect their means of delivery (in this case by letter), the less likely it is that a course of conduct amounting to harassment will be found. However, there is no rule and it will depend upon the facts of each individual case. In *Baron*, two letters sent some four-and-a-half months apart could be a course of conduct amounting to harassment, and therefore answer B is incorrect. Note it is alarm *or* distress; the court need only be satisfied that the behaviour involved one or the other (*DPP* v *Ramsdale* [2001] EWHC Admin 106), and therefore answer C is incorrect. Finally, the court in *Baron* refused to endorse the view that public service employees are less likely to be caused distress by threatening letters, and therefore answer A is incorrect.

General Police Duties, para. 4.9.4.1

Answer 9.6

Answer **A** — Under s. 1(1A) of the Protection from Harassment Act 1997, a person commits an offence if he/she pursues a course of conduct which involves harassment of two or more persons and which he/she knows or ought to know involves harassment of those persons and by which he/she intends to persuade any person not to do something which he or she is entitled or required to do, or to do something that he or she is not under any obligation to do.

Under s. 7(3)(b) of the Act, a course of conduct for this offence must involve, in the case of conduct in relation to two or more people, conduct on at least one occasion to each of those people. The fact that the letters were sent by two different people is irrelevant, because under s. 7(3A), a person's conduct may be aided and abetted by another, and both would commit this offence provided it can be shown they were acting together. Answer B is therefore incorrect.

Home Office Circular 34/2005 provides examples of offences which might be committed under s. 1(1A). In this guidance, it cites the example of an animal rights extremist sending a threatening email to an individual on one occasion working for one company and another similar letter to a different individual working for another company, with the intention of persuading them to stop supplying a third company with their products (similar to the circumstances in this question). Since the offence may be committed by sending different forms of communication to only one person from each company, answers C and D are incorrect (this is true even though the communications were sent by two different people).

General Police Duties, para. 4.9.4.1

Answer 9.7

Answer **C** — Section 1(2) of the Protection from Harassment Act 1997 states that for the purposes of this section:

> the person whose course of conduct is in question ought to know that it amounts to or involves harassment of another if a reasonable person in possession of the same information would think the course of conduct amounted to or involved harassment of the other.

This is an objective test as to whether that conduct was reasonable in the judgment of the jury/court—the test is not about whether the defendant 'knew' that the conduct amounted to harassment and answer D is incorrect.

The Court of Appeal has held that no characteristics of the defendant can be attached to the word 'reasonable' (*R v Colohan* [2001] EWCA Crim 1251) and answer B is incorrect.

Although the defendant's mental illness may be relevant to sentence, the protective and preventive nature of the Act together with the objective nature of the tests above means that such illness does not provide a defence. Answer A is incorrect.

General Police Duties, para. 4.9.4.2

Answer 9.8

Answer **A** — For an offence of putting people in fear of violence contrary to s. 4 of the Protection from Harassment Act 1997, it has to be shown that a course of conduct caused a person to fear, on at least two occasions, that violence would be used against them. The Divisional Court examined this issue in the case of *R (on the application of A)* v *DPP* [2004] EWHC 2454. In a case similar to the one in this question, the defendant argued that the victim had only been put in fear of violence by his threats to burn her house down on the second occasion; therefore the offence had not been made out. The Divisional Court disagreed and held that the magistrates were entitled to find that the two incidents had put the victim in fear of violence, notwithstanding her admission that, on the first occasion, she had not been too concerned. Answer B is therefore incorrect.

It must then be shown that the defendant knew or ought to have known that the victim would fear that violence would be used against them. Therefore answer D is incorrect. This is not an offence of 'intent' but is subject to a test of reasonableness against the standard of an ordinary person in possession of the same facts as the defendant, and therefore answer C is incorrect.

General Police Duties, para. 4.9.4.7

Answer 9.9

Answer **D** — Under ss. 3 and 3A of the Protection from Harassment Act 1997, the High Court *or* a county court may issue an injunction in respect of civil proceedings brought in respect of an actual *or* apprehended breach of s. 1(1) and (1A). Answers A and B are incorrect.

The effect of this is that a defendant may be made the subject of an injunction even though their behaviour has not amounted to an offence under the 1997 Act, or regardless of whether they were previously convicted of a s. 4 offence. Answer C is therefore incorrect.

General Police Duties, para. 4.9.4.9

Answer 9.10

Answer **A** — The extent to which the police (and local authorities) can use such publicity and include a photograph of the person made the subject of an anti-social behaviour order (ASBO) was clarified by the Divisional Court in *R (on the application of Stanley)* v *The Metropolitan Police Commissioner, Brent London Borough and the Secretary of State for the Home Department* [2005] EMLR 3. Following that decision the Home Office has produced guidance in relation to using such publicity. This guidance reflects the judgment of Lord Justice Kennedy, presiding judge in the case. The principles of this publicity are:

- Publicity is essential if local communities are to support agencies tackling anti-social behaviour. There is an implied power in the Crime and Disorder Act 1998 and the Local Government Act 2000 to publicise an order so that the order can be effectively enforced.

- ASBOs protect local communities. Obtaining the order is only part of the process; its effectiveness will normally depend on people knowing about the order.
- Information about ASBOs obtained should be publicised to let the community know that action has been taken in their area.
- A case-by-case approach should be adopted and each individual case should be judged on its merits as to whether or not to publicise the details of an individual subject to an ASBO—publicity should be expected in most cases.
- It is necessary to balance the human rights of individuals subject to an ASBO against those of the community as a whole when considering publicising ASBOs.
- Publicising should be the norm not the exception. An individual who is subject to an ASBO should understand that the community is likely to learn about it.

These principles do not relate to the age of the persons subject to the ASBO and clearly outline that publicity, including photographs, will be used. Therefore answers B, C and D are incorrect.

General Police Duties, para. 4.9.5

Answer 9.11

Answer **D** — Under s. 1C of the Crime and Disorder Act 1998, criminal courts may make an ASBO in respect of a defendant where he or she has been convicted of a criminal offence. The court can make an order of its own volition, irrespective of whether any specific application has been made by the relevant authority (which makes answer A incorrect). The order can only be made in addition to any sentence or conditional discharge (which makes answer B incorrect) (s. 1C(4)).

The issue of whether the same material should be used from a criminal trial to support the application of an ASBO was examined in the case of *S v Poole Borough Council* [2002] EWHC 244. In this case, the defendant had been convicted of several offences under the Education Act 1996, and objected to the same material being used from his criminal trial to support the application of an ASBO. He argued that the use of the ASBO had been intended as an alternative to prosecution. The Divisional Court did not find in favour of the appellant, and it held that it was 'perfectly proper' to use the same material in this way and that an ASBO is akin to an injunction in a civil court. Answer C is therefore incorrect.

General Police Duties, paras 4.9.5, 4.9.5.1

Answer 9.12

Answer **C** — The Drugs Act 2005 inserted ss. 1G and 1H into the Crime and Disorder Act 1998, and the sections relate to intervention orders. This type of order can be made alongside an ASBO when drug misuse has been a cause of the behaviour that led to the ASBO being made.

An intervention order sets out the specified activities and attendance requirements of a defendant, and the duration of the order cannot exceed six months (s. 1G). The breach of an order is a summary offence (s. 1H).

Answers A, B and D are therefore incorrect.

General Police Duties, para. 4.9.5.1

Answer 9.13

Answer **B** — Section 1(1) of the Crime and Disorder Act 1998 states that an application for an ASBO may be made by a relevant authority if it appears to the authority that the following conditions are fulfilled with respect to any person *aged 10 or over*. Answer C is therefore incorrect.

Under s. 1(1), the relevant authority must also show—

(a)   that the person has acted in an anti-social manner, that is to say, in a manner that caused or was likely to cause harassment, alarm or distress to one or more persons not of the same household as himself/herself; and

(b)   that such an order is necessary to protect relevant persons from further anti-social acts by him/her.

Since the behaviour must amount to harassment, alarm or distress to *one or more* persons not of the same household as himself/herself, answer D is incorrect. Further, there is no requirement for more than one *household* to be affected and answer A is incorrect.

General Police Duties, para. 4.9.5.1

Answer 9.14

Answer **B** — Section 1(1) of the Criminal Justice and Immigration Act 2008 provides that where a person aged under 18 is convicted of an offence, the court by or before which the person is convicted may make a Youth Rehabilitation Order (YRO) which can impose on the person any one or more of a number of requirements. The Order has a number of potential requirements each of which can operate as a standalone requirement or be combined with other requirements under the YRO. Examples of the type of requirements that may be made under a YRO include a supervision requirement, drug treatment requirement, curfew or unpaid work requirement.

The Act specifies that a person may only be made subject of an unpaid work requirement if he or she is 16 or 17 years of age. Answer D is incorrect, as there *are* restrictions on a person's age for some interventions.

However, there are no such restrictions in respect of a curfew requirement and answers A and C are incorrect.

General Police Duties, para. 4.9.5.2

Answer 9.15

Answer **B** — Exclusion orders may be granted under s. 205 of the Criminal Justice Act 2003 prohibiting a person from entering a place specified in the order, for a period specified but for a period of no more than two years. The order may specify different places for different periods or days.

Under s. 112(1) of the Serious Organised Crime and Police Act 2005, a constable may direct a person to leave a place if he or she believes, on reasonable grounds, that the person is in breach of an order.

A person who knowingly contravenes a direction given to him under this section is guilty of a summary offence (see s. 112(5)). Since the offence is committed when the person fails to comply with the direction (not when they simply breach the order), answers C and D are incorrect.

A direction under this section may be given orally (see s. 112(4)). Answer A is incorrect—there is no requirement to send a notice in writing.

General Police Duties, paras 4.9.5.4, 4.9.5.5

Answer 9.16

Answer **C** — Part 1A of the Anti-social Behaviour Act 2003, added by the Criminal Justice and Immigration Act 2008, makes provision for closure orders in respect of premises associated with persistent disorder or nuisance. Either the police or the local authority may apply for a closure order, provided they consult with each other.

If a closure order is applied for by the police, a constable (or a person authorised by the chief officer of police) may enter the premises and secure it against entry by any other person, using reasonable force if necessary. If the order has been applied for by the local authority, a person authorised by that authority may enter the premises and secure it against entry by any other person. Answers B and D are incorrect because entry must be made by the organisation which applied for the order, using reasonable force if necessary.

Section 11A(2) requires that the authorising officer must be satisfied that the local authority has been consulted and that reasonable steps have been taken to identify those living on the premises or with an interest in it before the authorisation for a closure notice is issued. However, the fact that the premises is privately owned will not bar the local authority from becoming involved, therefore answer A is incorrect.

General Police Duties, para. 4.9.5.10

Answer 9.17

Answer **D** — Part 1A of the Anti-social Behaviour Act 2003, added by the Criminal Justice and Immigration Act 2008, makes provision for closure notices in respect of premises associated with persistent disorder or nuisance. Either the police or the local authority may issue a closure notice, provided they consult with each other.

There must be reasonable grounds for believing that a person has engaged in anti-social behaviour on the premises *in the preceding three months* and that the premises are associated with significant and persistent disorder or persistent serious nuisance. The timescale is the same for both types of anti-social behaviour; therefore, answers A, B and C are incorrect.

General Police Duties, para. 4.9.5.10

Answer 9.18

Answer **D** — The Court of Appeal has expressed approval of the following definition of public nuisance:

> A common nuisance is an act not warranted by law or an omission to discharge a legal duty, which act or omission obstructs or causes inconvenience or damage to the public in the exercise of rights common to all of Her Majesty's subjects.

(*Attorney General* v *PYA Quarries Ltd (No. 1)* [1957] 2 QB 169)

This means that public nuisance can be committed by omissions, and therefore answer A is incorrect. It is not necessary to prove that every member within a class of people in the community has been affected by the defendant's behaviour, simply that a representative cross-section has been so affected (*PYA Quarries*). Therefore answer B is incorrect. There is no need to prove intent; the *mens rea*, therefore, is that the defendant is guilty of the offence charged 'if either he knew or he ought to have known' that the conduct would bring about a public nuisance (*R* v *Shorrock* [1994] QB 279). The fact that WATTS has refused to do anything about the house would be sufficient; answer C is therefore incorrect. The circumstances of this question have been held, in a fairly ancient case, to amount to a public nuisance (*R* v *Watts* (1757) 1 Salk 357).

General Police Duties, para. 4.9.6.1

Answer 9.19

Answer **B** — There are two offences covering *possession* of fireworks under the Fireworks Regulations 2004. First, an offence is committed by a person under the age of 18, who is in possession of an adult firework in a public place (reg. 4(1)). Adult fireworks are ordinary fireworks, which may be purchased by people over the age of 18, and will usually be used for families in their own homes on Bonfire Night. The second offence is committed where any person is in possession of a category 4 firework anywhere (reg. 5). Fireworks listed under category 4 are those which are more powerful than the ordinary ones referred to above, and are used in large displays.

However, both of the above offences are subject to the exception listed in reg. 6, which states that possession will not be unlawful if a person is in possession of fireworks in the course of his or her work or business, or where he or she has been properly authorised to conduct displays. Therefore, even though PLATT may not be authorised to conduct displays, he will be in possession of the fireworks as part of his work and does not commit the offence. Answer C is therefore incorrect. Also, because of this exception, it is irrelevant that he is under 18 (and answer A is incorrect). Answer D is incorrect, as PLATT has a defence not because he is not in a public place, but because of the above exception.

General Police Duties, para. 4.9.6.7

Answer 9.20

Answer **A** — The exception referred to in reg 7(2) of the Fireworks Regulations 2004 deals with three main types of firework display, namely:

- a 'permitted fireworks night';
- a firework display by a local authority; and
- a national public celebration or a national commemorative event.

Taking the first exception, the above restriction on using adult fireworks will not apply to use during permitted fireworks nights—an exception that has been built into the legislation to take account of the various festivals and celebrations that traditionally involve fireworks. The expression 'permitted fireworks night' means a period:

- beginning at 11 pm on the first day of the Chinese New Year and ending at 1 am the following day;
- beginning at 11 pm on 5 November and ending at 12 am the following day;
- beginning at 11 pm on the day of Diwali and ending at 1 am the following day; or
- beginning at 11 pm on 31 December and ending at 1 am the following day.

(See reg. 7(3).)

Applying these times means therefore that answers C and D are incorrect. The exception to a display by a local authority only applies to a person who is employed by a local authority, not a private firework company; answer B is therefore incorrect.

General Police Duties, para. 4.9.6.8

Answer 9.21

Answer **C** — The time as outlined in the Noise Act 1996 is 11 pm to 7 am. Therefore answers A, B and D are incorrect.

General Police Duties, para. 4.9.6.11

Answer 9.22

Answer **D** — Under s. 87(1) of the Environmental Protection Act 1990, a person is guilty of an offence if he or she throws down, drops or otherwise deposits any litter in any place to which this section applies and leaves it.

Section 87(1) applies to any place in the area of a principal litter authority (i.e. local council) other than a place to which the public does not have access (with or without payment) (see s. 87(3)). Although this section could be worded better, it means that the offence may only take place in an area covered by a local authority, to which the public has access (a public place) and which is in the open air. Answer A is incorrect as the public place must be 'in the open air'.

The offence may not be committed in any place in the open air (answer C is therefore incorrect), or in any place in the area of a local authority (this could take in private places also). Therefore answer B is incorrect.

It should be noted that the Clean Neighbourhoods and Environment Act 2005 clarifies that 'litter', for the purposes of Pt 4 of the Environmental Protection Act 1990, specifically includes cigarettes, cigars and like products and discarded chewing gum (including bubble gum).

General Police Duties, para. 4.9.6.12

Answer 9.23

Answer **A** — Section 3 of the Vagrancy Act 1824 creates the ancient offence of begging or gathering alms in streets and public places. A single act of approaching one person and asking for money is not, without more, enough to raise a *prima facie* case of begging (*R v Dalton* [1982] Crim LR 375). Answers B and C are therefore incorrect.

Where the person seeking money is doing something in exchange, such as singing as a busker, it has been held that this conduct does not amount to begging either (see *Gray v Chief Constable of Greater Manchester Police* [1983] Crim LR 45). Answers C and D are incorrect for this reason.

General Police Duties, para. 4.9.6.13

**Offences Involving
Communications**

STUDY PREPARATION

In the previous chapter, we studied the effects of more direct forms of harassment
and anti-social behaviour. This chapter deals with perhaps more subtle communications, forming a more personal type of abuse, which can be equally distress-
ing for the victim. The legislation covering these offences is varied, encompass-
ing the Postal Services Act 2000 and the Malicious Communications Act 1988
and deals with harassment by letter, telephone call, text and email.

The chapter also covers offences of communicating false information, under the
Anti-terrorism, Crime and Security Act 2001 and the Criminal Law Act 1977,
with the intention of inducing fear that people's lives are at risk.

QUESTIONS

Question 10.1

CORTEZ belonged to a hard-line group, which was protesting against the occupation of Middle Eastern countries by Western governments. At a pre-arranged time
during a demonstration, CORTEZ along with some other demonstrators sprayed
liquid in the faces of officers policing the demonstration, shouting that the substance was acid. In fact, the substance was a mild irritant, which produced no long-
term effects.

> What would the prosecution have to show in relation to CORTEZ and the others'
> states of mind, in order to convict them of an offence under s. 114 of the Anti-
> terrorism, Crime and Security Act 2001 (noxious substances etc.)?

A They intended that any person would fear either that his/her life was endangered, or that there would be a serious risk to human health.

B Only that they intended any person to fear that his/her life was endangered.

C They intended either to endanger life, or to create a serious risk to human health.

D They intended a particular person, or a particular group of people, to fear that their life/lives would be endangered.

Question 10.2

FISHER phones up the local radio station and says, 'There's a bomb going off in 10 minutes'; however, no actual location is given. FISHER is doing this as a joke and does not mean the station to take the matter seriously.

Has FISHER committed an offence contrary to s. 51(2) of the Criminal Law Act 1977 (communicating false information)?

A Yes, as the words spoken are sufficient.

B Yes, even though a specific location was not given.

C No, because it was only a practical joke.

D No, as there was no specific location given.

Question 10.3

Section 85 of the Postal Services Act 2000 deals with sending obscene articles through the post. MARSHALL has sent some indecent pictures, which have accidentally been delivered to a 65-year-old woman, who is a devout Christian.

In deciding if the pictures are 'obscene', what factors will the court take into account?

A The fact that they were sent to an old lady.

B The fact that she found them obscene.

C The fact that a reasonable person may find them obscene.

D The fact that the old lady has Christian views.

Question 10.4

FOSTER runs a post office and recently had problems with CHILTON because FOSTER had refused to cash a cheque that CHILTON had presented. CHILTON then refused to leave the Post Office and the police were called. CHILTON was removed from the premises and told by FOSTER not to attend there again. CHILTON has just walked into the premises and been told by FOSTER, 'I've already banned you; I want you to leave now'.

Which of the following statements is correct, in relation to s. 88 of the Postal Services Act 2000?

A   FOSTER is entitled to remove CHILTON from the premises if he refuses to leave.

B   FOSTER is entitled to remove CHILTON from the premises in these circumstances alone.

C   FOSTER is entitled to remove CHILTON from the premises if she suspects him of committing any offence under the Postal Services Act 2000.

D   FOSTER is entitled to remove CHILTON from the premises if he refuses to leave and FOSTER suspects him of committing an obstruction.

Question 10.5

BOLIN was expecting an important parcel, but was out of the house when it arrived. BOLIN drove into the street as a van belonging to a national parcel delivery service was being driven away. BOLIN followed the van to the next delivery address and approached the driver, QUINLAN, asking whether she had a parcel for him. QUINLAN stated that parcels could only be delivered to an address and that if BOLIN's was on the van, it would be delivered the next day. BOLIN became angry and blocked in QUINLAN's van, refusing to move until she handed over his parcel. QUINLAN called the police and Constable NORTON arrived a short while later.

Considering offences and powers under s. 88 of the Postal Services Act 2000, which of the following statements is correct?

A   Constable NORTON is required under this section to remove BOLIN from the scene, or assist QUINLAN to do so.

B   Constable NORTON is required under this section to remove BOLIN, or assist QUINLAN; however, QUINLAN had the power to do so herself.

C   BOLIN has committed an offence under this section by obstructing QUINLAN; however, the power to remove people only applies in a post office or related premises.

D   BOLIN has committed no offence under this section; the offence only relates to an obstruction caused in a post office or related premises.

Question 10.6

GARNER was recently fired by TOGHILL, the manager of the company GARNER worked for. GARNER was upset at the dismissal and in order to get revenge, arranged for a ton of horse manure to be delivered to TOGHILL's home address and dumped on the front lawn.

Considering the offence under s. 1 of the Malicious Communications Act 1988, which of the following statements is correct?

A Provided it can be shown that it was GARNER's intention to cause distress or anxiety to TOGHILL, the offence is complete.

B GARNER's behaviour would not amount to 'sending a communication'; the offence relates to sending letters or electronic communications.

C GARNER's behaviour would not amount to 'sending a communication', because the 'message' was delivered by someone else.

D The offence is complete in these circumstances alone, regardless of GARNER's intention.

Question 10.7

HEALD was infatuated with his neighbour, FARR and continually asked her out on dates. FARR was flattered and not at all threatened by this, but refused to go out with him. HEALD then made an indecent phone call to FARR in an effort to 'turn her on'. HEALD did not, however, intend FARR to be distressed by these calls. She was not threatened and found it all mildly amusing.

Consider the offence outlined in s. 127 of the Communications Act 2003 of improper use of a public electronic communications network. Has HEALD committed this offence?

A Yes, but only if it can be proved the phone call was grossly offensive.

B Yes, even though HEALD did not intend to cause distress and FARR was not distressed by the call.

C No, HEALD did not make persistent use of a public electronic communications network.

D No, FARR was not caused annoyance, inconvenience or needless anxiety by the call.

ANSWERS

Answer 10.1

Answer **A** — Under s. 114(1) of the Anti-terrorism, Crime and Security Act 2001, a person is guilty of an offence if he/she—

(a) places any substance or other thing in any place; or

(b) sends any substance or other thing from one place to another (by post, rail or any other means whatever);

with the intention of inducing in a person anywhere in the world a belief that it is likely to be (or contain) a noxious substance or other noxious thing and thereby endanger human life *or* create a serious risk to human health. Answer B is incorrect.

You do not have to show that the defendant had any particular person in mind in whom he/she intended to induce the belief in question (see the Anti-terrorism, Crime and Security Act 2001, s. 115(2) and the Criminal Law Act 1977, s. 51(3)). Answer D is therefore incorrect.

The key element to this offence is *not* any actual endangering of life or risk to human health, or an intention to do so; it is committing an act with the intention that someone else would believe such a thing would happen. Answer C is therefore incorrect.

General Police Duties, para. 4.10.2

Answer 10.2

Answer **C** — A call stating 'there is a bomb' is sufficient to comprise an offence contrary to s. 51(2) of the Criminal Law Act 1977, even though there is no reference to a place or location (*R v Webb* [1995] 92(27) LS Gaz 31), and answer D is therefore incorrect. Thus, answers A and B could both be correct. However, as this is an offence of 'specific intent', the defendant's intention is a factor. Although it is not necessary for FISHER to have any particular person in mind, this subsection states that the defendant has to have 'the intention of inducing in him or any other person a false belief that a bomb or other thing liable to explode or ignite is present in any place'. It is clear then that FISHER would have to intend that someone believed him, and a practical joke would not be covered by this section (answers A and B are therefore incorrect).

General Police Duties, para. 4.10.3

127

Answer 10.3

Answer **C** — Whether an article is obscene is a question of fact for the court to determine in each case. That test will not involve looking at the particular views or frailties of the recipient (answers A, B and D are therefore incorrect) but will be an objective test based on a reasonable bystander (*Kosmos Publications Ltd* v *DPP* [1975] Crim LR 345).

General Police Duties, para. 4.10.4.1

Answer 10.4

Answer **D** — Under s. 88(3) of the Postal Services Act 2000, a person commits an offence if without reasonable excuse, he/she fails to leave a universal postal service post office or related premises when required to do so by a person who is engaged in the business of a universal service provider, and the person reasonably suspects him/her of committing an offence under subs. (1).

A person who commits an offence under subs. (3) may be removed by any person engaged in the business of a universal service provider (s. 88(4)(b)).

Offences under s. 88(1) relate to obstructing a person engaged in the business of a universal service provider in the execution of his or her duty, or obstructing a person while in any universal postal service post office or related premises. There is no power under this section to remove a person who has committed *any* offence under the Postal Services Act 2000 and answer C is incorrect.

The power to remove a person is triggered only when the person who is engaged in the business of a universal service provider reasonably suspects that the person has committed an offence of obstruction *and* the person has failed to leave the premises. In the given scenario, the person has done neither and this power does not apply in the circumstances. Answers A and B are therefore incorrect.

General Police Duties, para. 4.10.4.2

Answer 10.5

Answer **C** — Under s. 88(1) of the Postal Services Act 2000, a person commits an offence if he/she obstructs a person engaged in the business of a universal service provider in the execution of his/her duty in connection with the provision of a universal postal service, *or* obstructs, while in any universal postal service post office or related premises, the course of business of a universal service provider. Since the obstruction offence may be committed in either of these circumstances, answer D is incorrect.

Under s. 88(5), a constable *shall* on demand remove, or assist in removing, any person who has committed an obstruction under this section and has without reasonable excuse failed to leave when required to do so by someone engaged in the postal provider's business. However, the power to remove a person only applies when he or she has committed an obstruction in a post office or related premises, and has refused to leave there. Answer A is incorrect (although, of course, there may be offences committed under other Acts of Parliament).

Finally, under s. 88(4), a person who commits an offence under subs. (3) *may* be removed by any person engaged in the business of a universal service provider. Again, this power only relates to an offence committed on post office or related premises and answer B is incorrect.

General Police Duties, para. 4.10.4.2

Answer 10.6

Answer **A** — Under s. 1(1)(a) of the Malicious Communications Act 1988, any person who sends to another person a letter, electronic communication or article of any description which conveys—

(i) a message which is indecent or grossly offensive;

(ii) a threat; or

(iii) information which is false and known or believed to be false by the sender;

commits an offence. GARNER's behaviour would not amount to an offence under s. 1(1)(a) above, because this subsection relates to the sending of a 'message'. However, under s. 1(1)(b), the sending of any *article* or electronic communication which is, in whole or part, of an indecent or grossly offensive nature amounts to an offence. GARNER's behaviour *would* be covered by this subsection, and answer B is incorrect.

Under s. 1, a person is guilty of an offence if his/her purpose, or one of his/her purposes, in sending it is that it should, so far as falling within paragraph (a) or (b) above, cause distress or anxiety to the recipient or to any other person to whom he intends that it or its contents or nature should be communicated. 'Purposes' is simply another way of saying 'intention' and since the prosecution would be required to prove intent, answer D is incorrect.

The offence can be committed by using someone else to send or transmit a message, or deliver an article (see s. 1(3)). Answer C is incorrect.

General Police Duties, para. 4.10.5

Answer 10.7

Answer **B** — Section 127 of the Communications Act 2003 contains two separate offences. Under s. 127(1), a person is guilty of an offence if he/she—

(a) sends by means of a public electronic communications network a message or other matter that is grossly offensive or of an indecent, obscene or menacing character; or

(b) causes any such message or matter to be so sent.

Since the offence may be committed by sending a message that is grossly offensive *or* of an indecent character, answer A is incorrect.

The offence under subs. (1) above is designed to deal with nuisance calls, and the offence is complete when the defendant sends the relevant message or other matter that is, as a matter of fact, indecent, obscene or menacing. There is no need to show intention on the part of the defendant, nor any resultant distress caused (answer D is therefore incorrect). The offence is complete by simply making an indecent phone call.

The separate offence under s. 127(2) of the Act *does* deal with causing annoyance, inconvenience or needless anxiety to another. Under this section, a person is guilty of an offence when they send or cause a message by means of a public electronic communications network that he/she knows to be false, or persistently makes use of such a network. However, since the behaviour of the person in this scenario is covered by s. 127(1), the offence is complete and answer C is incorrect.

General Police Duties, para. 4.10.6

11 | Terrorism and Associated Offences

STUDY PREPARATION

Changes in the terrorism legislation are clearly very important and highly relevant, particularly the additional police powers created by the Terrorism Act 2000. Until the events of 11 September 2001 and 7 July 2005, this was an area of policing left largely to highly specialist departments. The Terrorism Act 2006 amended and built on many of the provisions of the 2000 Act.

Areas covered in this chapter include the greatly extended definition of 'terrorism' and a 'terrorist' and police powers to deal with someone suspected of being one, as well as the obligations placed on members of the public to assist the authorities in identifying and dealing with terrorism.

Also dealt with here are the somewhat controversial powers given to courts to make derogating control orders against individuals suspected of being terrorists under the Prevention of Terrorism Act 2005 and the, still relevant, offences under the Explosive Substances Act 1883.

Finally, the chapter deals with the policing powers derived from the Serious Organised Crime and Police Act 2005 to deal with campaigners opposed to experiments with animals.

QUESTIONS

Question 11.1

CLEARY belongs to a hard-line group, which protests against the residency in the UK by Muslim extremists. CLEARY was convinced that a mosque near his home was a recruitment centre for terrorists and decided to take action. CLEARY discovered where the imam of the mosque lived and broke into his house one night armed with a firearm. CLEARY threatened the imam, stating that next time he would kill him if he did not clear out the terrorists from the mosque. CLEARY left the house without injuring anyone.

Would CLEARY's actions amount to terrorism, as defined in s. 1 of the Terrorism Act 2000?

A No, CLEARY's motive related to an ideological cause, not a political one.

B No, CLEARY's motive was not designed to influence the government or an international governmental organisation, or to intimidate the public.

C No, because CLEARY's actions amounted to a threat to use violence, not the actual use of it.

D Yes, CLEARY's actions amounted to an offence in these circumstances.

Question 11.2

MEAH arranged a private meeting in a hotel room between HASSAN, who is a member of a proscribed organisation, and SAIF, who is not. The intention of the meeting was to allow HASSAN to persuade SAIF, who is a wealthy businessman, to provide funds for the organisation. MEAH himself is not a member of the proscribed organisation and was not present at the meeting.

In these circumstances, has MEAH committed an offence under s. 12(2) of the Terrorism Act 2000 (arranging a meeting to further the activities of a proscribed organisation)?

A No, the meeting did not occur in a public place.

B No, the meeting only took place between two people.

C Yes, at least two people were present at the meeting.

D No, MEAH was not present at the meeting.

Question 11.3

GIRVAN is an employee of a well-known high street bank. Over the last few months she has been becoming increasingly suspicious of a customer's account and has started to collect information which she suspects demonstrates links between the customer's account and an animal rights group. She suspects, but has no evidence, that the customer is providing money that will be used for acts of terrorism. However, she has collected information relating to his personal bank account that she suspects to be important.

In relation to disclosing her suspicions to the police, which of the following statements is correct?

A She should disclose the information as soon as it amounts to admissible evidence.

B She must disclose the information now even if it does not amount to admissible evidence.

C She should disclose only her suspicions now, the information she collected is confidential.

D There is no obligation to disclose, it is a matter of choice.

Question 11.4

The police received information about a person who is suspected to be assisting in the commission of a terrorist act. The informant stated that a person had been seen covertly photographing a crowded shopping centre and that their behaviour was extremely suspicious. A surveillance operation took place and ZAFAR was identified and detained in the shopping centre. Officers confiscated a laptop and a camera, which contained hundreds of photographs of crowded areas and iconic sites.

The Terrorism Act 2000 creates a number of different offences. Which of the following statements is true in relation to s. 58 of the Act (collecting or making a record of information relating to terrorism)?

A It must be shown that the photographs were in ZAFAR's possession to encourage the commission of terrorist acts by any person.

B It must be shown that the photographs were in ZAFAR's possession to provide practical assistance to any person in relation to terrorist acts.

C There is no requirement to prove any intent on ZAFAR's behalf; simply being in possession of the photographs in these circumstances is an offence.

D It must be shown that the photographs were in ZAFAR's possession to provide practical assistance to himself in relation to terrorist acts.

Question 11.5

CHARTERIS lived in a flat in London and believed that the person living in the opposite flat was a wanted terrorist. CHARTERIS' suspicions were based on a picture released by the police of a person who escaped after attempting to blow up a bus. CHARTERIS is too scared to contact the authorities.

Could CHARTERIS commit an offence under s. 38B(2) of the Terrorism Act 2000, by failing to disclose information about the person living in the opposite flat?

A Yes, CHARTERIS must disclose this information to a police officer as soon as reasonably practicable.

B Yes, CHARTERIS must disclose this information to a police officer or a member of Her Majesty's forces as soon as reasonably practicable.

C No, CHARTERIS did not come into possession of the information through work or employment.

D No, this offence is only committed if a person fails to disclose information about an offence involving the commission, preparation or instigation of an act of terrorism.

Question 11.6

FARR has become associated with people who are in the process of being radicalised by a terrorist group. Some of the people have been sent to a training camp in the UK and FARR has been invited. Although FARR has not been directly involved in preparing for acts of terrorism, he suspects that the purpose of the training camp may be for his friends to receive instructions on bomb-making equipment and that he has been invited as a test of his loyalty.

If FARR does attend the training camp, what more would need to be shown regarding his intent, in order for him to be guilty of an offence under s. 8(1) of the Terrorism Act 2006 (attending a place used for terrorist training)?

A That FARR knew that at least one other person was present to receive training for the commission or preparation of acts of terrorism.

B That FARR knew the training was being delivered for the commission or preparation of acts of terrorism.

C That it would have been obvious to a reasonable person that the training was being delivered for the commission or preparation of acts of terrorism.

D That FARR knew or believed the training was being delivered for the commission or preparation of acts of terrorism, or that he could not reasonably have failed to understand the purpose of the training.

Question 11.7

PORTER has long been suspected of being involved in money laundering for a proscribed terrorist organisation. He has no previous convictions, neither is there any evidence at all that he is now committing, or that he has in the past committed, any specific offence.

Considering only the power of arrest under s. 41 of the Terrorism Act 2000, could the police arrest PORTER now?

A No, as he has no convictions for terrorism offences.

B No, as he is not reasonably suspected of committing a specific offence.

C Yes, provided he is reasonably suspected of being a terrorist.

D Yes, provided he is reasonably suspected of having links to terrorists.

Question 11.8

The Secretary of State has made an application to the court for a derogating control order to be made against MALIK, who has been under surveillance for some time and is suspected of instigating terrorist activities. The surveillance team has contacted the officer in charge with information that they believe MALIK intends to abscond before the control order is granted. The team has been ordered to arrest MALIK.

Which of the following statements is correct, in relation to where MALIK may be detained in these circumstances?

A MALIK must be taken to the nearest designated police station.

B MALIK must be taken to a police station, but this need not be the nearest designated police station.

C MALIK must be taken to the court where the control order is being considered.

D MALIK may be taken to a designated place the arresting officer considers most appropriate.

Question 11.9

OLIVER was a disaffected student who arranged to have some home-made bombs delivered to his house. He never got to use them, however, and stored them in the attic for future use. Three months later OLIVER moved out leaving his flatmate in the house. Two months after this new tenants moved in and found the items in the attic; not realising what they were they took them to the dump. An astute person at the dump found them and the police were called. An investigation led to locating OLIVER.

In relation to the offence of making or possessing explosive under suspicious circumstances contrary to s. 4 of the Explosive Substances Act 1883, which of the following is true?

A OLIVER was still in possession of the bombs when they were found at the dump and commits the offence.

B OLIVER loses possession when he leaves them with his flatmate and does not commit the offence.

C OLIVER loses possession when the new tenants move in and does not commit the offence.

D OLIVER loses possession when the bombs are discarded at the dump and does not commit the offence.

Question 11.10

TELLER created a home-made pipe bomb, using explosives drained from a number of fireworks, having found out how to do so on the Internet. TELLER boasted about making the pipe bomb on a social networking site and the police were informed. A warrant was executed at TELLER's house and the bomb was found. TELLER was subsequently prosecuted for an offence under s. 4 of the Explosive Substances Act 1883, but pleaded not guilty on the grounds that the bomb was made out of mere curiosity and there was no criminal intent.

What might the court take account of, when deciding whether or not TELLER was guilty of this offence?

A That the bomb was capable of being detonated.

B That the bomb was in TELLER's possession for a criminal purpose.

C That the bomb was in TELLER's possession unlawfully.

D That TELLER or some other person intended that the bomb should be detonated in some way.

Question 11.11

HIGGINS is a campaigner opposed to the exploitation of animals. HIGGINS has managed to arrange a meeting with O'SULLIVAN, the CEO of Eastshire Holdings, a company which HIGGINS believes is about to supply products to Westshire Sciences Institute (WSI). WSI is known to conduct experimentation work with animals. At the meeting, HIGGINS intends to peacefully persuade O'SULLIVAN not to enter into a contract with WSI on moral grounds.

Would HIGGINS commit an offence under s. 145(1) of the Serious Organised Crime and Police Act 2005, in these circumstances?

A Yes, HIGGINS has tried to induce O'SULLIVAN into not entering a contract.

B No, this offence does not apply to contractual issues between companies.

C No, the offence would only be complete if HIGGINS had tried to persuade O'SULLIVAN to break a contract already in place.

D No, HIGGINS' peaceful behaviour would mean that no offence has been committed in these circumstances.

ANSWERS

Answer 11.1

Answer **D** — Terrorism is defined in s. 1 of the Terrorism Act 2000 as:

(1) ... the use or threat of action where—
    (a) the action falls within subsection (2),
    (b) the use or threat is designed to influence the government or an international governmental organisation, or to intimidate the public or a section of the public, and
    (c) the use or threat is made for the purpose of advancing a political, religious, racial or ideological cause.

(2) Action falls within this subsection if it—
    (a) involves serious violence against a person,
    (b) involves serious damage to property,
    (c) endangers a person's life, other than that of the person committing the action,
    (d) creates a serious risk to the health or safety of the public or a section of the public, or
    (e) is designed seriously to interfere with or seriously to disrupt an electronic system.

Section 1(3) states that the use or threat of action falling within subs. (2) which involves the use of firearms or explosives is terrorism whether or not subs. (1)(b) is satisfied. This means that, where the relevant criminal activity involves the use of firearms or explosives, there is no further need to show that the behaviour was designed to influence the government or to intimidate the public or a section of the public. Answer B is incorrect.

Where the use or threat is made for the purpose of advancing a political, religious, racial or ideological cause, the offence will be complete (s. 1(1)(c)). Answer A is therefore incorrect.

Finally, a threat of serious violence will be sufficient to commit this offence, and answer C is incorrect.

General Police Duties, para. 4.11.2

Answer 11.2

Answer **B** — There are a number of serious terrorist offences arising out of proscribed organisations. In summary, these are:

- belonging or professing to belong to a proscribed organisation (s. 11(1));
- inviting support for a proscribed organisation (s. 12(1));
- arranging or managing (or assisting in doing so) a meeting of three or more people (in public or private) which the defendant knows is:
  — to support a proscribed organisation,
  — to further the activities of a proscribed organisation, or
  — to be addressed by a person who belongs or professes to belong to a proscribed organisation (s. 12(2));
- addressing a meeting to encourage support for a proscribed organisation or to further its activities (s. 12(3)).

Clearly, MEAH has arranged a meeting to support a proscribed organisation and/ or further the activities of a proscribed organisation; however, the conditions listed above are not all present. First, the meeting must be attended by three or more people; therefore, answer C is incorrect.

There is no requirement for the person who arranged the meeting to actually be present to commit the offence and answer D is incorrect.

Finally, the meeting may take place in public or private. Answer A is therefore incorrect.

General Police Duties, para. 4.11.2.1

Answer 11.3

Answer **B** — There are a number of offences contained in the Terrorism Act 2000, and some relate to money and its use for the purposes of terrorism. GIRVAN's suspicions about the customer's activities, if proved to be true, would amount to such an offence. Section 19 of the 2000 Act places a statutory duty on people who form a suspicion about activities they believe amount to the offences outlined here, if that belief/suspicion is based on information that comes to their attention in the course of their employment. The duty is to inform the police without delay of those suspicions, and answers A and D are therefore incorrect. They must also disclose the information on which it is based, and therefore answer C is also incorrect. Failure to comply with this duty is an offence, punishable with five years' imprisonment.

General Police Duties, para. 4.11.3

Answer 11.4

Answer **B** — Section 58 of the Terrorism Act 2000 creates an offence of collecting or making a record of information (including photographs and electronic records) of a kind likely to be useful to a person committing or preparing an act of terrorism, or possessing a document or record containing information of that kind (s. 58). Since the offence relates to the collection etc. of documents for any person, answer D is incorrect.

The document, etc. concerned must be of a kind that is likely to provide practical assistance to a person, rather than simply encouraging the commission of terrorist acts (*R* v *K* [2008] EWCA Crim 185). Answer A is incorrect.

Finally, simply possessing such documents, etc. will not amount to an offence in itself and answer C is incorrect.

General Police Duties, para. 4.11.3

Answer 11.5

Answer **A** — The Terrorism Act 2000, s. 38B states:

(1) This section applies where a person has information which he knows or believes might be of material assistance—
   (a) in preventing the commission by another person of an act of terrorism, or
   (b) in securing the apprehension, prosecution or conviction of another person, in the United Kingdom, for an offence involving the commission, preparation or instigation of an act of terrorism.

A person commits an offence if he/she does not disclose the information as soon as reasonably practicable (s. 38B(2)). This would include disclosing information which would lead to the arrest of a person for an offence involving the commission, preparation or instigation of an act of terrorism and answer D is incorrect.

In England, Wales or Scotland, disclosure must be made to a constable, whereas in Northern Ireland, disclosure must be made to a constable or a member of Her Majesty's forces (s. 38B(3)). Answer B is therefore incorrect.

Section 19 of the Act places a statutory duty on people who form a suspicion about terrorism offences, based on information that comes to their attention in the course of their employment. However, this is not the case for disclosure under s. 38B. Answer C is incorrect.

Note that it is a defence for a person charged with an offence under s. 38B(2) to prove that they had a reasonable excuse for not making the disclosure (s. 38B(4)).

General Police Duties, para. 4.11.3.1

Answer 11.6

Answer **D** — For the purposes of the Terrorism Act 2006, offences are grouped into three specific areas: encouragement etc. of terrorism; preparation of terrorist acts and terrorist training; and offences involving radioactive devices and materials and nuclear facilities and sites. The offences within the *preparation of terrorist acts and terrorist training* group are:

- preparation for terrorist acts (s. 5(1));
- providing instruction or training in any of the skills mentioned for the commission or preparation of acts of terrorism or Convention offences (s. 6(1));
- receiving instruction or training in any of the skills mentioned for the commission or preparation of acts of terrorism or Convention offences (s. 6(2));
- attendance at a place used for terrorist training (s. 8(1)).

In relation to the offences of providing or receiving instruction or training under s. 6, the skills mentioned include: the making, handling or use of a noxious substance, the use of any method or technique for doing anything capable of being done for the purposes of terrorism, and the design or adaptation for the purposes of terrorism of any method or technique for doing anything.

In *R v Da Costa* [2009] EWCA Crim 482, it was held that the person delivering the training had to know that one or more of those receiving it intended to use it for a terrorist purpose. However, this was the mens rea required to prove an offence by the person delivering training and not the person receiving it and answer A is incorrect.

In order to prove an offence under s. 8(1), it must be shown that the person *either knew or believed that the instruction or training was wholly or partly for purposes connected with the commission or preparation of acts of terrorism, or that the person could not reasonably have failed to understand the purpose of such instruction or training* (s. 8(2)). This is wider than simply 'knowing' the purpose of the training, and answer B is incorrect.

There is no mention of what would have been obvious to a reasonable person; therefore, answer C is incorrect.

General Police Duties, para. 4.11.4

Answer 11.7

Answer **C** — The Terrorism Act 2000 provides officers with an additional power of arrest in relation to 'terrorists'. This complements the existing powers under s. 24 of the Police and Criminal Evidence Act 1984 that exist for most of the offences connected with terrorist activities. It is a wide-ranging power in that it does not require reasonable suspicion of involvement in a specific offence, and therefore answer B is incorrect. It does not require evidence that the person is now, or has been in the past, a terrorist, and therefore answer A is incorrect. It is sufficient that the officer reasonably suspects the person to be a 'terrorist'. So what is a terrorist? Section 40 of the 2000 Act defines this as a person who:

- has committed an offence under any of ss. 11, 12, 15 to 18, 54 and 56 to 63; or
- is or has been concerned in the commission, preparation or instigation of acts of terrorism.

As far as the first statement is concerned, PORTER does not fit the definition in the fact pattern. However, where the officer has reasonable grounds to suspect him of being involved in the preparation of acts of terrorism through his money laundering activities, he may be justifiably arrested. This is true even though he is not suspected of a specific terrorist offence. Although it is a broad power, it requires more than mere links to terrorists, and answer D is therefore incorrect.

General Police Duties, para. 4.11.5

Answer 11.8

Answer **D** — Under s. 5(1) of the Prevention of Terrorism Act 2005, a constable may arrest and detain an individual if—

(a) the Secretary of State has made an application to the court for a derogating control order to be made against that individual; and

(b) the constable considers that the individual's arrest and detention is necessary to ensure that he is available to be given notice of the order if it is made.

If the Secretary of State has made an application for a control order to be made against an individual and a constable considers that the only way to ensure that he/she is available to be given notice of the order if it is made, the individual may be arrested and detained in order to appraise him/her of the terms of the order.

A constable who has arrested an individual under this section must take them to the designated place *that the constable considers most appropriate* as soon as practicable after the arrest (s. 5(2)). Answers A, B and C are therefore incorrect.

General Police Duties, para. 4.11.6.2

Answer 11.9

Answer **A** — The wording of this offence requires the prosecution—in cases of 'possession'—to prove that a defendant had the relevant article in his or her possession and that he or she knew the nature of it (see *R v Hallam* [1957] 1 QB 569). Clearly OLIVER knows the nature of the bombs and has possession when they are delivered to his address. At what point, if ever, does he lose possession of them?

However, the interpretation of 'in your possession' or 'under your control' is a wide one as demonstrated in a case where the defendant had moved out of his property and left home-made bombs and other articles in some boxes with a friend. New tenants in the property had discovered the boxes which later turned up on a rubbish tip. The defendant went to the police station after learning that he was a suspect and he claimed that he had collected the articles many years previously when he was too young to appreciate how dangerous they were. Although he had left the boxes with his friend he was nevertheless convicted of this offence as he still had the explosives under his control when he left the property (*R v Campbell* [2004] EWCA Crim 2309). There is also no need to show any criminal intent or an unlawful purpose on the part of the defendant (see *Campbell*).

OLIVER never loses possession; answers B, C and D are therefore incorrect.

General Police Duties, para. 4.11.7

Answer 11.10

Answer **C** — Section 4(1) of the Explosive Substances Act 1883 states:

> Any person who makes or knowingly has in his possession or under his control any explosive substance under such circumstances as to give rise to a reasonable suspicion that he is not making it or does not have it in his possession or under his control for a lawful object, shall, unless he can show that he made it or had it in his possession or under his control for a lawful object, be guilty of a felony …

Whether a person's purpose in having the items prohibited by these offences is a 'lawful object' will need to be determined in each case (see *R v Fegan* (1971) 78 Cr App R 189 and *R v G* [2009] UKHL 13).

In *R v Riding* [2009] EWCA Crim 892, a person alleged they had made a pipe bomb out of mere curiosity, using explosives drained from a number of fireworks. The defence contended that 'lawful object' meant the absence of a criminal purpose rather than a positive object that was lawful. However, the court was satisfied it meant the latter and mere curiosity could not be a 'lawful object' in making a lethal pipe bomb.

There is no requirement to show that the bomb was capable of being detonated, that it was in person's possession for a criminal purpose, or that the defendant or some other person intended that the bomb should be detonated in some way. Answers A, B and D are therefore incorrect.

General Police Duties, para. 4.11.7

Answer 11.11

Answer **D** — A person commits an offence under s. 145(1) of the Serious Organised Crime and Police Act 2005 if, with the intention of harming an animal research organisation, he or she:

(a)   does a relevant act, or

(b)   threatens that he or she or somebody else will do a relevant act,
in circumstances in which that act or threat is intended or likely to cause a second person to take any of the steps in subs. (2).

A 'relevant act' is an act amounting to a criminal offence, or a tortious act causing the other party to suffer loss or damage of any description.
   The steps referred to in subs. (2) above are:

(a)   not to perform any contractual obligation owed to a third person (whether or not such non-performance amounts to a breach of contract); or

(b)   to terminate any contract; or

(c)   not to enter into a contract with a third person.

Since the circumstances in the question are covered by s. 145(2)(c) above, answers B and C are incorrect.
   Under s. 145(3)(b), no offence is committed if the only relevant tortious act is an inducement to break a contract. This means that no offence is committed by people peacefully arguing, or representing, that one person should cease doing business with another on the basis of the other's involvement with an animal research organisation. Answer A is therefore incorrect.

General Police Duties, para. 4.11.9.1

12 | Public Disorder

STUDY PREPARATION

This chapter addresses the maintenance of public order using the increasingly wide range of offences and powers that are available to the police. In tackling that law, it is important to know the elements of the main offences and also the features that distinguish one event from another, whether the offence is committed by an individual or by more than one person.

The police have extended powers to give directions in order to prevent intimidation or harassment towards people in their own homes, under the Criminal Justice and Police Act 2001, while the Anti-social Behaviour Act 2003 provides police officers with powers to disperse groups behaving in an anti-social manner. The Criminal Justice and Immigration Act 2008 provides additional powers to remove a person who is causing nuisance or disturbance on NHS premises.

The long-established legislation dealing with public meetings, assemblies, demonstrations and processions is also dealt with here.

QUESTIONS

Question 12.1

DENNIS owns an off-licence and had just closed the premises late at night, locking the door. HUDSON arrived at the premises in a drunken state demanding to be let in to buy a bottle of wine. DENNIS refused to allow HUDSON in and HUDSON began shouting, 'If you don't let me in, I'll smash all these windows'. HUDSON then sat on the wall waiting for DENNIS to open the shop door.

Assuming that an arrest may be necessary in these circumstances, does DENNIS have the power to arrest HUDSON for a breach of the peace, contrary to common law?

A No, the threats were made towards DENNIS' property, not DENNIS.

B Yes, provided DENNIS reasonably believed HUDSON would carry out the threat.

C Yes, provided DENNIS reasonably believed HUDSON was capable of carrying out the threat.

D No, only a police officer has the power of arrest to prevent a breach of the peace that has not yet occurred.

Question 12.2

ANDREWS is out in town one day with his wife, who is wearing a fur coat, when BROWN, an animal rights protestor, approaches them and says, 'You murderer, how many animals have died to clothe you?' BROWN is calm and makes no threat. ANDREWS is infuriated and starts a heated argument. Constable WILLIAMSON is nearby and hears the commotion and goes to investigate. On arrival, ANDREWS tells the officer what had happened and says, 'If this clown isn't taken out of my sight I will not be responsible for my actions'. The officer fears that a breach of the peace will take place and that there will be violence.

Which of the following actions is appropriate or available to the officer?

A Arrest ANDREWS for breach of the peace.

B Arrest BROWN for breach of the peace.

C Arrest neither, as breach of the peace is not taking place currently.

D Arrest both for breach of the peace.

Question 12.3

A group of 20 people have been charged with the offence of riot, following a serious incident of disorder on a housing estate. The Crown Prosecution Service intends introducing evidence that at least 15 of the defendants were threatening violence towards people from a minority ethnic group, while five defendants actually used violence towards them. Other evidence shows that at least ten other people were gathered near those charged. These people did not take part in the threats or violence, but their presence added to the intimidation.

According to s. 1 of the Public Order Act 1986, who can be found guilty of riot in these circumstances?

A Any of the people present who were not victims of the incident.

B Any of the defendants who used or threatened to use unlawful violence.

C The five defendants who actually used unlawful violence.

D None of the people present, as only five defendants actually used violence.

Question 12.4

A large group of people are appearing in Crown Court to answer a charge of riot, contrary to s. 1(1) of the Public Order Act 1986. The court has heard objections from the defence relating to the evidence provided by the Crown Prosecution Service regarding the defendants' 'common purpose'.

What evidence would the court require, relating to the issue of a 'common purpose'?

A That the defendants used simultaneous violence for a common purpose.

B That the defendants had an agreed common purpose.

C That the defendants had an unlawful common purpose.

D Only that the defendants had a common purpose.

Question 12.5

HOWLEY has been charged along with a number of other people, with an offence of violent disorder, under s. 2 of the Public Order Act 1986. HOWLEY intends to use the defence that he was intoxicated at the time of the incident, and that he was not aware of his actions.

What does s. 6 of the Public Order Act 1986 state in relation to the defence of intoxication?

A It cannot be used as a defence in relation to this offence, or an offence under s. 1.

B HOWLEY *may* use this defence if he can show either that his intoxication was not self-induced, or it was caused solely by taking a substance in the course of medical treatment.

C HOWLEY *may* use this defence, but only if he can show that his intoxication was not self-induced.

D HOWLEY *may* use this defence, but only if he can show that his intoxication was caused solely by taking a substance in the course of medical treatment.

Question 12.6

WORTON, CAMERON and MAHROOF appeared in Crown Court for violent disorder, contrary to s. 2 of the Public Order Act 1986, following a fight in a pub. After hearing the evidence, the jury acquitted WORTON of the offence.

Could CAMERON and MAHROOF still be convicted of the offence in these circumstances?

A Yes, only two people are required to have used or threatened unlawful violence for this offence.

B No, when a defendant is acquitted of this offence, all other defendants must also be acquitted.

C Yes, when a defendant is acquitted of this offence, the other defendants may still be convicted.

D Only if it can be shown that CAMERON and MAHROOF actually used violence (as opposed to threatening violence).

Question 12.7

Constable CARLISLE attended a report of a stolen vehicle being driven around a housing estate. On arrival, the officer saw SALTER getting out of the stolen vehicle. Constable CARLISLE arrested SALTER, who began violently to resist arrest. While the officer was waiting for back-up, a crowd of about eight people gathered around and each of them threatened violence towards Constable CARLISLE. Some of the people then started to punch and kick the officer to aide SALTER's escape.

Has an offence of violent disorder, under s. 2 of the Public Order Act 1986, been committed in these circumstances?

A Yes, if it can be shown that the people were present together, using or threatening unlawful violence.

B Yes, but only in respect of the people who were present together, using unlawful violence.

C Yes, if it can be shown that the people were present together, using or threatening unlawful violence simultaneously.

D Yes, if it can be shown that SALTER and the other people were deliberately acting together, to use or threaten unlawful violence.

Question 12.8

WEBB and CAHILL were in dispute about a boundary between their gardens. One day, CAHILL returned from work as WEBB was about to cut down a tree, which was in the disputed boundary area. CAHILL, who owned an Alsatian dog that lived in a kennel in the rear garden, saw what was happening and shouted at WEBB, 'Stop that or I'll set the dog on you and it will cause you serious injury'. The dog was still in the kennel, but WEBB was genuinely in fear that CAHILL would carry out the threat. At the time, WEBB was alone in one enclosed garden, and CAHILL was alone in the other. There were no other people present at the scene.

Could CAHILL be guilty of an offence under s. 3 of the Public Order Act 1986 (causing an affray) in these circumstances?

A No, there was no likelihood of another person being present at the scene, who would fear for their safety.

B Yes, CAHILL threatened WEBB with immediate personal violence.

C No, CAHILL would have to threaten or use personal violence towards WEBB, rather than making a threat with the dog.

D Yes, had a person of reasonable firmness been at the scene, they would have feared for their safety.

Question 12.9

LOADER had recently split up from his wife, GAIL, and one day he saw her in a car in the street, accompanied by her new partner, ANWAR. GAIL got out of the car and LOADER approached her, angry that she was with another man. He shouted at her, 'That's the man you left me for; I'm going over there to smash his face in'. During the conversation, ANWAR remained in the car.

Has LOADER committed an offence contrary to s. 4 of the Public Order Act 1986 in these circumstances?

A Yes, if he intended that GAIL would believe violence would be used against ANWAR.

B Yes, but only if GAIL believed violence would be used against ANWAR.

C Yes, regardless of his intent, the offence is complete.

D No, because the threat was to use violence against ANWAR, who was not present.

Question 12.10

SADIQUE, who is Asian but from Uganda, has bought a product, which has failed to work. He returns it to the shop and is dealt with by AKANJI, a shop assistant who is Nigerian by birth. Less than happy with the service, SADIQUE calls AKANJI 'an African twat' and 'an African bitch'. AKANJI is very distressed by this and contacts the police.

Has SADIQUE committed an offence contrary to s. 31(1)(b) of the Crime and Disorder Act 1998 (racially aggravated intentional harassment, alarm or distress)?

A No, as 'African' does not describe a racial group.

B No, as SADIQUE is from the same racial group as AKANJI.

C Yes, provided SADIQUE intended to distress AKANJI.

D Yes, there is no need to prove intent, provided distress is caused.

Question 12.11

RICHARDS was caught using a video camera near a school and the evidence obtained indicated that he had been committing an offence contrary to s. 5 of the Public Order Act 1986. When viewed, the video showed that he was dancing naked in front of the school whilst children played in the background. The children were unaware that they were being filmed and no one had seen or heard the behaviour.

Has an offence contrary to s. 5 of the Public Order Act 1986 been committed?

A Yes, a person of reasonable firmness would have been distressed had they been present.

B Yes, a person of reasonable firmness would have been distressed had they seen the video.

C No, as the defendant's behaviour was not seen or heard by anyone.

D Yes, but only if the prosecution could produce a witness who saw or heard the behaviour.

Question 12.12

Constable ROBINSON was on patrol in a shopping centre, when she saw INCE walking along, shouting and swearing in a loud voice. There were a number of shoppers in the area and Constable ROBINSON approached INCE and advised him to stop swearing and annoying people. INCE ignored Constable ROBINSON and walked away, continuing to swear loudly at passers-by. Constable ROBINSON decided that it was necessary to issue INCE with a Disorder Penalty Notice for an offence contrary to s. 5 of the Public Order Act 1986.

What would have to be proved in relation to INCE's state of mind, for the offence under s. 5 to be made out?

A That he ought to have been aware that his behaviour was insulting.

B That he intended his behaviour to be insulting, or was aware that it was.

C That someone was actually insulted by his behaviour.

D That he intended his behaviour to be insulting and was aware that it was.

Question 12.13

Inspector LOTT has been called to a residential property because a group of animal rights protesters have gathered outside. The group have followed PRICE to the house, believing that he lives there; however, he does not. The group is protesting against PRICE, who works at a local laboratory where they believe experiments take place involving animals. The group's intention is to intimidate PRICE into giving up his job at the laboratory. Also in the house is PRICE's friend, BLUNT, the house owner. BLUNT and PRICE have asked Inspector LOTT to move the protesters away from the premises.

What would Inspector LOTT reasonably have to believe in order to utilise his powers under s. 42 of the Criminal Justice and Police Act 2001, to direct the group to leave the area?

A That their presence amounts to, or is likely to amount to, the harassment of PRICE.

B That their presence amounts to, or is likely to amount to, the harassment of PRICE or BLUNT.

C That their presence amounts to, or is likely to amount to, the harassment of any person in the dwelling.

D That their presence amounts to, or is likely to amount to, the harassment of BLUNT.

Question 12.14

IRWIN was treated in the casualty department of a hospital, after falling and spraining a wrist. Although the injuries were not serious, IRWIN was convinced that the arm was broken. IRWIN returned to the hospital about four hours after being discharged and insisted on receiving further treatment. IRWIN began causing a disturbance and because the hospital staff were worried about their safety, they called the police. POWELL, the on-duty security guard, became aware of the disturbance and decided to deal with IRWIN before the police arrived. POWELL was a duly authorised NHS staff member.

Would POWELL have the authority to remove IRWIN from the premises before the arrival of the police?

A No, only a constable could do so, because IRWIN was a patient, waiting for medical advice.

B Yes, either POWELL, a constable or any NHS staff member could do so, because IRWIN was not a patient, waiting for medical advice.

C Yes, either POWELL or a constable could do so, because IRWIN was not a patient, waiting for medical advice.

D No, having received treatment less than eight hours ago, IRWIN may not be ejected from the premises.

Question 12.15

HALSTEAD is the chair of a city centre traders' association. Every Monday morning at 8.30 am, HALSTEAD organises a group of between 30–40 traders, who park their cars on the outskirts of the city centre and ride to work on bicycles. The group's aims are to highlight the harm caused by carbon emissions, and to ease traffic congestion. Due to the number of cyclists, some disruption is inevitably caused to vehicular traffic.

Considering s. 11 of the Public Order Act 1986 (public processions), as the organiser of the group, is HALSTEAD required to notify the local police?

A No, this legislation applies to demonstrations or protests; therefore, notice is not required.

B Yes, provided the bicycles follow a set route and a set time.

C Yes, this is a procession to publicise a cause or a campaign; therefore, notice is required.

D No, this legislation does not apply to commonly and customarily held processions, such as this.

Question 12.16

Constable JEFFERS, who is in full uniform, has been deployed to deal with a trespassory assembly, in respect of which an order under s. 14A of the Public Order Act 1986 has been obtained prohibiting it taking place. The officer is four-and-a-half miles from the monument where the assembly was due to take place, and is carrying out powers granted by s. 14C of the 1986 Act, preventing access to the site. The officer has stopped a vehicle, and has directed the occupants not to proceed in the direction of the assembly.

Are the officer's actions lawful?

A Yes, as the officer was in uniform the actions are lawful.

B Yes, the actions are lawful; it is immaterial that the officer was in uniform.

C No, the officer is outside the radius set by the Act at four miles.

D No, the officer has no power to stop vehicles under this section.

Question 12.17

Constable DONAHUE is the community beat officer on a housing estate, which has been suffering an ongoing youth annoyance problem outside a small shopping centre. One bank holiday weekend, the police were called to the location to deal with intimidation and annoyance towards shopkeepers and customers, on average 20 times a day. Constable DONAHUE was on duty on the bank holiday Monday and visited the shopping centre during the afternoon. There were two youths present who the officer knew were the main instigators. After speaking to the shopkeepers, Constable DONAHUE formed the opinion that there would be further harassment that afternoon and evening. Constable DONAHUE asked the control room if they could contact the on-duty superintendent, to consider whether an order should be given under s. 30 of the Anti-social Behaviour Act 2003, to disperse the two youths before the problem escalated again.

Would the on-duty superintendent be able to authorise such a request in the circumstances?

A No, because there are only two people present.

B Yes, because there are two or more people present.

C No, this power may not be used at such short notice.

D Yes, this is a significant and persistent problem; it is irrelevant how many people are present.

Question 12.18

A dispersal order under s. 30 of the Anti-social Behaviour Act 2003 is in place in a shopping centre, because of anti-social behaviour that had been caused by youths drinking excessively, intimidating shoppers and committing a number of robberies. One Saturday, a group of 20 people attended the shopping centre to stage a protest against America's involvement in Iraq. The group had not notified the police of their intention to protest. Their target was a large food hall area, which contained several American-owned fast food outlets. They intended preventing people from entering the shops and persuading them not to buy food there. They began shouting at shoppers who were entering the food hall and many people felt harassed and intimidated by their actions. The police were called to deal with the incident.

Would the officers attending the scene be able to use powers under s. 30(4) of the Anti-social Behaviour Act 2003 to disperse the protesters, by virtue of the order already in place?

A No, this would be an abuse of power; the order was in place for unrelated incidents of anti-social behaviour.

B Yes, but they would need the superintendent who gave the original order to extend the criteria to include the protest.

C No, a fresh dispersal order will need to be applied for by any superintendent to take in the behaviour by the protesters.

D Yes, the protesters may be dispersed using the powers granted by the first dispersal order.

Question 12.19

Constable LONGMAN was working in an area in which an order had been given under s. 30 of the Anti-social Behaviour Act 2003, enabling officers to disperse people from the locality, because of persistent harassment and intimidation from young people. Constable LONGMAN was patrolling the relevant area in uniform one evening, when he saw a group of ten young people. One member of the group appeared to be intimidating a person who was walking past them. Constable LONGMAN recognised the people as being local residents.

What powers does Constable LONGMAN have to deal with the people, under s. 30(3) of the Anti-social Behaviour Act 2003, in these circumstances?

A He may give a direction to the youth concerned not to come back to the locality for 24 hours.

B He may give a direction to the whole group to disperse from the area immediately.

C He may give a direction to the whole group not to come back to the locality for 24 hours.

D He may not give a direction, as only one person was involved in the intimidation.

Question 12.20

Constable DARCH was on patrol at 9.30 pm in a housing estate where, following incidents of significant and persistent anti-social behaviour, a dispersal order was in place. Constable DARCH saw PURSE, aged 15, staggering around shouting loudly and clearly drunk. PURSE refused to go home and even though there were no other young people in the area, Constable DARCH was concerned that PURSE would continue to act in an anti-social manner if left at the location.

Would Constable DARCH have the power to take PURSE home by force in these circumstances, utilising powers under s. 30(6) of the Anti-social Behaviour Act 2003 (power to remove people to their place of residence)?

A Yes, in order to prevent PURSE from committing anti-social behaviour.

B No, these powers only apply between the hours of 10 pm and 6 am.

C No, this power may only be used to protect young people at risk of anti-social behaviour by others.

D No, there is no power to use force under this section.

Question 12.21

The residents association on a housing estate has become increasingly concerned about gang-related activity in the area on most evenings. Young people have formulated into two rival gangs and there is evidence of regular violence taking place between them. Some of the gang members are as young as 12 years of age, and this has prompted members of the committee to approach the police to establish whether any action could be taken to prevent the gangs from continuing their activities.

Section 34 of the Policing and Crime Act 2009 deals with measures that can be taken to prevent gang-related activities. Which of the following statements is correct in relation to the members of the gang involved in the activities?

A Measures can be taken against any person under the age of 18.

B Measures can be taken against any person over the age of 14.

C Measures can be taken against any person who satisfies the conditions, regardless of their age.

D Measures can be taken against any person between the ages of 14 and 17.

ANSWERS

Answer 12.1

Answer **B** — A breach of the peace was defined specifically in *R* v *Howell* [1982] QB 416. A breach of the peace generally occurs when an act is done, or threatened to be done:

- which harms a person or, in his or her presence, his or her property; or
- which is likely to cause such harm; or
- which puts someone in fear of such harm.

Since DENNIS was in fear that harm would be done to the shop, answer A is incorrect.
A constable or any other person may arrest without warrant any person:

- who is committing a breach of the peace;
- whom he or she reasonably believes will commit a breach of the peace in the immediate future; or
- who has committed a breach of the peace, where it is reasonably believed that a recurrence of the breach of the peace is threatened.

The power of arrest is given to a constable or any other person (answer D is incorrect). There is no requirement for the person to reasonably believe that the person is capable of carrying out the threat, merely that the threat may be carried out. Answer C is incorrect.

General Police Duties, paras 4.12.2, 4.12.2.4

Answer 12.2

Answer **A** — Police officers are expected to focus their attention on those who are likely to present the actual threat of violence or disorder, which was the approach taken by the Divisional Court in the case of *Redmond-Bate* v *DPP* [1999] Crim LR 998. The court held that in this case, where preachers who were antagonising passers-by were unlawfully arrested for breach of the peace, the officers should have directed their attention to the passers-by from whom the threat of violence was emanating. The Court of Appeal, in *Bibby* v *Chief Constable of Essex Police* [2000] EWCA Civ 113, set out conditions that must be met before the power to arrest for breach of the peace should be used:

- The common law power to arrest for breach of the peace should be exercised only in the clearest circumstances.
- The threat must come from the person to be arrested.
- His or her conduct must clearly interfere with the rights of others.
- The person to be arrested must be acting unreasonably so as to give rise to a well-founded fear that a breach of the peace will be occasioned.

The second point in the above list makes B and D incorrect as BROWN is not making any threats. Also, as the power of arrest can be used to prevent a future breach of the peace, answer C is incorrect. Arresting ANDREWS would fit the test in *Bibby* and would be lawful. As BROWN has made no threat, arresting him would be unlawful, as it does not fit the test in *Bibby*.

General Police Duties, paras 4.12.2.3, 4.12.2.4

Answer 12.3

Answer **C** — Under s. 1(1) of the Public Order Act 1986:

> Where 12 or more persons who are present together use or threaten unlawful violence for a common purpose and the conduct of them (taken together) is such as would cause a person of reasonable firmness present at the scene to fear for his personal safety, each of the persons using unlawful violence for the common purpose is guilty of riot.

The offence of riot may be made out in these circumstances against the five defendants who actually used violence (answer D is therefore incorrect). However, only those defendants who actually used violence will be guilty and answers A and B are incorrect. Of course, other defendants present may also be guilty of other serious Public Order Act offences.

General Police Duties, para. 4.12.4

Answer 12.4

Answer **D** — Under s. 1(1) of the Public Order Act 1986:

> Where 12 or more persons who are present together use or threaten unlawful violence for a common purpose and the conduct of them (taken together) is such as would cause a person of reasonable firmness present at the scene to fear for his personal safety, each of the persons using unlawful violence for the common purpose is guilty of riot.

There must be a common purpose, but this need not be part of a pre-determined plan, nor be unlawful in itself. Answers B and C are incorrect.

Section 1(2) states that it is immaterial whether or not the 12 or more use or threaten unlawful violence simultaneously. Therefore, answer A is incorrect.

General Police Duties, para. 4.12.4

Answer 12.5

Answer **B** — Section 6(5) of the Public Order Act 1986 states:

> For the purposes of this section a person whose awareness is impaired by intoxication shall be taken to be aware of that of which he would be aware if not intoxicated, unless he shows either that his intoxication was not self-induced or that it was caused solely by the taking or administration of a substance in the course of medical treatment.

The defence under s. 6(5) applies to all of the general Public Order Act offences; therefore, answer A is incorrect.

The defence may be raised either when the defendant claims intoxication was not self-induced or that it was caused solely by the taking or administration of a substance in the course of medical treatment. Answers C and D are therefore incorrect.

General Police Duties, para. 4.12.4.2

Answer 12.6

Answer **C** — Section 2(1) of the Public Order Act 1986 states:

> Where 3 or more persons who are present together use or threaten unlawful violence and the conduct of them (taken together) is such as would cause a person of reasonable firmness present at the scene to fear for his personal safety, each of the persons using or threatening unlawful violence is guilty of violent disorder.

Section 2(1) requires three or more persons who are present together to use or threaten unlawful violence and answer A is incorrect.

In order to convict any defendant of this offence, it must be shown that there were three or more people using or threatening violence. However, where two of the defendants are acquitted, the remaining defendant can be convicted (see *R v Mahroof* (1988) 88 Cr App R 317). Answer B is incorrect.

For an offence of riot, under s. 1 of the Act, only the persons who actually used violence may be convicted. This is not the case for an offence under s. 2; therefore, answer D is incorrect.

General Police Duties, para. 4.12.5

Answer 12.7

Answer **A** — Under s. 2(1) of the Public Order Act 1986, where three or more persons who are present together use or threaten unlawful violence and the conduct of them (taken together) is such as would cause a person of reasonable firmness present at the scene to fear for their personal safety, each of the persons using or threatening unlawful violence is guilty of violent disorder. Unlike the offence of riot (under s. 1 of the Act), for this offence each of the persons using *or* threatening unlawful violence may be guilty of the offence; therefore, answer B is incorrect.

Under s. 2, there is no requirement to show that the persons using or threatening unlawful violence did so simultaneously (unlike the offence under s. 1) and answer C is incorrect.

The circumstances in this question are similar to the case of *R* v *NW* [2010] EWCA Crim 404. In that case, a person was violently resisting arrest by a police officer, during which time a crowd gathered and various members of the crowd used or threatened violence. The Court of Appeal held that for the purposes of this section, it was not necessary for a person to deliberately act in combination with at least two other people present at the scene, but that it is sufficient that at least three people be present, each separately using or threatening unlawful violence. Answer D is therefore incorrect.

General Police Duties, para. 4.12.5

Answer 12.8

Answer **A** — Under s. 3(1) of the Public Order Act 1986, a person is guilty of affray if he/she uses or threatens unlawful violence towards another and his/her conduct is such as would cause a person of reasonable firmness present at the scene to fear for his or her personal safety.

However, in order to prove this offence, the threat cannot be made by words alone (s. 3(3)). CAHILL has not committed an act of violence towards WEBB (either personally or with the dog) in these circumstances as the behaviour merely amounted to a verbal threat. Answer B is therefore incorrect.

The 'action' by the defendant *may* consist of utilising something else such as a dog to threaten the violence (*R v Dixon* [1993] Crim LR 579). Answer C is therefore incorrect.

Finally, for this offence to be complete, the House of Lords has held that, in order to prove the offence of affray, the threat of unlawful violence has to be towards a person (or persons) present at the scene (*I v DPP* [2001] UKHL 10). This means that there does have to be *someone* other than the defendant at the scene.

Once this element has been proved, it will be necessary to prove the second element, namely whether the defendant's conduct would have caused a hypothetical person present at the scene to fear for his/her personal safety (see *R v Sanchez* (1996) 160 JP 321 and *R v Carey* [2006] EWCA Crim 17).

However, where the likelihood of a hypothetical person of reasonable firmness being present was low this element of the offence was not satisfied. In *R (On the Application of Leeson) v DPP* [2010] EWHC 994 (Admin) a woman had issued a drunken threat to kill her long-term partner whilst holding a knife, in a bathroom, in an otherwise unoccupied house. In these circumstances the court held that there was no possibility of a hypothetical bystander fearing for their safety.

The most recent case (*Leeson* above) places a different perspective on the 'hypothetical' third person, and in the example given in this question, the two parties were in separate enclosed gardens, with very little likelihood of another person being affected by the behaviour (as opposed to a situation in a pub, for example, where several people could be injured). This makes answer A correct, and answer D incorrect.

General Police Duties, para. 4.12.6

Answer 12.9

Answer **A** — A person is guilty of an offence under s. 4(1) if he or she uses towards another person threatening, abusive or insulting words or behaviour, with intent to cause that person to believe that immediate and unlawful violence would be used against him or her, or another. Since LOADER has threatened to use immediate and unlawful violence towards ANWAR, and he is in a position to do so as ANWAR is nearby, the offence is complete (and answer D is incorrect). It is immaterial that ANWAR was not present when the threat was made, or that he was not even aware of the threat.

Under s. 6(3) of the Act, a person is guilty of an offence only if he or she *intends* his or her words or behaviour to be threatening, abusive or insulting, or is aware that they may be, therefore answer C is incorrect. It is LOADER's intent that counts, not whether GAIL actually believed that violence would be used. Answer B is therefore incorrect.

General Police Duties, para. 4.12.7

Answer 12.10

Answer **C** — This question loosely follows the circumstances of *R* v *White (Anthony Delroy)* [2001] 1 WLR 1352, where the Court of Appeal upheld White's conviction for this offence. The court held that the words used are to be construed as they are generally used in England and Wales; and on that basis the word 'African' described a racial group defined by reference to race and therefore answer A is incorrect. The word 'Asians' has been similarly recognised (see *DPP* v *Rishan Kumar Pal* [2000] Crim LR 756). This offence can be committed towards people from the same racial group as the accused and answer B is therefore incorrect. This is a crime of 'specific intent' and as such does require the intent to be proven, and therefore answer D is incorrect.

General Police Duties, para. 4.12.8

Answer 12.11

Answer **C** — The Public Order Act 1986, s. 5 states:

(1) A person is guilty of an offence if he—
    (a) uses threatening, abusive or insulting words or behaviour, or disorderly behaviour, or
    (b) displays any writing, sign or other visible representation which is threatening, abusive or insulting,
    within the hearing or sight of a person likely to be caused harassment, alarm or distress thereby.

This requirement was confirmed in *Taylor* v *DPP* [2006] EWHC 1202 (Admin) where it was held that there must be at least evidence that there was someone who could see, or could hear, at the material time, what the individual was doing; answers A and B are therefore incorrect.

However, there was no requirement for the prosecution to call evidence that someone did actually hear the words spoken or see the behaviour. Answer D is incorrect.

General Police Duties, para. 4.12.9

Answer 12.12

Answer **B** — Section 6 of the Public Order Act 1986 states that a person is guilty of an offence under s. 5 only if:

> ... he intends his words or behaviour, or the writing, sign or other visible representation, to be threatening, abusive or insulting, or is aware that it may be threatening, abusive or insulting, or (as the case may be) he intends his behaviour to be or is aware that it may be disorderly.

This is a case of either/or: INCE would either have to intend his behaviour to be insulting, or he would have to be aware that it was (answer D is incorrect). There is no requirement for some person actually to have been insulted by the behaviour (although in the fact pattern of this question, there were many shoppers in the area who could provide useful evidence of their feelings at the time of the offence), therefore answer C is incorrect.

The fact that a person ought to have known that his or her behaviour was insulting is immaterial, making answer A incorrect. The person's state of mind is often ignored when it comes to charging people with offences under s. 5 (and s. 4 above). Occasionally, defence solicitors make a point of insisting that their client be interviewed before charge. While it may be impractical to interview all offenders for these offences, it may be worth considering when the facts are unclear.

General Police Duties, para. 4.12.9.1

Answer 12.13

Answer **D** — Section 42 of the Criminal Justice and Police Act 2001 gives the police certain powers to give directions in order to prevent intimidation or harassment. The legislation is designed to prevent protesters causing harassment to people in their own homes, as happened in this question. The most senior police officer present at the scene has discretionary powers to give directions to people in the vicinity, including a direction to leave the area.

In order to give a direction under s. 42, the officer must believe, on reasonable grounds, that the persons present are there for the purposes of persuading the resident or anyone else that they should not do something they are entitled or required to do, or that they should do something they are not obliged to do. The officer must also believe, on reasonable grounds, that the person's presence amounts to or is likely to result in the harassment of the resident, or is likely to cause alarm or distress to the resident. Therefore, in this question, even though the group's hostility is directed at PRICE, the outcome must be the harassment of BLUNT, the resident. Answers A, B and C are incorrect for this reason.

General Police Duties, para. 4.12.9.3

Answer 12.14

Answer **C** — Section 119(1) of the Criminal Justice and Immigration Act 2008 creates an offence of causing a nuisance or disturbance to an NHS staff member who is working on NHS premises and then failing to leave when required to do so by a constable or an NHS staff member. This section will only apply to people who are not on the NHS premises for the purpose of obtaining medical advice, treatment or care for themselves.

Section 120 of the 2008 Act provides a power for a constable or authorised person to remove a person who has committed an offence under s. 119. Although a non-authorised NHS staff member may ask a person to leave, this does not extend to a power of removal of a person who refuses. Answer B is incorrect.

An authorised officer cannot remove the person if it is reasonably believed they are in need of medical advice, etc. or that such removal would endanger their mental or physical health (s. 120(4)).

However, a person ceases to be on NHS premises for the purpose of obtaining medical advice, treatment or care for himself or herself in the following two circumstances:

- once the person has received the medical advice (s. 119(3)(a));
- if the person has received the medical advice, etc. during the last eight hours (s. 119(3)(b)).

Having received treatment less than eight hours previously, IRWIN is not a patient and may be ejected from the premises. Answers A and D are therefore incorrect.

It should be noted that this legislation is only in force in relation to NHS premises in England at this time (and not Wales).

General Police Duties, para. 4.12.10

Answer 12.15

Answer **D** — Section 11 of the Public Order Act 1986 places certain obligations on the organisers of public processions that are intended:

- to demonstrate support for, or opposition to, the views or actions of any person or body;

- to publicise a cause or campaign; or
- to mark or commemorate an event.

Since the legislation applies to processions that are intended to publicise a cause or campaign, or to mark or commemorate an event, in addition to demonstrations, answer A is incorrect.

If a public procession is to be held for any of these purposes, the organisers must give written notice, by delivering it to a police station in the relevant police area, unless it is not reasonably practicable to do so (s. 11(1) and (4)). Under s. 11(3), the notice must specify:

- the date and time of the proposed procession;
- the proposed route; and
- the name and address of the person(s) proposing to organise it.

If such a procession is held without compliance with these requirements, or if a procession takes place on a different date, time or route, each of the people organising it commits a summary offence (s. 11(7)).

However, it was held that this did not apply to commonly and customarily held processions, for example, an organised cycle ride that started at the same time and place on the last Friday of every month, even though there was no fixed, settled or predetermined route, end-time or destination (*R (on the application of Kay)* v *Commissioner of Police of the Metropolis* [2008] UKHL 69). Answers B and C are therefore incorrect.

General Police Duties, para. 4.12.11.1

Answer 12.16

Answer **D** — Under s. 14A of the Public Order Act 1986, the chief officer of police has the power, if he or she reasonably believes that it is intended to hold a trespassory assembly which may result in serious disruption to the life of the community or significant damage to land or a building or monument which is of historical, archaeological or scientific importance, to apply to the district council for an order prohibiting for a specified period the holding of all trespassory assemblies in the district or part of it. The order must not last for more than four days and must not apply to an area greater than that represented by a circle of five miles radius from a specified centre, and therefore answer C is incorrect. A constable, who must be in uniform, has power to stop someone he or she reasonably believes to be on his or her way to an assembly prohibited by an order under s. 14A and to direct him or her not to proceed in the direction of the assembly, and therefore answer B is incorrect. This power, however, does not apply to vehicles and is restricted to 'stop that person', and answer A is therefore incorrect. Other powers exist to stop the vehicle, however.

General Police Duties, paras 4.12.11.7, 4.12.11.9

Answer 12.17

Answer **C** — A written order may be given under s. 30 of the Anti-social Behaviour Act 2003, authorising the dispersal of groups of people if the relevant officer (a superintendent) has reasonable grounds for believing that any members of the public have been intimidated, harassed, alarmed or distressed as a result of the presence or behaviour of groups of two or more persons in public places. Answer A is incorrect, as an order may be given even if only two people are present. Answer D is incorrect as there must be at least two people present. The relevant officer must also be satisfied that the anti-social behaviour is a significant and persistent problem in the relevant locality (which would be the case in the circumstances given).

However, because of the implications of such an authorisation on the human rights of members of the public, further conditions are attached to the order; for example, the order may not be given without the consent of the local authority (s. 31(2)). More significantly, the authorisation must be given publicly, for example by notifying the local newspaper or by placing posters in a conspicuous place (s. 31(3)). The publicity must be given before the specified date on which the powers of dispersal are due to begin (see s. 31(2)).

Note that in accordance with the Crown Prosecution Service: Anti-Social Behaviour Guidance (May 2008), the validity of the authorisation must be proved at court, both as regards the reasons for making the authorisation and that proper publicity has been given (*Carter* v *Crown Prosecution Service* [2009] EWHC 2197 (Admin)).

Clearly, these powers may not be utilised in matters of urgency and appropriate planning must take place beforehand. Answer B is therefore incorrect.

General Police Duties, para. 4.12.12.1

Answer 12.18

Answer **D** — A written order granted by a superintendent must be in place before the police can act under s. 30(4) of the Anti-social Behaviour Act 2003 and order the group to disperse. If the order is in place, a constable in uniform, who has reasonable grounds for believing that the presence or behaviour of two or more persons in a public place has resulted, or is likely to result, in any members of the public being intimidated, harassed, alarmed or distressed, may issue directions:

(a) requiring the people in the group to disperse (either immediately or by such time and in such a way as the officer may specify);

(b) requiring any of those people whose place of residence is not within the relevant locality to leave the relevant locality (or any part of it) either immediately or by such time and in such a way as the officer may specify; and

(c) prohibiting any of those people whose place of residence is not within the relevant locality from returning to the relevant locality (or any part of it) for such period (not exceeding 24 hours) from the giving of the direction as the officer may specify.

In *R (on the application of Singh)* v *Chief Constable of West Midlands* [2005] EWHC 2840, it was held that the use of s. 30(4) powers to disperse a group of protesters of two or more people who were causing harassment, alarm or distress to members of the public, was lawful even though the order which was already in force related to quite different anticipated anti-social behaviour. Therefore, the police in this question may use their powers to disperse the group, without applying to the superintendent who originally granted the order, or any other superintendent. Answers A, B and C are all incorrect for this reason.

In addition, because of the implications of such an authorisation for the human rights of members of the public, further conditions are attached to the order; for example, the order may not be given without the consent of the local authority (s. 31(2)). More significantly, the authorisation must be given publicly, for example by notifying the local newspaper or by placing posters in a conspicuous place (s. 31(3)). The publicity must be given before the specified date on which the powers of dispersal are due to begin (see s. 31(2)). This means that these powers may not be given in matters of urgency, as in the scenario, and that appropriate planning must take place beforehand. Answers B and C are also incorrect for this reason.

General Police Duties, paras 4.12.12.1, 4.12.12.2

Answer 12.19

Answer **B** — Under s. 30(3) of the Anti-social Behaviour Act 2003, a written order must first have been given by a superintendent, authorising the dispersal of groups of people from a locality. If the order is in place, a constable in uniform, who has reasonable grounds for believing that the presence or behaviour of two or more persons in a public place has resulted, or is likely to result, in any members of the public being intimidated, harassed, alarmed or distressed, may exercise the following powers granted by s. 30(4):

(a) require the people in the group to disperse either immediately or by such time as the officer may specify; *or*

(b) require any person whose place of residence is not within the locality, to leave the locality immediately (or within a specified time); *and*

(c) prohibit any person whose place of residence is not within the locality from returning within a specified period of time (not exceeding 24 hours).

Since the people in the group were all local residents, the officer will only be able to deal with them under s. 30(4)(a) above, and will not be able to prohibit them from returning within 24 hours (but he will be able to require the people in the group to disperse immediately). Answers A and C are therefore incorrect.

Any reference to the presence or behaviour of a group of people will include any one or more of those people. Therefore, even though only one of the group was actually intimidating a member of the public, the officer has the power to disperse the whole group in these circumstances. Answers A and D are incorrect for this reason.

General Police Duties, para. 4.12.12.2

Answer 12.20

Answer **A** — Section 30(6) of the Anti-social Behaviour Act 2003 states that if, between the hours of 9 pm and 6 am, a constable in uniform finds a person in any public place in the relevant locality whom he has reasonable grounds for believing:

(a) is under the age of 16; and

(b) is not under the effective control of a parent or a responsible person aged 18 or over, he may remove the person to the person's place of residence unless he has reasonable grounds for believing that the person would, if removed to that place, be likely to suffer significant harm.

Since the incident occurred at 9.30 pm, it is within the timescales and answer B is incorrect.

In *R (W)* v *Metropolitan Police Commissioner* [2006] EWCA Civ 458 it was held that the word 'remove' in s. 30(6) naturally and compellingly means 'take away using reasonable force if necessary'. However, this is not an arbitrary power and, within a designated dispersal area, a constable must only use this power (a) to protect children under 16 from the physical and social risks of anti-social behaviour by others, *or* (b) to prevent children from themselves participating in anti-social behaviour. Since force may be used in either of the above circumstances, answers C and D are incorrect.

General Police Duties, para. 4.12.12.3

Answer 12.21

Answer **B** — The Policing and Crime Act 2009 provides courts with the power to grant injunctions in relation to gang-related violence. Under s. 34(1), a court may grant an injunction against a respondent aged *14 or over*, if the relevant conditions are met, relating to the prevention of the respondent from engaging in, or encouraging or assisting, gang-related violence, or alternatively, to protect the respondent from gang-related violence.

It should be noted that the full measures of this Act are not yet in place. In December 2010 the Home Office published 'Statutory Guidance: Injunctions to Prevent Gang-Related Violence' to help local partners apply for and manage gang injunctions effectively and appropriately. Currently gang injunctions are being piloted for those aged 14–17.

Answers A, C and D are therefore incorrect.

General Police Duties, para. 4.12.12.5

Sporting Events

STUDY PREPARATION

The maintenance of public order at sporting events is an important area of responsibility for the police and the service has a far more sophisticated range of measures to help deal with football hooliganism than it did in the 1970s and 1980s. Large sporting events can tie up significant numbers of officers and the emphasis today is on more preventative measures to control spectators.

The Sporting Events (Control of Alcohol etc.) Act 1985 and the Football (Offences) Act 1991 create offences relating to drunkenness and rowdy behaviour at designated sporting events, while the Football Spectators Act 1989 provides the courts with significant powers to issue banning orders against those who are involved with football-related disorder, in connection with regulated football matches both inside and outside the United Kingdom.

The police rely heavily on football clubs to regulate the sale of tickets at major sporting events. The final part of the chapter deals with offences created by the Criminal Justice and Public Order Act 1994 to deal with 'ticket touts', whose actions can undermine attempts to separate home and away supporters.

QUESTIONS

Question 13.1

GREEN was a football fan attending a designated football match. GREEN was caught on CCTV climbing over a fence from the away supporters end into a sterile area which was designed to keep the two sets of fans separated.

Which of the following statements is correct, in relation to offences under s. 4 of the Football (Offences) Act 1991 (going onto the playing area)?

A The offence is committed by a person who goes onto the playing area only.

B The offence is committed by a person who goes onto the playing area, or an area to which spectators are not generally admitted.

C The offence is committed by a person who goes onto the playing area, or an area to which other spectators are admitted.

D The offence is committed by a person who goes onto any area of the ground to which spectators are not generally admitted.

Question 13.2

HARDING was convicted of criminal damage and affray in the car park of a Premier League football ground. HARDING attacked a coach belonging to away supporters with a baseball bat, smashing several windows. The incident occurred at the end of a game, while fans were inside the ground. HARDING, who had left the ground early to cause the damage, pleaded guilty, admitting having been involved in a long-standing dispute with supporters of the other club.

Which of the following statements would be correct in relation to the imposition of a banning order, under s. 14A of the Football Spectators Act 1989?

A The court is now under a statutory duty to make an order against HARDING.

B The court is now under a statutory duty to consider making an order against HARDING.

C The court is under a statutory duty to consider making an order, but only if requested to do so by the prosecution.

D The court is under no statutory duty to consider making an order because HARDING was not convicted of a violent offence against a person.

Question 13.3

The police have been looking for JENSEN to serve a notice on him prior to applying for a banning order against him, because of his violent behaviour at Premiership football matches. JENSEN has so far evaded the police, however, officers working at a home tie of a UEFA Champions League match have been circulated his photograph. JENSEN is spotted outside the ground at the end of the game by Constable BARNETT and because the next game for the club is in two weeks' time, which is the return leg abroad, the officer is keen to detain JENSEN before he disappears again.

Would Constable BARNETT be entitled to detain JENSEN in these circumstances, using powers under s. 21A(2) of the Football Spectators Act 1989?

A No, there is no power of detention at this time because this is not within the control period.

B Yes, JENSEN could be detained for up to a maximum of six hours while a decision is being made whether to serve a notice on him.

C No, JENSEN has not yet been served with a notice outlining that a banning order is to be applied for.

D Yes, JENSEN could be detained for up to a maximum of four hours while a decision is being made whether to serve a notice on him.

Question 13.4

CORTEZ is appearing in the magistrates' court due to his part in organising a violent confrontation during a European Champions League football match in Italy. As a result of an undercover operation, the police have been able to demonstrate that CORTEZ was the organiser of violence between fans from an English Premier League club and an Italian club. However, the police have been unable to produce evidence that CORTEZ actually took part in the violence in Italy. An application is being made for a banning order against CORTEZ.

Could such an order succeed in these circumstances?

A Yes, and if it makes an order, the court must require CORTEZ to surrender his passport.

B No, a banning order may only be made when the person has been convicted of a relevant offence.

C Yes, and if it makes an order, the court may require CORTEZ to surrender his passport.

D No; because the incidents of violence occurred abroad, the court must be satisfied that CORTEZ actually took part.

Question 13.5

HUNTER was driving a public service vehicle containing a number of passengers who support an English Premier League club. HUNTER was driving the supporters home from a match against another Premier League club. The vehicle was stopped on the motorway by the police, who found that many of the passengers were either in possession of alcohol or drunk. HUNTER admitted stopping at a shop, to allow the passengers to buy alcohol, which they brought onto the vehicle.

Which of the following statements is correct, in relation to offences that may have been committed under the Sporting Events (Control of Alcohol etc.) Act 1985?

A No offences were committed under this Act, as the supporters were not on their way to a designated sporting event.

B HUNTER committed the offence, along with anyone who was drinking alcohol in the vehicle.

C HUNTER committed the offence, along with anyone who was drunk in the vehicle.

D HUNTER committed the offence, along with anyone who was in possession of alcohol or who was drunk in the vehicle.

Question 13.6

CRIBBINS supports an English Premier League club, which has reached the final of the European Champions League tournament. The football match is being played in Paris. CRIBBINS owns a mini-bus which is designed to carry 12 passengers and has agreed to drive ten friends to the match free of charge. The vehicle was stopped near the ferry port by police, who found that most of the passengers were completely drunk and CRIBBINS admitted that alcohol had been brought onto the vehicle and had been consumed on the way to the port.

Have any offences been committed under the Sporting Events (Control of Alcohol etc.) Act 1985, in these circumstances?

A Yes, CRIBBINS committed the offence, as well as any people who were either in possession of alcohol or drunk.

B No, offences under this Act do not apply to people attending a designated sporting event in another country.

C No, the vehicle was not a public service vehicle; therefore the offence was not committed.

D Yes, but because the vehicle was not a public service vehicle, only CRIBBINS is guilty of the offence.

Question 13.7

DAWKINS is entering a designated sports ground and has been searched by a police officer. The officer finds a hip flask on DAWKINS, which contains malt whisky. When questioned, DAWKINS said he had it with him to drink from and did not intend using it to harm anyone.

Has DAWKINS committed an offence contrary to s. 2 of the Sporting Events (Control of Alcohol etc.) Act 1985 (alcohol at sports grounds)?

A No, as he has no intention of using the article to cause injury.

B No, because the article is not of the kind normally discarded.

C Yes, because the article contains alcohol.

D Yes, because the article is capable of causing injury to a person.

Question 13.8

WINGROVE supports a football team which is a member of the English Football League, which has qualified for the Champions League. WINGROVE has managed to buy 50 tickets for an away game in Germany and has advertised them for sale on a website. WINGROVE intends making a profit by selling the tickets at more than their market value.

Does WINGROVE commit an offence under s. 166 of the Criminal Justice and Public Order Act 1994, in these circumstances?

A No, the offence does not apply to football matches abroad.

B No, the offence will only be committed when WINGROVE actually sells a ticket.

C No, the offence only applies to international football matches abroad.

D Yes, provided WINGROVE is not authorised by the organisers of the match.

ANSWERS

Answer 13.1

Answer **B** — Under s. 4 of the Football (Offences) Act 1991, it is an offence for a person at a designated football match to go onto the playing area, *or any area adjacent to the playing area to which spectators are not generally admitted,* without lawful authority or lawful excuse (which shall be for him to prove). The standard of proof will be that of the balance of probabilities.

Answers A, C and D are therefore incorrect.

General Police Duties, para. 4.13.2.1

Answer 13.2

Answer **B** — Under s. 14A of the Football Spectators Act 1989, the court may make a banning order against a person who is convicted of a relevant offence. The relevant offences are set out in sch. 1 and include offences relating to drunkenness, violence or threats of violence, or public order offences committed at or in connection with a football match or when travelling to or from a football match (whether or not the match was actually attended by the offender).

Violence includes violence towards property and disorder includes stirring up racial hatred (see s. 14C). Answer D is therefore incorrect.

Rather than simply having the power to make such orders, courts are under a statutory duty to pass such orders if they are satisfied that there are reasonable grounds to believe that the orders would help prevent violence or disorder at/in connection with a 'regulated football match'. If the court does *not* pass an order, it must state in open court its reasons for not doing so. Therefore, while the court has a statutory duty to *consider* an order (using the above guidelines), it is not under such a duty to automatically make one because of a person's conviction and answer A is incorrect.

On the other hand, the court is the responsible authority in these circumstances and it should consider making an order *whether or not* it has been requested to do so by the prosecution. Answer C is therefore incorrect.

General Police Duties, para. 4.13.3

Answer 13.3

Answer **A** — Under s. 21A of the Football Spectators Act 1989, if a constable in uniform

(a) has reasonable grounds for suspecting that the condition in s. 14B(2) is met in the case of a person present before him, and

(b) has reasonable grounds to believe that making a banning order in his case would help to prevent violence or disorder at or in connection with any regulated football matches,

the constable may detain the person in his custody (whether there or elsewhere) until he has decided whether or not to issue a notice under s. 21B, and shall give the person his reasons for detaining him in writing. (The condition under s. 14B(2) referred to is that the person has at any time caused or contributed to any violence or disorder in the United Kingdom or elsewhere.)

Answer C is incorrect as there is no requirement to serve a notice on a person *before* detaining them under s. 21A(2). The actual purpose of the power is to detain a person in order to decide whether or not to serve a notice of a banning order on him/her.

A person may not be detained under subs. (2) above for more than four hours or, with the authority of an officer of at least the rank of inspector, six hours (s. 21A(3)). Therefore, the *maximum* period of detention while deciding whether or not to serve the notice is six hours and answer D is incorrect.

Finally, both answers B and D are also incorrect because the power under s. 21A(2) is only applicable during any control period in relation to a regulated football match outside the United Kingdom or an external tournament. 'Control period' means, in relation to a regulated football match outside England and Wales, the period:

(a) beginning five days before the day of the match, and

(b) ending when the match is finished or cancelled.

This means there is no power to detain JENSEN at this time; however, the opportunity to do so will come before the next game for the club, in the five-day period leading up to the second leg.

General Police Duties, para. 4.13.3.2

Answer 13.4

Answer **A** — Banning orders may be made under s. 14A or s. 14B of the Football Spectators Act 1989. Under s. 14A, the court may make a banning order against a person who is convicted of a relevant offence. The relevant offences are set out in sch. 1 and include offences relating to drunkenness, violence or threats of violence, or public order offences. Under s. 14B, the Chief Officer of police or the Director of Public Prosecutions may submit a request to the court, by way of complaint, to make such an order, even when the person has not been convicted of a relevant offence. Answer B is incorrect.

On application to the court under s. 14B, the magistrates may make an order if the person has at any time *caused or contributed to* any violence or disorder in the United Kingdom or elsewhere. Therefore, since the police are able to produce evidence that CORTEZ caused or contributed to violence abroad, answer D is incorrect.

Finally, if the court imposes a banning order in connection with regulated football matches outside the United Kingdom, it *must* require the surrender of the person's passport and/or identity card (s. 14E(3)). Answer C is therefore incorrect.

General Police Duties, para. 4.13.3

Answer 13.5

Answer **D** — Section 1 of the Sporting Events (Control of Alcohol etc.) Act 1985 applies to people who are being conveyed in public service vehicles or railway passenger vehicles, which are being used for the principal purpose of carrying passengers to *or from* designated sporting events (s. 1(1)). Answer A is therefore incorrect.

Under s. 1(2), a person who knowingly causes or permits alcohol to be carried on a vehicle to which the section applies is guilty of an offence (which makes HUNTER guilty of the offence). Other offences are committed by any person who has alcohol in his/her possession while on a vehicle to which this section applies (s. 1(3)), or to a person who is drunk on such a vehicle (s. 1(3)). Since the offence applies to both classes of people, answer C is incorrect.

Section 1 does not actually mention people who are *drinking* alcohol whilst in a vehicle to which this section applies (although by implication, such people are likely to be in possession of alcohol). Since the wording is incorrect (and the offence applies both to people who have alcohol in their possession *and* who are drunk), answer B is incorrect.

General Police Duties, para. 4.13.4

Answer 13.6

Answer **A** — Section 1 of the Sporting Events (Control of Alcohol etc.) Act 1985 creates offences which may be committed by people who are either in possession of alcohol or drunk, whilst being conveyed in public service vehicles or railway passenger vehicles, which are being used for the principal purpose of carrying passengers to or from designated sporting events.

However, s. 1A(1) of the Sporting Events (Control of Alcohol etc.) Act 1985 applies to a motor vehicle which is *not* a public service vehicle but is adapted to carry more than eight passengers, and is being used for the purpose described above.

Section 1A(2)(a) states that a person who knowingly causes or permits alcohol to be carried on a motor vehicle to which this section applies is guilty of an offence if he or she is its driver (or its keeper or the keeper's servant or agent, or the servant or agent of a person to whom it is so made available). Therefore, even though the vehicle was not a public service vehicle, CRIBBINS is still guilty of the offence. Answer C is incorrect.

Further offences are committed under s. 1A(3) and (4), by a person who has alcohol in his/her possession or who is drunk, while on a motor vehicle to which this section applies. Answer D is therefore incorrect.

Finally, offences under s. 1 and s. 1A apply to 'designated' or 'regulated' football matches, *outside the United Kingdom*, including any match involving a club whose national football association is a member of FIFA, where the match is part of a competition or tournament organised by or under the authority of FIFA or UEFA, and where the competition or tournament is one in which a club from the Football League, the Football Association Premier League, the Football Conference or the League of Wales is eligible to participate or has participated. Answer B is therefore incorrect.

General Police Duties, para. 4.13.4

Answer 13.7

Answer **C** — An offence under s. 2 of the Sporting Events (Control of Alcohol etc.) Act 1985 is committed by 'a person who has alcohol or an article to which this section applies in his possession'.

The article to which s. 2 applies is defined as any article capable of causing injury and there is no need to prove intention, and therefore answer A is incorrect. However, this article is further defined as:

- bottles, cans or other portable containers (including ones that are crushed or broken); *which*

- are for holding any drink; *and*
- are of a kind which, when empty, are normally discarded or returned to, or left to be recovered by, the supplier.

As the hip flask does not fit this definition, answer D is incorrect. The fact that DAWKINS is in possession of alcohol makes him liable; it does not have to be an article to which this section applies. So he commits the offence even though the hip flask is not an article to which s. 2 applies, and therefore answer B is incorrect.

General Police Duties, para. 4.13.4.2

Answer 13.8

Answer **D** — It is an offence under s. 166(1) of the Criminal Justice and Public Order Act 1994 for an unauthorised person to sell a ticket for a designated football match, or otherwise to dispose of such a ticket to another person. A person is 'unauthorised' unless he or she is authorised in writing to sell or otherwise dispose of tickets for the match by the organisers of the match (s. 166(2)(a)).

Section 166(2)(aa) outlines the criteria for 'selling' a ticket, which includes offering to sell a ticket, exposing a ticket for sale and advertising that a ticket is available for purchase. Answer B is therefore incorrect.

For the purposes of s. 166(2)(c) a 'designated football match' is described in art. 2(2) of the Ticket Touting (Designation of Football Matches) Order 2007 (SI 2007/790) as an association football match in England and Wales; whereas art. 2(3) designates association football matches *outside* England and Wales involving a national team (of England or Wales), or a team representing a club which is a member of the Football League, the Football Association Premier League, the Football Conference or League of Wales, or matches in competitions or tournaments organised by or under the authority of FIFA or UEFA, in which any of such English or Welsh domestic or national teams is eligible to participate or has participated. Answers A and C are therefore incorrect.

General Police Duties, para. 4.13.6

14 | Weapons

STUDY PREPARATION

While the definition contained in s. 1 of the Prevention of Crime Act 1953 appears quite simple, you need to know the component parts to fully understand the offence. Learn the meaning of 'lawful authority', 'reasonable excuse', 'has with him' and 'public place'; there are many decided cases to assist (or confuse) you. You must also, of course, learn the three categories of offensive weapons.

Commonly, people tend to confuse the offence under the 1953 Act with the offence of carrying a bladed or sharply pointed article, especially in relation to folding pocket-knives and the length of blades. Remember also where the evidential burden lies in relation to proof for both offences, and the special defences under the Criminal Justice Act 1988.

One of the greatest problems in this very relevant area is separating the different statutory requirements. It is essential to be able to distinguish between the requirements relating to offensive weapons (in the Prevention of Crime Act 1953) and those relating to pointed or bladed instruments as regulated by the Criminal Justice Act 1988. Unless you are very clear about these differences, life will get very confusing. Further legislation in this chapter relates to the carrying of weapons on educational premises and the powers given to staff in such places.

Also, you must be able to tell the difference between an 'offensive weapon' and a 'weapon of offence', as contained in the offence of trespassing with a weapon of offence, under the Criminal Law Act 1977. The manufacture and sale of weapons receive attention, with a long list of weapons that may not be manufactured or sold, etc. Further offences may be committed by selling and marketing knives and articles to children under 16. Do not forget to learn about crossbows and the three offences contained in the Crossbows Act 1987. Also, pay attention to the powers given to a constable to search people and vehicles.

Apart from that, it is very straightforward!

QUESTIONS

Question 14.1

Constable LEACH stopped BERTRAND, who was driving a motor vehicle on a road, and conducted a search under s. 1 of the Police and Criminal Evidence Act 1984. The officer discovered a flick-knife underneath BERTRAND's seat. BERTRAND was arrested and charged with having an offensive weapon with him in a public place, contrary to s. 1(1) of the Prevention of Crime Act 1953. BERTRAND has pleaded not guilty, stating that he had a 'good reason' for having the weapon; that he had been threatened recently and was carrying the knife for his own protection.

In relation to BERTRAND's claim to have a reasonable excuse, which of the following statements is correct?

A The prosecution must show beyond reasonable doubt that BERTRAND did not have a 'good reason' for having the weapon.

B Carrying a weapon in self-defence could not amount to a 'good reason' for having it; BERTRAND has no defence to this charge.

C Carrying a weapon in self-defence could amount to a 'good reason' for having it; BERTRAND must show on the balance of probabilities that he had a reasonable excuse for having it.

D Carrying a weapon in self-defence could amount to a 'good reason' for having it; BERTRAND must show beyond reasonable doubt that he had a reasonable excuse for having it.

Question 14.2

FAWCETT was driving home from work when he caused another car, being driven by GRANT, to brake sharply. GRANT followed him, shouting obscenities and sounding his horn. When FAWCETT stopped at traffic lights, GRANT got out of his car and ran towards him. FAWCETT got out of his own car and picked up a steering wheel lock, and threw it at GRANT, intending to injure him.

Is the steering wheel lock an 'offensive weapon' in these circumstances?

A No, FAWCETT formed the intention to use the article after it came into his possession.

B Yes, as soon as FAWCETT formed the intention to use the article.

C Yes, because FAWCETT used the article, intending to injure GRANT.

D Yes, as soon as FAWCETT picked the article up with the intention to use it.

Question 14.3

Constable BAKER was on patrol when she stopped a vehicle owned and being driven by CLEMENT. HARVEY was in the front passenger seat. Constable BAKER made a search of the vehicle and discovered a flick-knife in the glove compartment.

Could HARVEY and CLEMENT be guilty of an offence under the Prevention of Crime Act 1953?

A No, only CLEMENT may commit the offence, being the owner of the car.

B Yes, the offence is complete against both; no further proof is required.

C No, it is not possible for two people to have the same weapon with them.

D Yes, provided they both knew that the other person had it with him at the time.

Question 14.4

PENFOLD was stopped and searched on his way to a football match while he was walking in High Street. The searching officer, Constable MARRIOTT, discovered in PENFOLD's pocket a number of 50 pence pieces that had been sharpened around the edges. Believing that they were offensive weapons, the officer lawfully arrested PENFOLD.

In order to prove that PENFOLD was guilty of possessing an offensive weapon would Constable MARRIOTT need to prove intent by PENFOLD to use the coins to cause injury?

A No, provided it can be shown that the coins have been made to cause injury.

B Yes, because there is no apparent victim in these circumstances.

C Yes, because the coins are not offensive weapons *per se*.

D No, provided it can be shown the coins have been adapted to cause injury.

Question 14.5

BARRY was stopped and searched in the street by Constable ROCH. The officer found a pocket-knife in BARRY'S pocket, which had a 4-inch blade. BARRY admitted that he was on his way to a football match and intended to use the knife in a fight with rival fans.

Is this weapon an offensive weapon under the Prevention of Crime Act 1953?

A Yes, as the blade is more than 3 inches long.
B Yes, a folding pocket-knife with a blade of more than 3 inches will always be an offensive weapon.
C Yes, it is an offensive weapon regardless of the length of the blade.
D No, a folding pocket-knife will not be an offensive weapon regardless of the length of the blade.

Question 14.6

BROOKER was stopped and searched by the police in a public place, whilst on the way to a football match. At the time, BROOKER was carrying a butter knife, which was not sharpened, and which had a blade of at least 3.5 inches in length.

Could BROOKER commit an offence under s. 139 of the Criminal Justice Act 1988 in these circumstances?

A No, because the blade was not sharp.
B Yes, because the knife was a bladed instrument.
C Yes, because the knife was a bladed instrument more than 3 inches long.
D No, because it is unlikely that the blade was capable of causing injury.

Question 14.7

Constable WARREN was on duty on a Sunday evening when he stopped MOHAMMED, who was driving a car on the road. Constable WARREN conducted a search of the vehicle and found a meat cleaver under the seat. MOHAMMED stated that he worked as a chef in a restaurant and that he used the meat cleaver as part of his work. He further stated that he had put it in his car the previous night, intending to take it to be sharpened on Monday morning.

Would MOHAMMED have a defence to a charge under s. 139 of the Criminal Justice Act 1988 (having a bladed or sharply pointed article) in these circumstances?

A Yes, the statutory defence of 'good reason'.
B Yes, because he had it for use in his work.

C No, the offence is complete in these circumstances.

D Yes, the statutory defence of 'lawful authority'.

Question 14.8

HUTCHINGS visited his friend, CARTER, who lives with his parents in the caretaker's house of a primary school. When he arrived, both boys played in the garden of the caretaker's house. Both boys were playing with flick-knives.

Who would commit an offence of having with him an offensive weapon on school premises in these circumstances?

A Neither, because they are not on school premises.

B Both, because they are on school premises.

C HUTCHINGS only, because he does not reside on the premises.

D Both, because they are not in a dwelling on school premises.

Question 14.9

A report was received by the police of a disturbance in a high school. The first person to arrive was Constable SANCHEZ, who was in plain clothes. He was told that two pupils had threatened a teacher and that one of them had a knife. After a search, Constable SANCHEZ found the two youths in the street outside.

What powers would Constable SANCHEZ have under the Criminal Justice Act 1988 in these circumstances?

A He has no powers under the 1988 Act and must use his powers under the Police and Criminal Evidence Act 1984.

B He has a power under the 1988 Act to search the youths for an offensive weapon.

C He has no powers under the 1988 Act as the pupils were not trespassing.

D He has no powers under the 1988 Act as he is not in uniform.

Question 14.10

PIETERSEN, a head teacher of a high school, was contacted by a member of staff stating that SNACHEZ, a pupil at the school, had been seen carrying a knife on school premises. The teacher kept SNACHEZ under observation until PIETERSEN arrived. Utilising powers under s. 550AA of the Education Act 1996, PIETERSEN searched SNACHEZ but did not find the knife. SNACHEZ was carrying a bag and the member of staff suggested that SNACHEZ may have hidden the knife inside it.

What authority would PIETERSEN have to search SNACHEZ's possessions under this legislation?

A None, possessions may not be searched under this legislation, only a pupil may be searched.

B A pupil's possessions may be searched, but only in the pupil's presence and in the presence of another member of staff.

C A pupil's possessions may be searched, but only in the presence of another member of staff and with the pupil's permission.

D A pupil's possessions may be searched, but only in the presence of another member of staff.

Question 14.11

MEARS was a high school pupil on a field trip. The teacher in charge, SMITH, was told by another pupil that MEARS had taken a flick-knife on the trip and had hidden it in a coat pocket. SMITH told MEARS to hand over the weapon; however, MEARS denied being in possession of a knife.

What powers, if any, would SMITH have to search for the weapon, under s. 550AA of the Education Act 1996?

A SMITH may have searched MEARS, using force if necessary.

B None, as they were not on school premises.

C None, only a head teacher may search a pupil under this legislation.

D SMITH may have searched MEARS, but not by the use of force.

Question 14.12

FLANNAGAN is the head teacher of a high school and was informed that a 15-year-old pupil, HEATLEY, had been seen in the classroom with a knife by the teacher, BOYD. FLANNAGAN made his way to the class and spoke to BOYD, who stated he had seen HEATLEY hide the knife down the front of his trousers. FLANNAGAN has entered the room, however, HEATLEY has denied being in possession of a knife and told FLANNAGAN he would have to find the knife himself.

What action is FLANNAGAN entitled to take in order to search for the knife?

A FLANNAGAN may search HEATLEY, provided BOYD is present.

B FLANNAGAN may search HEATLEY, provided BOYD is present and the search is conducted in private.

C As the head teacher, FLANNAGAN has the power to search HEATLEY whether BOYD is present or not.

D FLANNAGAN has no power to search HEATLEY in these circumstances, and will have to call the police if he wishes to recover the knife.

Question 14.13

CRUZ was employed as a computer software programmer, but was sacked for selling material to a rival company. CRUZ returned to the company offices one night, entering the gated compound using an electronic pass that had not been confiscated. CRUZ's intention was to sabotage the company software, by loading a virus onto the server. CRUZ was in possession of a knife, intending to use it to threaten the night security guard if necessary. However, CRUZ was unable to get into the main company building as the electronic pass did not work. CRUZ was disturbed by the security guard and ran off.

Has CRUZ committed an offence contrary to s. 8(1) of the Criminal Law Act 1977 (trespassing with a weapon of offence)?

A No, CRUZ has not entered a dwelling with a weapon of offence.
B Yes, CRUZ has entered premises with a weapon of offence.
C No, CRUZ has not entered a building with a weapon of offence.
D No, CRUZ has not entered a dwelling, or land adjacent to a dwelling with a weapon of offence.

Question 14.14

ANDREWS owned a house which was being renovated. One day he visited it and found HARVEY squatting inside. ANDREWS asked HARVEY to leave. However, HARVEY was carrying a knife and threatened ANDREWS with it. The police were called and Constable RAMAN arrived, and was considering how to deal with HARVEY.

Which of the following is the definition of a weapon of offence under s. 8 of the Criminal Law Act 1977?

A Any article made or adapted for use for causing injury to or incapacitating a person, or intended by the person having it with him or her for that use.
B Any article made or adapted for use for causing injury to or intended by the person having it with him or her for that use.
C Any article intended by the person having it with him or her for the purpose of causing injury.
D Any article made or adapted for use for causing injury to or incapacitating a person.

Question 14.15

STONE owns a shop which sells second-hand goods and has a reputation for being able to supply unusual weapons. COLLINS entered the shop looking for some weapons for himself and his friends for a football match the following week. STONE indicated that he could get his hands on some knuckle dusters, which he could sell at a good price. COLLINS agreed to return three days later to buy them.

At what point, if any, would STONE commit an offence under the Criminal Justice Act 1988?

A Not until he actually sells the weapons to COLLINS.

B Not until he is in possession of the weapons with intent to sell them.

C When he offered to sell the weapons to COLLINS.

D Not until he has the weapons with him with intent to sell them.

Question 14.16

FAHEY is aged 18 and works in a hardware shop. McKAY, aged 17, came into the shop one day and selected a pocket-knife from the display, intending to buy it. The pocket-knife had a blade with a cutting edge of 3.5 inches.

Considering offences under s. 141A of the Criminal Justice Act 1988, could FAHEY lawfully sell this pocket-knife to McKAY?

A Yes, because FAHEY is over 18.

B Yes, because McKAY is over 16.

C No, because McKAY is under 18.

D Yes, this offence does not apply to folding pocket-knives.

Question 14.17

GUY, aged 15, was in the back garden of his parents' house, and had with him a crossbow. He was using it to fire at a target in the garden, and was accompanied at the time by PREECE, aged 18. At no time did any of the bolts fired from the crossbow leave the garden.

Has GUY committed an offence in these circumstances?

A No, because he was accompanied by a person over 18.

B No, because he was not in a public place.

C No, because none of the missiles was allowed to leave the property.

D Yes, because he was not accompanied by a person over 21.

Question 14.18

EMMERSON, aged 16, was at home one day when a friend brought a bag containing an old crossbow to the house. When the friend left, EMMERSON took the crossbow into the back garden and discovered that the crossbow was not assembled, though it appeared that all the component parts were present to re-assemble it. Whilst alone in the garden, EMMERSON began attempting to re-assemble the crossbow.

Has EMMERSON committed an offence under s. 3 of the Crossbows Act 1987, in these circumstances?

A No, not until the crossbow has been re-assembled.

B Yes, because EMMERSON is under 17.

C Yes, provided the crossbow can be re-assembled.

D No, because EMMERSON was not in a public place.

Question 14.19

Constable SHAPIRO received a complaint of persons dangerously firing a crossbow in the back garden of a dwelling. On arrival, neighbours showed the officer some bolts from the crossbow, which had penetrated the hedge separating their gardens. Constable SHAPIRO could see BARRYMORE alone in the garden, but there was no sign of a crossbow. BARRYMORE appeared to be about 14 years of age.

Does Constable SHAPIRO have the power to enter BARRYMORE's garden to search for the crossbow in these circumstances?

A Yes, there is a power to enter any land other than a dwelling house in order to conduct such a search.

B No, there is no power to enter land, which forms part of a dwelling under this legislation.

C Yes, there is a power to enter any premises or vehicle in order to conduct such a search.

D No, a constable only has the power to search a person or a vehicle under this legislation.

ANSWERS

Answer 14.1

Answer **C** — To prove an offence contrary to s. 1(1) of the Prevention of Crime Act 1953, the prosecution must first show, beyond reasonable doubt, that the defendant had an offensive weapon with him—which in these circumstances should cause no problem. The burden of proof then shifts to the defendant to show that he or she had 'good reason' or a reasonable excuse for having the weapon. Answer A is incorrect, as the prosecution bears no further burden once it can be shown the person has an offensive weapon with him/her.

The burden of proof on the defendant will be judged on the balance of probabilities, and not beyond reasonable doubt; therefore, answer D is incorrect.

The defendant *may* show that he/she had 'good reason' or 'lawful authority' for having the article in a public place (s. 139(4) and (5) of the Criminal Justice Act 1988), which could in some circumstances be carrying the weapon in self-defence (see *R v Emmanuel* [1998] Crim LR 347). Similarly, in *R v McAuley* [2009] EWCA Crim 2130 it was held that it could amount to a 'good reason' if the appellant was carrying the knife for his own protection and he could show on the balance of probabilities that he was in fear of an imminent attack. Answer B is incorrect.

General Police Duties, paras 4.14.2, 4.14.3.1

Answer 14.2

Answer **A** — The expression 'has with him' will not in most cases include circumstances where a person has an 'innocent' article, which he or she uses offensively. The purpose of the Prevention of Crime Act 1953 is to prevent people from arming themselves for some future event, and the intention of the Act is to deal with preventative issues.

The case of *Ohlson v Hylton* [1975] 1 WLR 724 demonstrates this. The defendant had a bag of tools with him in the course of his trade. He produced a hammer from the bag and used it to hit someone. The court held that, as he had formed the intention to use the hammer *after* it came into his possession, the offence was not made out (answers B and C are therefore incorrect). This decision was followed by several other similar cases (*Bates v Bulman* [1979] 1 WLR 1190, *R v Dayle* [1974] 1 WLR 181 and *R v Humphreys* [1977] Crim LR 225).

This is not to say that 'innocent' articles may never become offensive weapons, such as people carrying screwdrivers to defend themselves; it depends on the immediacy of the conversion from one to another, and therefore answer D is incorrect.

General Police Duties, para. 4.14.2

Answer 14.3

Answer **D** — It is possible for more than one person to have the same weapon 'with them' (*R* v *Edmonds* [1963] 2 QB 142), and therefore answers A and C are incorrect. It would be necessary to prove that they knew of the existence of the weapon in the hands of the other.

In this case it was decided that both parties knew of the existence of the weapon and that they knew the other party had it 'with him' at the time of the offence. Answer B is incorrect as the offence is not complete until this is proved.

General Police Duties, para. 4.14.2

Answer 14.4

Answer **D** — The prosecution would have to show that the coins have been adapted to cause injury in order to show that they are offensive weapons. However, once the prosecution have proved this, there is no need to show an intention to use them to cause injury (*Davis* v *Alexander* (1970) 54 Cr App R 398).

Answer A is incorrect because the coins have not been 'made' to cause injury; they are not offensive weapons *per se*. However, the fact that they are not offensive weapons *per se* still does not place a burden upon the prosecution to prove intent to use them (*Davis* v *Alexander*), which is why answer C is incorrect.

Answer B is incorrect because it is the adaptation of the article that is relevant, not the intention of the person carrying it (*Bryan* v *Mott* (1976) 62 Cr App R 71).

If PENFOLD were charged under the third leg of the definition, where the weapon is intended to cause injury, the prosecution would have to prove an intention to cause injury by PENFOLD. This would obviously be a harder case to prove than adaptation in the above circumstances.

General Police Duties, para. 4.14.2

Answer 14.5

Answer **C** — Under the Prevention of Crime Act 1953, an offensive weapon is an article which is made, intended or adapted for causing injury. The weapon in question will be an offensive weapon because BARRY intends that it will be used to cause injury.

Under the 1953 Act, it is irrelevant what length the blade happens to be. However, under s. 139 of the Criminal Justice Act 1988, a person commits an offence if he or she has a bladed or sharply pointed instrument in a public place—unless the instrument is a folding pocket-knife with a blade of less than 3 inches. Do not mix the two Acts.

Answers A and B are incorrect as they refer to the length of the blade as being relevant. Answer D is incorrect because a folding pocket-knife may be an offensive weapon, depending on the circumstances.

General Police Duties, para. 4.14.2

Answer 14.6

Answer **B** — Under s. 139 of the Criminal Justice Act 1988, a person commits an offence if he or she has a bladed or sharply pointed instrument in a public place. The Act provides for a person either carrying a sharply pointed instrument or a bladed instrument. There is no requirement for a bladed instrument to be sharp and in *Brooker* v *DPP* (2005) 169 JP 368, it was held that a blunt butter knife fell within s. 139. Answer A is therefore incorrect.

(Note that in a similar case, *R (On the Application of the Royal Borough of Windsor and Maidenhead)* v *East Berkshire Justices* [2010] EWHC 3020 (Admin), it was held that a grapefruit knife is not just a gadget but a knife within the meaning of s. 141A(2)(a) of the Criminal Justice Act 1988.)

Under the Act, a folding pocket-knife is excluded, provided the cutting edge of the blade is less than 3 inches long. This does not apply to all bladed instruments and the length of the blade of any other bladed instrument is irrelevant, which is why answer C is incorrect.

There is no requirement under the Act to prove that the instrument was capable of causing injury, and therefore answer D is incorrect.

General Police Duties, para. 4.14.3

Answer 14.7

Answer **C** — A defendant charged with an offence under s. 139(1) of the Act may claim either that he or she had a 'good reason' for having the weapon with him or her, or that he or she had 'lawful authority'. Further, the defendant may also claim that he or she had the weapon for use at work.

The circumstances in the question mirror those in the case of *Mohammed* v *Chief Constable of South Yorkshire* [2002] EWHC 406 (Admin). The defendant appealed against his conviction for an offence under s. 139(1), claiming that he had the meat cleaver with him for a 'good reason' (*per* s. 139(4)), or alternatively that he had it with him for use in his work (*per* s. 139(5)). The appeal failed in the Administrative Court, which held that the defendant had not shown that he had a 'good reason' for having the weapon, as the 'ultimate lawful purpose' claimed was too far distant from the time when the defendant was caught with the article. Answer A is incorrect.

The court also held that the defendant did not have the cleaver for use at work; he had it for the purposes of *rendering it possible* to use at work. The court held that he could have taken the cleaver directly from work on the Monday morning to be sharpened. Answer B is therefore incorrect.

'Lawful authority' means those occasions where people are required to carry weapons as a matter of duty, such as police officers or members of the armed forces (*Bryan* v *Mott* (1976) 62 Cr App R 71). In these circumstances, MOHAMMED could not claim this defence and answer D is incorrect.

General Police Duties, para. 4.14.3.1

Answer 14.8

Answer **A** — This offence was added to the Prevention of Crime Act 1953, and a further offence was added to the Criminal Justice Act 1988 of having a sharply pointed or bladed instrument on school premises. The definitions of weapons mirror the original offences; therefore, it follows that a flick-knife will be an offensive weapon *per se*.

Under the definition of 'school premises', the offence may only be committed on premises providing primary or secondary education, or both, whether full-time or part-time.

The offence will not be committed on land occupied solely as a dwelling by a person employed at the school. This means a caretaker's house in a school. Answer B is incorrect for this reason.

The fact that one of the people was not a resident is not relevant (which is why answer C is incorrect), and the exemption applies to both the land and the dwelling (therefore, answer D is also incorrect).

General Police Duties, para. 4.14.4

Answer 14.9

Answer **A** — Under the Criminal Justice Act 1988, an offence is committed when a person has an offensive weapon with him or her on school premises.

Under the Act, a constable may enter school premises and search those premises and any person for an offensive weapon. Note that the power under the Act only enables a constable to enter and search premises and search people on the premises. The power is not extended to searching people off school premises. The officer may, of course, use his power under s. 1 of the Police and Criminal Evidence Act 1984 to search the youths. This is why answer A is correct and answer B is incorrect.

There is no requirement for the constable to be in uniform, and therefore answer D is incorrect.

A person may commit an offence under this Act whether he or she is on the premises lawfully or not, and therefore answer C is incorrect.

General Police Duties, para. 4.14.4.2

Answer 14.10

Answer **B** — Section 550AA(1) of the Education Act 1996 states that a member of the staff of a school who has reasonable grounds for suspecting that a pupil at the school may have with him or her or in his or her possession:

(a) an article to which section 139 of the Criminal Justice Act 1988 applies (knives and blades etc.), or

(b) an offensive weapon (within the meaning of the Prevention of Crime Act 1953),

may search that pupil or his possessions for such articles and weapons.

(Answer A is incorrect.)

A pupil's possessions may not be searched under this section except in their presence and in the presence of another member of the staff. Since the pupil needs to be present, answer D is incorrect. However, the search may take place without the pupil's permission—indeed, as much force as is reasonable may be used in exercising this power (see s. 550AA(8)). Answer C is therefore incorrect.

Note that the person carrying out a search may only require the removal of outer clothing; they must be of the same sex and carry out the search in the presence of another member of staff also of the same sex as the pupil (s. 550AA(5)).

General Police Duties, para. 4.14.4.3

Answer 14.11

Answer **A** — Section 550AA(1) of the Education Act 1996 states that a member of the staff of a school who has reasonable grounds for suspecting that a pupil at the school may have with him or her or in his or her possession:

(a) an article to which section 139 of the Criminal Justice Act 1988 applies (knives and blades etc.), or

(b) an offensive weapon (within the meaning of the Prevention of Crime Act 1953), may search that pupil or his possessions for such articles and weapons.

Under s. 550AA(2), a search may be carried out only where the member of the staff and the pupil are on school premises; or they are elsewhere and the member of the staff has lawful control or charge of the pupil. Answer B is therefore incorrect.

A person may carry out a search under this section only if he or she is the head teacher of the school; or he or she has been authorised by the head teacher to carry out the search (see s. 550AA(3)). Answer C is therefore incorrect.

Finally, such a search may take place without the pupil's permission—indeed, as much force as is reasonable may be used in exercising this power (see s. 550AA(8)). Answer D is therefore incorrect.

General Police Duties, para. 4.14.4.3

Answer 14.12

Answer **D** — Section 550AA(1) of the Education Act 1996 states that a member of the staff of a school who has reasonable grounds for suspecting that a pupil at the school may have with him or her or in his or her possession:

(a) an article to which section 139 of the Criminal Justice Act 1988 applies (knives and blades etc.), or

(b) an offensive weapon (within the meaning of the Prevention of Crime Act 1953), may search that pupil or his possessions for such articles and weapons.

A search under this section may only be conducted by a head teacher, or a person authorised by the head teacher. Section 550AA(5) of the Act places certain restrictions on the conduct of the search. The person carrying out the search must be of the same sex and *must* carry out the search in the presence of another member of staff of the same sex. Answer C is incorrect.

A further restriction provided by s. 550AA(5) is that any search of the pupil may only require the removal of outer clothing. Therefore, if the person has hidden the weapon in somewhere more private, the staff at the school will have no power to search for the weapon, whether the search is conducted in private or not. Unless the pupil gives up the weapon voluntarily, the only option available to the head teacher would be to call a constable to conduct the search utilising their powers under the Criminal Justice Act 1988. Answers A, B and C are incorrect for this reason.

General Police Duties, para. 4.14.4.3

Answer 14.13

Answer **B** — Under s. 8(1) of the Criminal Law Act 1977, a person who is on any premises as a trespasser, after having entered as such, is guilty of an offence if, without lawful authority or reasonable excuse, he/she has with him/her on the premises any weapon of offence.

'Premises' for this purpose means:

(1) any building; or

(2) any part of a building under separate occupation;

(3) *any land adjacent to and used/intended for use in connection with a building;*

(4) the site comprising any building(s) together with ancillary land;

(5) any fixed structure;

(6) any movable structure, vehicle or vessel designed or adapted for residential purposes.

(s. 12 of the 1977 Act.)

Any building, or land adjacent to a building (not just a dwelling), is covered by s. 8(1), therefore CRUZ has committed the offence and answers A, C and D are incorrect.

General Police Duties, para. 4.14.5

Answer 14.14

Answer **A** — For an offence contrary to s. 8 of the Criminal Law Act 1977 the definition of 'weapon of offence' is the same as that for aggravated burglary, namely any article made or adapted for use for causing injury to or incapacitating a person, or intended by the person having it with him or her for that use (s. 8(2)). This is answer A; therefore answers B, C and D are incorrect.

General Police Duties, para. 4.14.5

Answer 14.15

Answer **C** — Section 141 of the Criminal Justice Act 1988 makes it an offence to manufacture, sell, hire, offer for sale or hire, expose, have in possession for the purpose of sale or hire, or lend or give to another person, any weapon listed in the schedule to the Act (knuckle dusters are included).

The offence may be committed by making an offer—the Act makes no mention of being in possession of the article when the offer is made, which is why answer C is correct (this is similar to a case of offering to supply drugs under the Misuse of Drugs Act 1971).

Although offences would be made out in answers A and B, the offence has already been committed.

Answer D would be an incorrect answer in any circumstances, as unlike the original 1953 Act, which requires a person to have the weapon with him, this offence deals with possession for the purpose of sale or hire.

General Police Duties, para. 4.14.6

Answer 14.16

Answer **C** — Under s. 141A of the Criminal Justice Act 1988, it is an offence for any person to sell to a person under 18 a knife, blade, razor blade, axe, or any article which has a blade or sharp point and is made or adapted for causing injury.

Previously, a person would have committed an offence by selling such an article to a person under the age of 16 (and no offence would have been committed in these circumstances). However, the Violent Crime Reduction Act 2006 increased the age limit, so that a sale to any person under the age of 18 is an offence and answer B is incorrect.

The offence does not apply to a razor blade in a cartridge, where not more than 2 mm of the blade is exposed or to a folding pocket-knife with a blade of less than 3 inches. Since the blade in this question was 3.5 inches, it is covered by s. 141A and answer D is incorrect.

The age of the person making the sale is not relevant (which is why answer A is incorrect).

General Police Duties, para. 4.14.7.1

Answer 14.17

Answer **D** — Under s. 3 of the Crossbows Act 1987, a person under the age of 18 who has with him or her a crossbow (or parts of a crossbow) capable of discharging a missile is guilty of an offence, unless accompanied by a person who is over 21 (which makes answer A incorrect).

There is no requirement for the person to be in a public place and therefore answer B is incorrect. Answer C is incorrect, as the statement is taken from the Firearms Act 1968 in relation to air weapons.

(Note that the Violent Crime Reduction Act 2006 increased the age from under 17 to under 18.)

General Police Duties, para. 4.14.8

Answer 14.18

Answer **C** — Under s. 3 of the Crossbows Act 1987, a person under the age of 18 who has with him or her—

(a)   a crossbow which is capable of discharging a missile, or

(b)   parts of a crossbow which together (and without any other parts) can be assembled to form a crossbow capable of discharging a missile

is guilty of an offence, unless he/she is under the supervision of a person who is 21 years of age or older.

Since s. 3 applies either to a working crossbow which is capable of discharging a missile, or parts of a crossbow which together (and without any other parts) can be assembled to form a crossbow capable of discharging a missile, answer A is incorrect.

There is no requirement for the person to be in a public place, therefore answer D is incorrect. Finally, the Violent Crime Reduction Act 2006 increased the age from under 17 to under 18, therefore, EMMERSON commits the offence by being under 18 (not under 17) and answer B is incorrect.

General Police Duties, para. 4.14.8

Answer 14.19

Answer **A** — Under s. 3 of the Crossbows Act 1987, a person under the age of 18 who has with him a crossbow which is capable of discharging a missile, or parts of a crossbow which together (and without any other parts) can be assembled to form a crossbow capable of discharging a missile, is guilty of an offence, unless he is under the supervision of a person who is 21 years of age or older.

Under s. 4(1), if a constable reasonably suspects a person is committing or has committed an offence under s. 3, they may search the suspected person or their vehicle for the crossbow (or part of a crossbow). Under s. 4(4), for the purposes of exercising the powers under s. 4(4), a constable may also enter any land other than a dwelling house in order to conduct the search.

In contrast to searches conducted under s. 1 of PACE (where a person cannot be searched in their own garden), the term 'dwelling house' under the Crossbows Act 1987 appears to mean just that—a house. Therefore, while there is no power to enter a person's dwelling house to conduct a search under this section (answer C is incorrect), there is a power to enter other land which is not a dwelling house (such as a garden) in order to do so. Answer B is incorrect.

Lastly, the powers of search under this legislation are not restricted to a search of a person or their vehicle. Answer D is therefore incorrect.

General Police Duties, para. 4.14.8.1

15 Civil Disputes

STUDY PREPARATION

After the wealth of detail covered by the previous few chapters, this one may come as something of a relief.

Although the title would tend to suggest that the police have little interest or involvement, civil disputes are nevertheless a significant feature of police patrol work. The area of domestic violence has received a great deal of political and legislative attention over recent years.

In addition to the various statutory measures in place to govern civil disputes, it is in this area that some of the most difficult 'balancing acts' in relation to human rights issues take place. These issues should be borne in mind when addressing questions in this chapter.

QUESTIONS

Question 15.1

Inspector BHARWANI was called to the house of Constable URQUART who was accused of assaulting his wife. A criminal investigation began and evidence was gathered. This evidence was insufficient for a criminal charge; however Constable URQUART stands charged with 'general conduct' misconduct.

What sanction can Constable URQUART expect if found guilty at a misconduct hearing?

A He can expect any sanction except dismissal/requirement to resign as he was not convicted of a criminal offence.

B He can expect a fine higher than normal due to the aggravating factor of domestic violence.

C He can expect to be dismissed/required to resign, as this is guidance from the Association of Chief Police Officers.

D He could be dismissed/required to resign, at the presiding officer's discretion.

Question 15.2

VIVIERS recently ended a five-year relationship with SIMMS because of SIMMS' alcoholism. SIMMS has a 14-year-old daughter, CLAIRE, from a previous relationship; CLAIRE has no contact with her father. VIVIERS assumed parenting responsibility for CLAIRE while he lived with her, although he did not formally adopt her. CLAIRE is still in regular contact with VIVIERS and has recently disclosed that SIMMS is regularly violent towards her, but she does not wish to contact the police. VIVIERS has contacted a solicitor in relation to taking out a non-molestation order against SIMMS, on CLAIRE's behalf.

Under the Family Law Act 1996, can VIVIERS apply for a non-molestation order in these circumstances?

A No, because he is not CLAIRE's natural or adopted parent.

B No, because he does not have current parental responsibility for CLAIRE.

C Yes, because he had previous parental responsibility for CLAIRE.

D Yes, but only if the court agrees that VIVIERS should have parental responsibility for the child and he is applying for such.

Question 15.3

DANIELS and EVERSHAM used to share a house as friends, but not as co-habitants. Over a period of time, DANIELS became fixated with EVERSHAM. The behaviour caused EVERSHAM considerable distress and she eventually moved out. DANIELS then began following EVERSHAM home from work and she genuinely feared for her safety. EVERSHAM visited a solicitor with a view to obtaining a non-molestation order against DANIELS.

Would EVERSHAM be likely to succeed in obtaining such an order, under s. 42 of the Family Law Act 1996?

A No, DANIELS has not been made subject to a court order under this Act.

B Yes, an application may be made in these circumstances.

C No, DANIELS and EVERSHAM were not co-habitants, or spouses or related to each other.

D No, such an order may only be made to prevent the molestation of a child.

Question 15.4

HANSEN has been made subject of a non-molestation order under the Family Law Act 1996. The family court made the order ex parte, in HANSEN's absence, following evidence from the petitioner, BAIG. The terms of the order state that HANSEN must not contact BAIG in any way. HANSEN has breached the order by telephoning BAIG.

What action could be taken, in respect of HANSEN's breach of the non-molestation order?

A HANSEN could be arrested for a criminal offence, but a lack of knowledge of the order may provide a defence.

B HANSEN can be arrested for a criminal offence; lack of knowledge is no defence—this is an absolute offence.

C No action can be taken, as HANSEN was not in court when the order was made.

D BAIG must return to the family court and request that a power of arrest is attached to the order before HANSEN can be arrested.

Question 15.5

When the full provisions of s. 24 of the Crime and Security Act 2010 are in place, the power to issue a domestic violence protection notice (DVPN) will be provided in order to protect vulnerable people from domestic violence.

In relation to this power, which of the following statements is correct?

A The DVPN must be issued by a police officer, of at least the rank of superintendent.

B The DVPN must be issued by a police officer, of at least the rank of inspector.

C The DVPN must normally be issued by a police officer, of at least the rank of inspector; however, in urgent cases, the notice may be issued by any police officer.

D The DVPN must be issued by a magistrate, following the application of a police officer of at least the rank of inspector.

Question 15.6

Under s. 24 of the Crime and Security Act 2010 the issuing of a domestic violence protection notice (DVPN) will be the trigger point for an application of a domestic violence protection order (DVPO), which will allow authorities time to put specific intervention/protection measures in place.

In relation to the issuing of a DVPO, which of the following statements is correct?

A A DVPO should not last longer than seven days.

B A DVPO should not last longer than 14 days.

C A DVPO will last between 14 and 28 days.

D A DVPO must be issued to last a minimum of 28 days.

Question 15.7

ASHTON has been sacked from his job at an aeronautical factory. He complains to his union, which takes four weeks to decide his case. The union eventually decides to authorise industrial action and to picket the aeronautical factory. In the intervening period, however, the firm has moved premises and no longer occupies the premises where ASHTON worked. A considerable amount of land at the new factory is private.

In relation to picketing, which of the following is true?

A The pickets cannot enter the private land to picket.

B The pickets could picket the new premises as it is still technically ASHTON's place of work.

C There would be a maximum of six pickets allowed at any one time.

D The right to picket outside the factory is an absolute right and cannot be overridden.

Question 15.8

Employees of a company are currently on strike; however a few have remained at work. One employee, HIGGINS, who is still working, is followed home by two of the strikers; they call him a 'scab' and a 'strike breaker'. They also whistle and jeer at him. HIGGINS is very distressed by this behaviour. Consider the offence of intimidation or annoyance by violence or otherwise contrary to s. 241 of the Trade Union and Labour Relations (Consolidation) Act 1992.

Has this offence been committed?

A No, because there need to be more than two people following HIGGINS.

B No, because they are not threatening or intimidating HIGGINS or using violence.

C Yes, provided the strikers intended to compel HIGGINS to join the strike.

D Yes, provided the strikers intended to cause the distress that HIGGINS suffered.

ANSWERS

Answer 15.1

Answer **C** — The area of domestic violence has received a great deal of political and legislative attention, bringing about important changes that affect the police. First, the Domestic Violence, Crime and Victims Act 2004 makes significant changes to the law. In addition, the Association of Chief Police Officers has issued a policy document setting out the approach to be adopted where police officers are personally involved in domestic violence and advocating a 'presumption towards dismissal' where an officer is convicted of a domestic violence-related offence. In addition, any officer whose conduct is found to have fallen below the required standard in respect of domestic violence/abuse can expect to be dismissed or required to resign despite not having attracted a criminal conviction. The expectation is that he or she will have to leave the service; answers A and B are therefore incorrect. And this is not at the presiding officer's discretion; answer D is therefore incorrect.

General Police Duties, para. 4.15.2

Answer 15.2

Answer **C** — Section 42 of the Family Law Act 1996 provides for 'non-molestation' orders. Under s. 42(1), a 'non-molestation order' means an order containing either or both of the following provisions—

(a) provision prohibiting a person ('the respondent') from molesting another person who is associated with the respondent;

(b) provision prohibiting the respondent from molesting a relevant child.

Section 62(3) of the Act describes 'associated' persons who may either be the petitioner or respondent for a non-molestation order. A non-molestation order may be applied for by anyone who is 'associated' with the respondent, including former cohabitants.

Under s. 62(4), a person will be 'associated' with a child if—

(a) he is a parent of the child; or

(b) he has or has had parental responsibility for the child.

Therefore, the fact that VIVIERS does not currently have parental responsibility for CLAIRE, or is not her natural or adopted parent is irrelevant and he may apply for an order. Answers A and B are incorrect.

There is no mention in s. 42 or s. 62 of the petitioner having to apply for a formal parental role in relation to children before an order can be made—this is about preventing an individual from molesting another and answer D is incorrect.

General Police Duties, para. 4.15.2.3

Answer 15.3

Answer **B** — Under s. 42(1) of the Family Law Act 1996, a 'non-molestation order' means an order containing a provision prohibiting a person ('the respondent') from molesting another person who is associated with the respondent or from molesting a relevant child. Since the provisions do not only apply to children, answer D is incorrect.

Under s. 42(2)(a), the court may make a non-molestation order when an application has been made by a person who is associated with the respondent whether or not any other family proceedings have been instituted. Answer A is therefore incorrect.

Section 62 contains a long list of people who are 'associated' with the respondent, including relatives, children, spouses, co-habitants and civil partners (and people who formerly enjoyed such a status). Under s. 62(3)(c), they also include people who live, or have lived, in the same household, otherwise than merely by reason of one of them being the other's employee, tenant, lodger or boarder. Answer C is therefore incorrect.

General Police Duties, para. 4.15.2.3

Answer 15.4

Answer **A** — Section 42A of the Family Law Act 1996 was introduced by the Domestic Violence, Crime and Victims Act 2004 and states—

(1) A person who without reasonable excuse does anything that he is prohibited from doing by a non-molestation order is guilty of an offence.

(2) In the case of a non-molestation order made by virtue of s. 45(1), a person can be guilty of an offence under this section only in respect of conduct engaged in at a time when he was aware of the existence of the order.

Consequently, this provides a power of arrest for the breach of a non-molestation order under the provisions of s. 24(1) of the Police and Criminal Evidence Act 1984. Answer D is incorrect as there is no longer a requirement to attach a power of arrest to an order before a person can be arrested.

In relation to subs. (2) above, non-molestation orders made by virtue of s. 45(1) are ex parte orders where the respondent has not been present at the proceedings when the order was made. This section makes it clear that if the defendant was not in court *and* he or she was not aware of its existence, he or she cannot be found guilty of the offence—but this does not mean that the person cannot be arrested until the facts have been established. Answers B and C are therefore incorrect.

General Police Duties, para. 4.15.2.4

Answer 15.5

Answer **A** — At this time the provisions under s. 24 of the Crime and Security Act 2010 have only been commenced providing for pilot schemes to be conducted to allow for an assessment of the effectiveness of the provisions of the domestic violence protection notice (DVPN) and domestic violence protection order (DVPO) in practice.

A DVPN must be issued by a police officer, of at least the rank of superintendent (s. 24(1)); therefore, answers B, C and D are incorrect.

General Police Duties, para. 4.15.2.5

Answer 15.6

Answer **C** — At this time the provisions under s. 24 of the Crime and Security Act 2010 have only been commenced providing for pilot schemes to be conducted to allow for an assessment of the effectiveness of the provisions of the domestic violence protection notice (DVPN) and domestic violence protection order (DVPO) in practice.

The issuing of a DVPN triggers an application for a DVPO. This is an order lasting *between 14 and 28 days*, which prohibits P from molesting V and may also make provision about access to shared accommodation (ss. 27 to 30). Answers A, B and D are incorrect.

General Police Duties, para. 4.15.2.5

Answer 15.7

Answer **A** — Although picketing is lawful under s. 220 of the Trade Union and Labour Relations (Consolidation) Act 1992, there are some restrictions. It is lawful to picket your former place of work if the action is as a result of the termination of your employment. However, a person's place of work does not include new premises of an employer who has moved since dismissing the people picketing (*News Group Newspapers Ltd* v *SOGAT '82 (No. 2)* [1987] ICR 181), and therefore answer B is incorrect. The 1992 Act does not place restrictions on the number of pickets; the number six is from the agreed Code of Practice on picketing which has no legal force, and therefore answer C is incorrect. Note, however, that if numbers are large enough, there might be a presumption that the pickets intend to intimidate others, which would make it unlawful (*Broome* v *DPP* [1974] AC 587). If there is a real danger of any offence (e.g. public disorder) being committed, the pickets have no right to attend at the factory to picket under s. 220 (*Piddlington* v *Bates* [1960] 1 WLR 162), and therefore answer D is incorrect. Section 220 does not authorise pickets to enter onto private land (*British Airports Authority* v *Ashton* [1983] 1 WLR 1079).

General Police Duties, para. 4.15.3.1

Answer 15.8

Answer **C** — This is an offence of 'specific intent', and as such there has to be an element of intention to bring about a specific outcome. It is committed by someone who follows the victim with 'two or more other persons' (therefore answer A is incorrect), where they follow the victim 'in a disorderly manner in or through any street or road'. There does not have to be a threat or use of violence; disorder would be sufficient, and therefore answer B is incorrect. Their intention must be to compel HIGGINS to join the strike, and not simply to cause distress, and therefore answer D is incorrect. (Note that if the circumstances were reversed and HIGGINS was on strike, the offence would still be committed by compelling him to return to work.)

General Police Duties, para. 4.15.3.3

16 | Offences Relating to Land and Premises

STUDY PREPARATION

The Criminal Justice and Public Order Act 1994 created several offences which have the effect of allowing the criminal courts to deal with offences of trespass. This chapter deals with offences such as trespassing with intent to disrupt lawful activities, trespassing with intent to reside on land, raves and residing in vehicles on land, all of which are very topical. Each offence has several elements to it, but there are common themes throughout, such as authorising officers, offences of failing to leave land when directed to do so and returning within three months of a direction being given.

The Criminal Law Act 1977 makes up the bulk of the second part of the chapter. Offences under s. 6 and s. 7 of the Act are rarely used, but remain useful pieces of legislation, especially that of using violence for securing entry to premises.

Lastly, do not ignore the offences of being found on enclosed premises and causing a nuisance on educational premises; both are useful offences to remember.

QUESTIONS

Question 16.1

A new football stadium is being built on the outskirts of a town. Vehicles belonging to the building company have been parked in an enclosed warehouse situated adjacent to the building site, which is due to be demolished after the stadium is completed. Environmental protestors have been attempting to stop the building work. The builders arrived for work one morning and as they opened the doors to the warehouse, a number of protestors stormed in and chained themselves to the vehicles. Building work was disrupted for several hours as the police were called to remove them. It was a peaceful protest; no property was damaged and no one was threatened.

Have the protesters committed an offence under s. 68 of the Criminal Justice and Public Order Act 1994 (aggravated trespass), in these circumstances?

A No, as the protestors were not on land in the open air.

B Yes, the offence is complete in these circumstances.

C No, as the protestors were not on land where the building work was due to take place.

D No, as the protestors did not threaten or intimidate the builders, or cause damage.

Question 16.2

PARSONS, a farmer, agreed to allow a family of travellers to stay on his land for a week. Between them, the travellers had two caravans and two cars. After two weeks, they were still on the land and PARSONS asked them to leave. When they refused, he contacted the police.

Would the officers have the power, under s. 61 of the Criminal Justice and Public Order Act 1994, to direct the family to leave the land?

A No, because the family did not have more than 12 vehicles between them.

B Yes, they could direct the family to leave the land, with their vehicles.

C No, because the family were originally given permission to stay by the landowner.

D No, because the family have not caused damage or used threatening/insulting behaviour.

Question 16.3

HARNEY worked as a security guard on a building site, which was due to be developed for housing. HARNEY was employed by the company which owned the land, as there had been persistent problems with travellers setting up an unofficial site. One day, O'CONNER drove onto the site in his car. He was alone at the time, and HARNEY recognised him as a traveller who had stayed at the site some time ago. HARNEY spoke to O'CONNER, who admitted that his family were due at the site in a few hours, and that they intended staying there for a while. HARNEY then contacted the police to assist.

Would the officer attending the scene have the power to direct O'CONNER to leave the land, under s. 62A of the Criminal Justice and Public Order Act 1994, in these circumstances?

A Yes, because he has at least one vehicle with him.

B No, because he does not have a caravan with him.

C Yes, provided there is a suitable site elsewhere for him to go to.

D No, because O'CONNER was unaccompanied at the time.

Question 16.4

On a Saturday morning, the police received complaints from residents about a group of people gathered on a beach. The group had arrived the previous evening and were partying all night. The police attended and saw 20 people listening to loud, amplified music. The group stated they intended staying until the Monday as it was a bank holiday weekend and that the music would carry on that night and on the Sunday.

Would a senior officer have sufficient evidence at this stage to reasonably believe that a 'gathering' is taking place, as defined in s. 63(1) of the Criminal Justice and Public Order Act 1994?

A Yes, there were at least ten people gathering at the site of a rave.

B No, the people gathering were not trespassing on land.

C Yes, there is sufficient evidence at this time to define this as a 'gathering'.

D No, s. 63(1) does not apply in the daylight hours, the senior officer would have to wait until night time to make this decision.

Question 16.5

Detective Constable WU was in plain clothes one evening, when he responded to an assistance call from a uniformed officer, Constable HOLMES. When he arrived, Constable HOLMES informed Detective Constable WU that a gathering was taking place three miles away, which had been declared as a 'rave'. Constable HOLMES had stopped 20 vehicles and was attempting to get them to turn around. Until further assistance arrived, Constable HOLMES continued to stop vehicles, while Detective Constable WU spoke to the drivers suspected of attending the rave and directed them not to proceed.

Were the directions given by Detective Constable WU lawful in the circumstances?

A Yes, he has acted correctly in these circumstances.

B No, he was outside the required radius from the rave to be able to give the directions.

C No, he was inside the required radius from the rave to be able to give the directions.

D No, he should have been in uniform when giving the directions.

Question 16.6

McDOWELL formed a relationship with SANDERS and invited him to live in her home with her three children. SANDERS began inflicting significant domestic abuse on McDOWELL and she asked him to leave, which he did. However, because of continued harassment, McDOWELL had to seek refuge in a hostel with the children. While she was at the hostel, SANDERS managed to get into her home and despite several attempts by the police, he refused to leave. McDOWELL attended court and was granted an interim possession order for one month, to allow her to return to the premises. A copy of the order was fixed to the premises in line with the court's instructions.

In relation to such an order, what does s. 76 of the Criminal Justice and Public Order Act 1994 state about SANDERS' liability?

A SANDERS must leave the premises immediately.

B SANDERS must leave the premises immediately and commits an offence if he returns within one month.

C SANDERS must leave the premises within 24 hours.

D SANDERS must leave the premises within one month.

Question 16.7

TOM and CAROL live together, but TOM has been violent towards her after drinking heavily. One evening, when TOM was in a pub, CAROL double locked the front door of their house to stop him getting in. When he got home, TOM lost his temper and began kicking the door to get in. CAROL was scared and called the police.

Would TOM be guilty of an offence under s. 6 of the Criminal Law Act 1977 (using violence for securing entry)?

A No, because CAROL is not a trespasser on the property.

B Yes, but he would have a defence as a displaced residential occupier.

C Yes, but he would have a defence as a protected intending occupier.

D Yes, if it can be shown that he was aware CAROL was on the premises.

Question 16.8

GREEDY is a landlord who wishes to regain possession of one of his flats, the tenant of which is refusing to leave. GREEDY is unhappy that the tenant has moved in three of her friends. GREEDY turns up at the front door for the purpose of gaining possession of the property, using violence if necessary. He threatens to kick the front door down, he then threatens to enter and use violence against any person in the house, he then specifically threatens violence against the tenant. The tenant inside is obviously opposed to this entry and GREEDY knows this is the case.

At what point is an offence contrary to s. 6 of the Criminal Law Act 1977 first committed?

A When GREEDY first attends at the premises with the purpose of using violence to gain possession.

B When GREEDY threatened violence to property, i.e. the door.

C When GREEDY threatened violence to any person, i.e. any of the persons in the flat.

D When GREEDY threatened violence to a specific person, i.e. the tenant.

Question 16.9

TILLEY owned a printing business, which was located in a shop premises. TILLEY owned the building, and lived in a flat above the shop. Business was slow and TILLEY had to lay off his assistant, CARNE. CARNE kept his keys to the premises and while TILLEY was away on business the following week, CARNE moved into his flat. When TILLEY returned, CARNE refused to leave the flat, stating that he was homeless as a result of losing his job. TILLEY contacted the police, claiming to be a displaced residential occupier. When the police arrived, CARNE refused to leave.

Given that the flat in question is situated in a business premises, what defence is available to CARNE under s. 7 of the Criminal Law Act 1977 (person failing to leave premises)?

A None, failing to leave premises when requested in these circumstances is an absolute offence.

B None, but the prosecution must show that this part of the premises was used mainly for residential purposes.

C CARNE has a defence, unless the prosecution can show that this part of the premises was used mainly for non-residential purposes.

D CARNE has a defence if he can show that this part of the premises was used mainly for non-residential purposes.

Question 16.10

MARKS intended to frighten his neighbour KAREN on Halloween night. He wore a mask and climbed into her garden, which was enclosed on three sides by hedges. He approached the kitchen window, where KAREN was standing, and pressed his face against the glass. KAREN was frightened and screamed loudly. She was heard by other neighbours who contacted the police.

Could MARKS be guilty of the offence of being found on enclosed premises in these circumstances?

A Yes, MARKS' behaviour would amount to an offence under s. 4 of the Vagrancy Act 1824.

B Yes, but only if it can be shown MARKS intended committing a criminal offence at that time.

C No, MARKS' behaviour would only amount to trespassing, which is not a criminal act.

D No, as MARKS was not on the premises for an unlawful purpose.

Question 16.11

The police attended an alarm at an office building in a city centre. They made a search of the premises and found PECK, who was hiding in one of the offices. The officers recognised PECK as a homeless person with whom police regularly had dealings. Following questioning, the officers decided that there was insufficient evidence to arrest PECK for burglary. PECK was then arrested for being found on enclosed premises.

Would the premises that PECK was found on amount to an 'enclosed premises', for the purposes of offences under s. 4 of the Vagrancy Act 1824?

A No, 'enclosed premises' will only include outhouses and land ancillary to buildings.

B No, if the person is found in a building, that building must be a dwelling for the purposes of this offence.

C Yes, providing the person is found in a building, or outhouse or land ancillary to a building, it doesn't matter what type of building.

D No, a room within an office building will not amount to an enclosed area for the purposes of this offence.

Question 16.12

BRENT lived in a property owned by Western Housing Association. BRENT owned several abandoned cars which were in a dangerous condition and were parked in a communal parking area at the rear of the property, owned by the association. The association served a notice to remove the cars; however, BRENT refused to do so and attended the company's offices, threatening to tow the cars across the entrance of the parking area to barricade them in. The association was concerned that this action might cause distress to other residents.

Would BRENT's threats be sufficient to merit an application by the association for an anti-social behaviour injunction, under s. 153A of the Housing Act 1996?

A No, the conduct was not directed at a person living in the vicinity of the house.

B Yes, provided the company named the people likely to be affected in the injunction.

C No, as the conduct occurred in the association's offices and not in the vicinity of the house.

D Yes, regardless of where the conduct occurred, or whether the company can name the people likely to be affected in the injunction.

Question 16.13

EASTWOOD is a caretaker at a school maintained by a local authority. He received a call from teachers that some youths from a different school were on the playing fields shouting and swearing at them. EASTWOOD telephoned the police and made his way to the field. He arrived before the police to find several youths sitting next to a classroom quietly.

Which statement will be correct in relation to the youths causing a nuisance on educational premises?

A They may be removed from the premises by either EASTWOOD or the police.

B EASTWOOD has no powers to deal with the youths; he must wait for the police to arrive.

C EASTWOOD has no powers to deal with the youths, as the disturbance has ceased.

D EASTWOOD has a power to detain the youths until the police arrive at the school.

ANSWERS

Answer 16.1

Answer **B** — Under s. 68(1) of the Criminal Justice and Public Order Act 1994, a person commits the offence of aggravated trespass if he/she trespasses on land and, in relation to any lawful activity which persons are engaging in or are about to engage in on that or adjoining land, does there anything which is intended by him to have the effect—

(a) of intimidating those persons or any of them so as to deter them or any of them from engaging in that activity,

(b) of obstructing that activity, or

(c) of disrupting that activity.

Therefore, even though the protestors did not threaten or intimidate the builders, or cause damage, their actions were sufficient to obstruct and disrupt the activity. Answer D is incorrect.

The offence is committed when a person trespasses on land where the activity is due to take place or on *adjoining* land (which makes answer C incorrect).

Section 68 originally included the phrase 'in the open air' but it was removed by the Anti-social Behaviour Act 2003. In *DPP* v *Chivers* [2010] EWHC 1814 (Admin) it was held that the purpose and effect of this amendment was quite plainly to include buildings. Answer A is incorrect.

Note that in order to establish the offence of aggravated trespass under s. 68, you must prove that the defendant had committed the act(s) complained of in the physical presence of a person engaged or about to engage in the lawful activity with which the defendant wished to interfere (*DPP* v *Tilly* [2001] EWHC Admin 821).

General Police Duties, para. 4.16.4

Answer 16.2

Answer **C** — To prove the offence under s. 61 of the Criminal Justice and Public Order Act 1994, you need to show that at least two people are trespassing on land with a common purpose of residing there and reasonable steps have been taken to ask them to leave.

If the above conditions are apparent, you must then show that:

- they have damaged land; *or*
- they have used threatening, etc. behaviour; *or*
- they have between them *six* or more vehicles.

As none of these apply, answers B and D are incorrect. Under s. 61(2), if the people had been given permission to stay on the land but had subsequently become trespassers, the officers would have to satisfy themselves that one of the conditions in s. 61(1) had occurred after they had become trespassers.

The original 1994 Act specified 12 vehicles, but this has been amended to six and therefore answer A is incorrect.

(It should be noted that the Home Office has issued guidance to the police on the use of the powers under s. 61. It advises that the police must be able to demonstrate that all eviction and enforcement decisions are 'proportionate' in weighing individual harm against the wider public interest.)

General Police Duties, para. 4.16.5

Answer 16.3

Answer **D** — Section 62A of the Criminal Justice and Public Order Act 1994 provides an alternative power to police officers to the one contained in s. 61 of the Act. In order to use the powers under this section, the senior officer at the scene may direct persons to leave the land and remove any vehicles if the following conditions are met:

- that the person and one or more others (i.e. *at least* two people) are trespassing on land;
- that they have at least one vehicle between them;
- that they are present with a common purpose of residing there; *and*
- that the occupier or a person acting on his or her behalf has asked the police to remove the trespassers.

Since there must be at least two persons present on the land, and O'CONNER was alone, the police officer attending the scene would have had no powers under this section, regardless of how many vehicles were present, which makes answer A incorrect.

If the people have one or more caravans in their possession or control, and there is a suitable pitch on a relevant caravan site elsewhere, there is a further condition requiring the senior officer to consult with the local authority and ascertain if there is a suitable pitch on a relevant caravan site for each of the caravans. However, this is an additional power, and s. 62A may still be used if the people do not have a caravan with them, which means that answers B and C are incorrect.

General Police Duties, para. 4.16.6

Answer 16.4

Answer **C** — The elements of a 'gathering' for a rave are found in s. 63(1) of the Criminal Justice and Public Order Act 1994. The senior officer (a superintendent) would have to be satisfied that these elements are present before giving a direction for people to leave under this section. Those elements are that:

- the gathering is on land in the open air;
- the gathering is likely to be attended by 20 or more persons (whether or not they are trespassers);
- amplified music is played during the night (with or without intermissions), which by reason of its loudness and duration and the time at which it is played, is likely to cause serious distress to the inhabitants of the locality.

Taking matters in order, the superintendent must first believe that a gathering of 20 people is likely to take place—not ten. This is the figure described in s. 63(2)(b), which is the preventative element of this section, where officers can tell people to leave to prevent the rave from taking place. Answer A is incorrect.

It is irrelevant whether the gathering is trespassing and answer B is incorrect. (Note that s. 63(1A) of the Act deals specifically with gatherings where people are trespassing.)

Generally, the amplified music must be played during the night; however, there will be occasions where raves take place over several days. This is provided for in s. 63(1)(a), which states that this section applies when:

> such a gathering continues during intermissions in the music and, where the gathering extends over several days, throughout the period during which amplified music is played at night (with or without intermissions).

Therefore, as the officers attending the scene (and their superintendent) had reason to believe that a rave would take place the same evening, they would not have to wait until the evening before taking action. Answer D is incorrect.

General Police Duties, para. 4.16.7.1

Answer 16.5

Answer **D** — Under s. 65 of the Criminal Justice and Public Order Act 1994, where a constable in uniform reasonably believes a person is on his or her way to a gathering to which s. 63(2) applies (direction to leave land in respect of a rave), the officer may stop the person and direct him or her not to proceed in the direction of the gathering. Unlike other directions under this Act, a direction under s. 65 must be given by a constable in uniform, and answer A is incorrect.

The power may be exercised within *five* miles of the boundary of the site of the gathering. Answers B and C are incorrect, as the officers were inside this radius; and had Detective Constable WU been in uniform, the directions not to proceed would have been lawful.

General Police Duties, para. 4.16.7.6

Answer 16.6

Answer **C** — Section 76 of the Criminal Justice and Public Order Act 1994 states:

(1) This section applies where an interim possession order has been made in respect of any premises and served in accordance with rules of court; and references to 'the order' and 'the premises' shall be construed accordingly.

(2) Subject to subsection (3), a person who is present on the premises as a trespasser at any time during the currency of the order commits an offence.

As SANDERS is on the premises without McDOWELL's permission, and the court has granted the order, he is likely to be a trespasser and will fall within this legislation and as a trespasser, commits an offence.

However, s. 76(3) states that no offence under subs. (2) is committed by a person if—

(a) he leaves the premises within 24 hours of the time of service of the order and does not return; or

(b) a copy of the order was not fixed to the premises in accordance with rules of court.

Since the notice was fixed on the premises, that particular aspect is satisfied. This means that SANDERS must leave the premises within 24 hours to avail himself of this defence. Answers A, B and D are incorrect.

Note that under s. 76(4), a person who was in occupation of the premises at the time of service of the order but leaves them commits an offence if he re-enters the premises as a trespasser or attempts to do so after the expiry of the order but within the period of one year beginning with the day on which it was served.

General Police Duties, para. 4.16.8.3

Answer 16.7

Answer **D** — A person is guilty of an offence if he or she uses or threatens violence for the purpose of securing entry to premises, provided there is someone on the premises who is opposed to the entry and the person using/threatening the violence knows that this is the case (s. 6(1) of the Criminal Law Act 1977).

The person would have a defence if he or she could show that he or she was either a displaced residential occupier (DRO) or a protected intended occupier (PIO).

To be a DRO, a person would have to show that he or she was occupying premises immediately before being excluded by a person who entered those premises as a trespasser. As CAROL is not a trespasser, TOM would not be a DRO and would have no defence. Answer B is therefore incorrect.

To be a PIO, a person must have a freehold/leasehold interest in a property with two years to run. He or she must intend to use the property for his or her own occupation as a residence and, as above, must have been excluded by a person who has entered the premises as a trespasser. As CAROL is not a trespasser, answer C is incorrect.

The fact that CAROL is not a trespasser is the reason for TOM having no defence, which is why answer A is incorrect.

General Police Duties, paras 4.16.9.3, 4.16.9.4

Answer 16.8

Answer **B** — Section 6 the Criminal Law Act 1977 states:

(1) Subject to the following provisions of this section, any person who, without lawful authority, uses or threatens violence for the purpose of securing entry into any premises for himself or for any other person is guilty of an offence, provided that—

    (a) there is someone present on those premises at the time who is opposed to the entry which the violence is intended to secure; and

    (b) the person using or threatening the violence knows that that is the case.

It is immaterial whether the violence used/threatened is against a person or property, or whether the purpose of the entry is to gain possession of the premises or any other purpose (s. 6(4)). So the offence is complete only after violence is first used or threatened, not when it is intended; answer A is therefore incorrect. Although answers C and D would amount to an offence contrary to s. 6 the question asked at what point will the offence first be committed, and that is when the threat of violence was made against the front door; answers C and D are therefore incorrect within the confines of this question.

General Police Duties, para. 4.16.9.3

Answer 16.9

Answer **D** — The offence of failing to leave a premises when requested is covered by s. 7(1) of the Criminal Law Act 1977. The offence is complete, because CARNE entered the premises as a trespasser and refused to leave when requested by a displaced residential occupier (TILLEY).

A defence is provided under s. 7(3)(a) of the Act (and answer A is incorrect); it is for the accused to prove that the premises are or formed part of premises used mainly for non-residential purposes. Answers B and C are incorrect. (Whether CARNE would be able successfully to claim this defence is doubtful, as the flat is clearly a residential premises.)

General Police Duties, para. 4.16.9.5

Answer 16.10

Answer **A** — It is a summary offence under s. 4 of the Vagrancy Act 1824 for any person to be found in or upon any dwelling house, warehouse, coach house, stable or outhouse or in any enclosed yard, garden or area for *any unlawful purpose*. The unlawful purpose must be to commit some specific criminal offence as opposed to simply trespassing with a purely immoral purpose, and without more will not suffice (*Hayes* v *Stevenson* (1860) 3 LT 296).

The case of *Smith* v *Chief Superintendent of Woking Police Station* (1983) 76 Cr App R 234 dealt with the issue of 'unlawful purpose'. The defendant was convicted after being found in the garden of a house peering through a window trying to frighten the woman inside. Had there not been any intention to frighten, the 'unlawful' purpose would probably not have been made out. This mirrors the circumstances in this question and the behaviour could easily amount to a criminal offence under the Public Order Act 1986. Answers C and D are incorrect.

There is no need to show that the person intended to carry out a criminal offence at the particular time that he or she was found (or even at that particular place). Answer B is therefore incorrect.

General Police Duties, para. 4.16.9.6

Answer 16.11

Answer **D** — It is a summary offence under s. 4(1) of the Vagrancy Act 1824 for any person to be found in or upon any dwelling house, warehouse, coach house, stable or outhouse or in any enclosed yard, garden or area for *any unlawful purpose*. This ancient offence was created to prevent vagrancy and the original definition gives a clue as to the type of premises that might be considered enclosed—

(i) every person wandering abroad and lodging in any barn or outhouse, or in any deserted or unoccupied building, or in the open air, or under a tent, or in any cart or wagon, and not giving a good account of himself or herself;

(ii) every person being found in or upon any dwelling house, warehouse, coach-house, stable, or outhouse, or in any enclosed yard, garden, or area, for any unlawful purpose;

commits an offence.

Answers A and B are incorrect as the Act covers many buildings that are not merely dwellings or outhouses and land ancillary to buildings.

However, a room within an office building has been held *not* to amount to an enclosed area for the purposes of this offence (*Talbot* v *Oxford City Justices* [2000] 1 WLR 1102). Answer C is therefore incorrect.

General Police Duties, para. 4.16.9.6

Answer 16.12

Answer **D** — Under s. 153A(3) of the Housing Act 1996, a court may, on the application of a relevant landlord, grant an anti-social behaviour injunction if:

the person against whom the injunction is sought is engaging, has engaged or threatens to engage in housing-related conduct capable of causing a nuisance or annoyance to:

(a) a person with a right (of whatever description) to reside in or occupy housing accommodation owned or managed by a relevant landlord,

(b) a person with a right (of whatever description) to reside in or occupy other housing accommodation in the neighbourhood of housing accommodation mentioned in paragraph (a),

(c) a person engaged in lawful activity in, or in the neighbourhood of, housing accommodation mentioned in paragraph (a), or

(d) a person employed (whether or not by a relevant landlord) in connection with the exercise of a relevant landlord's housing management functions.

Therefore, as the conduct can be directed at a person employed by the company, answer A is incorrect. Further, it is immaterial where conduct to which this section applies occurs (answer C is incorrect).

Finally, an injunction may be granted without a particular individual being named as someone adversely affected by the conduct referred to in the injunction, and in respect of conduct that is not described by reference to any person or persons at all. If conduct is described in an injunction by reference to a person or persons, these may be persons generally, or persons of a particular description, or a specified person. Answer B is therefore incorrect.

General Police Duties, para. 4.16.9.7

Answer 16.13

Answer **A** — Where a person has caused a nuisance, disturbance or annoyance on educational premises, a police constable, or a person authorised by the local authority, may remove that person from the premises (s. 547(3) of the Education Act 1996). The power is to remove, not to detain, which is why answers B and D are incorrect.

Answer C is incorrect because the power to remove a person may be used even when the disturbance has ended.

General Police Duties, para. 4.16.9.8

17 Licensing and Offences Relating to Alcohol

STUDY PREPARATION

The Licensing Act 2003 brought licensing and licensed premises into line with the Government's effort to place crime and disorder matters at the top of the policing agenda. Licensing matters are dealt with by licensing authorities (made up of local authority members).

Operating schedules place the emphasis firmly on the holders of personal licences to run orderly premises, taking into account such matters as crime and disorder, public safety and protection of children. Knowledge of the different types of licences and the new system of objecting to them is critical. You should also learn the powers to enter premises and, once inside, how to deal with offences and/or drunkenness.

Ages are important, and most of the original offences of under-age drinking under the 1964 Act have remained.

The Confiscation of Alcohol (Young Persons) Act 1997 first introduced the concept of confiscating alcohol from young people in public places. The Criminal Justice and Police Act 2001 introduced a similar power to confiscate alcohol from people in designated public places.

Further powers of enforcement are provided, allowing the courts and the police to make an order requiring licensed premises to be closed.

The Gambling Act 2005 reformed the laws relating to gambling and introduced a licensing system to regulate operating licences, personal licences, premises licences and temporary use of premises notices. The responsibility for granting licences is shared between the Gambling Commission and local licensing authorities.

QUESTIONS

Question 17.1

The Licensing Act 2003, sch. 2 makes provision in relation to 'late night refreshment'.

Between which hours must refreshments be supplied in order for a person to qualify as a provider of 'late night refreshment'?

A 11 pm and 5 am.

B 10 pm and 5 am.

C 11 pm and 5.30 am.

D 9 pm and 5.30 am.

Question 17.2

Constable KHAN was on duty as part of a plain-clothes team of police officers, working with LEWIS, a licensing officer from the local authority and a person authorised under the Licensing Act 2003. The team was tasked with visiting public houses in the locality to identify licensing offences. They arrived at the Royal Oak public house at 10.50 pm and identified themselves to GEORGE, the door supervisor, and asked to enter the premises. GEORGE refused, stating the premises were about to close. The operating schedule stated that the premises should close at 11 pm.

Does either Constable KHAN or LEWIS have the power to enter the premises using reasonable force under the Licensing Act 2003?

A No, the power to enter by reasonable force is restricted to uniformed officers only.

B Constable KHAN only; LEWIS does not have a power to enter by force in these circumstances.

C Yes, both have the power to enter using reasonable force in these circumstances.

D Yes, but only if they have reason to believe that offences are being committed.

Question 17.3

Section 19(4) of the Licensing Act 2003 allows the Secretary of State to impose mandatory conditions for all relevant premises licences, for the promotion of the licensing objectives.

Which of the following statements is correct, in respect of the power to impose such conditions under the Act?

A The number of mandatory conditions that may be set must not exceed 9.

B The number of mandatory conditions that may be set must not exceed 15.

C The number of mandatory conditions that may be set must not exceed 20.

D The number of mandatory conditions that may be set is unlimited, provided the promotion of the licensing objectives is the primary reason for setting them.

Question 17.4

An application has been submitted to open a new licensed premises in a city centre. The licensing authority for the area is concerned that the number of licensed premises that are in the area has already reached saturation point. There have been no objections from interested parties in respect of the application.

Would members of the licensing authority be entitled to act as interested parties in respect of this application?

A No, members of the relevant licensing authority may only act as interested parties in respect of a licensing review, not a licensing application.

B No, a public authority acting as an interested party would be a breach of Art. 6 of the European Convention on Human Rights.

C No, the notion of interested parties is meant to be restricted to such people as members of the public who could be directly affected by the premises.

D Yes, members of the relevant licensing authority may act as interested parties in such circumstances.

Question 17.5

A request has been made by the local police for an accelerated review of the conditions of the licence of the Horse and Jockey public house, because of the number of serious disorder incidents that have occurred there recently.

Within what period of time must such an application be considered?

A Within 24 hours.

B Within 36 hours.

C Within 48 hours.

D Within 7 days.

Question 17.6

In the last four weeks, the police have been called to numerous violent incidents at the Railway public house, which re-opened two months ago after refurbishment, with a new personal licence holder and extended opening times. During this period, two people have been stabbed and this weekend another person received serious facial injuries after being hit with a beer glass. The police are considering making a request for an accelerated review of the conditions of the licence because of the serious disorder.

How must an application be pursued under the terms of s. 53A of the Licensing Act 2003?

A A senior police officer or a senior representative of the local authority must present the application to the licensing authority.

B A senior police officer must present the application to the licensing authority.

C A senior police officer must present the application to the magistrates' court.

D A senior representative from any responsible authority must present the application to the licensing authority.

Question 17.7

SWANSON has recently been granted a personal licence to sell alcohol at the Rat and Carrot public house.

According to s. 111 of the Licensing Act 2003, how long will SWANSON's personal licence be valid?

A Two years, unless it is revoked or surrendered.

B Five years, unless it is revoked or surrendered.

C Ten years, unless it is revoked or surrendered.

D No limit, unless it is revoked or surrendered.

Question 17.8

Section 57(5) of the Licensing Act 2003 outlines the obligations for the production of a club premises certificate (or a certified copy of it).

Who may demand the production of such a certificate?

A A constable only.

B A constable in uniform only.

C A constable or an authorised person.

D A constable in uniform or an authorised person.

Question 17.9

Section 97 of the Licensing Act 2003 provides a power of entry for a constable to enter and search any premises which holds a club premises certificate.

What restrictions are placed on this power of entry during normal opening hours?

A Entry is allowed to detect licensing offences or to prevent a breach of the peace only.

B Entry is allowed to prevent a breach of the peace only.

C Entry is allowed to detect licensing offences, to search for offences relating to the supply of drugs, or to prevent a breach of the peace.

D Entry is allowed to search for offences relating to the supply of drugs, or to prevent a breach of the peace only.

Question 17.10

FRENCH intends holding a musical event over a bank holiday weekend. FRENCH has managed to persuade a number of local bands to play live music over the period and intends applying for a temporary licence to serve alcohol during the course of the event.

Which of the following statements is correct, in relation to the application that FRENCH must make for such temporary activities?

A If the number of people attending the event exceeds 500, the total length of the event must not exceed 36 hours.

B The number of people attending the event may not exceed 200; the total length of the event must not exceed 48 hours.

C The number of people attending the event may not exceed 500; the total length of the event must not exceed 96 hours.

D If the number of people attending the event exceeds 500, the total length of the event must not exceed 96 hours.

Question 17.11

GEORGES has served a temporary event notice on the local authority, indicating an intention to hold a disco in the local youth club. Within the notice, GEORGES has outlined that the club intends selling alcohol at the disco, but only to people that members of staff know to be over 18. The licensing officer, Constable LEONARD, has received a copy of the notice. Constable LEONARD intends objecting to the sale of alcohol, due to the previous history of such events, when a substantial amount of damage was caused to local shops and vehicles by youths leaving the premises.

What must Constable LEONARD do now, in order to object to the granting of the temporary event notice?

A Send a notice of objection to the relevant licensing authority.

B Send a notice of objection to the relevant licensing authority and GEORGES.

C Send a notice of objection to the owner of the premises, who would qualify as the premises user.

D Send a notice of objection to GEORGES.

Question 17.12

RICHARDS entered the Horse and Groom public house in an intoxicated condition and was served a pint of beer by HOPKINS. RICHARDS walked away from the bar and began abusing other customers. RICHARDS was ejected from the premises before drinking any of the beer. HOPKINS is a bar worker and is neither the holder of a premises licence nor the designated premises supervisor.

Has HOPKINS committed an offence by selling alcohol to a person who is drunk, under s. 141 of the Licensing Act 2003?

A Yes, HOPKINS would commit the offence in these circumstances.

B No, the offence will only be committed by the holder of a premises licence and the designated premises supervisor.

C No, as RICHARDS did not consume the drink.

D No, the offence will only be committed by the holder of a premises licence.

Question 17.13

HOULIE was in the Glendale public house one evening and was asked to leave by GREEN, the holder of the premises licence. HOULIE was drunk and abusive towards the bar staff. HOULIE left the premises voluntarily. However, once outside, he began banging on the door trying to get back into the pub. GREEN ignored HOULIE and contacted the police and when they arrived, HOULIE was walking away from the premises.

Has HOULIE committed an offence under s. 143 of the Licensing Act 2003 in these circumstances?

A No, because HOULIE has not actually re-entered the premises after being asked to leave.

B No, as no one has requested that he not re-enter the pub.

C Yes, as he was trying to regain entry to the pub in which he was drunk and disorderly.

D Yes, as it is an offence to be or have been drunk and disorderly on licensed premises.

Question 17.14

Constable TERRY was called to the garden of a house in the early hours of the morning. On arrival, Constable TERRY found COYLE drunk and asleep in a flowerbed. COYLE woke up as a result of being prodded by the officer. COYLE stood up, but was clearly unsteady and out of concern for his safety, Constable TERRY took hold of COYLE by the arm and led him out of the garden. Once they reached the street, COYLE became violent and disorderly towards Constable TERRY. The officer then decided to arrest COYLE for being drunk and disorderly.

Would COYLE's behaviour amount to an offence of drunk and disorderly, under s. 91(1) of the Criminal Justice Act 1967?

A No, the original incident took place in a private place, where the offence cannot be committed.

B Yes, COYLE's disorderly behaviour occurred before being arrested by Constable TERRY.

C No, COYLE's disorderly behaviour occurred after being taken hold of by the officer, which amounts to an arrest.

D Yes, it is irrelevant where Constable TERRY took hold of COYLE, this offence may be committed in a private place, as well as a public place.

Question 17.15

JENKINS is a heavy drinker, and is well known for being able to handle his liquor. One night he is out drinking with his friends and as a prank one of them drops amphetamine powder into JENKINS' pint of lager. Two hours later, in the street outside the pub, JENKINS begins to shout and swear at people. JENKINS is drunk, having consumed ten pints of lager. Police officers approach him and he shouts and physically threatens the officers. They arrest JENKINS for being drunk and disorderly. At court, it is argued that his disorderly behaviour was due entirely to the drug, of which he had no knowledge, and that he is not guilty.

In relation to this offence, which of the following statements is correct?

A He may be guilty, as alcohol is a partial cause of his intoxication.

B He is guilty, as it is immaterial what caused the intoxication.

C He is not guilty, as this offence is not made out where there are several causes of the incapacitated state.

D He is not guilty, as the cause of his intoxication was not self-induced.

Question 17.16

APPLEBY is 16 years old and in a public house which is open for the purposes of supplying alcohol for consumption on those premises. She is passing through the main area to go to the toilet as there is no other way to get into there. She is not accompanied by anyone as her parents are outside in the beer garden.

Has an offence been committed contrary to the Licensing Act 2003?

A Yes; as she is 16 and unaccompanied, the licensee commits an offence of allowing her to be in there.

B Yes; as she is 16 and unaccompanied, both APPLEBY and the licensee commit an offence.

C No; because she is 16, neither APPLEBY nor the licensee commits the offence.

D No, because she is only passing through the premises, there being no other way to get to the toilet.

Question 17.17

JABLONOWSKI is working in the Masons Arms public house. She serves TINNEY who is aged 16 and, generally speaking, looks his age. JABLONOWSKI believes TINNEY is 18 years of age, but asks for identification to impress her boss and TINNEY produces a student ID card stating he is 18; the card however is a very poor fake and should have been easily perceived as such. JABLONOWSKI, however, serves TINNEY alcohol.

Which of the following is true in relation to selling alcohol to someone under 18?

A JABLONOWSKI has a defence in that she honestly believed that TINNEY was over 18.

B JABLONOWSKI has a defence in that she asked for evidence of his age and it was produced.

C JABLONOWSKI has a defence in that she believed TINNEY was over 18 *and* she asked for evidence of his age.

D JABLONOWSKI has no defence as TINNEY produced fake evidence and it should have been obvious to her it was fake.

Question 17.18

In the Horse and Jockey public house, GILES, aged 18, went to the bar and ordered a pint of beer for himself, and another for his friend HARRISON, whom he knew was aged 17; both were consuming table meals. PARRY, who was serving at the time, provided the beer, but was not aware one of them was for HARRISON whom she knew was aged 17. HARRISON drinks his beer.

In relation to offences under the Licensing Act 2003, who of the above, if any, have committed offences?

A No offences have been committed, as HARRISON was consuming a table meal and can drink beer in such circumstances.

B Only GILES, of buying alcohol on behalf of an individual aged under 18.

C GILES, of buying alcohol on behalf of an individual aged under 18, and PARRY for serving it.

D All three; GILES for buying, PARRY for selling and HARRISON for consuming the drink, which was not cider or wine.

Question 17.19

During the summer months, DENNIS organised a series of 20/twenty cricket matches. DENNIS was granted temporary event notices to sell alcohol at each of the matches. After the first week, the police received information that alcohol was being sold to young people. They conducted test purchase operations over the next two weeks and on two occasions, alcohol was sold to different young people, under the age of 18. DENNIS was responsible for both sales.

Would DENNIS be guilty of an offence under s. 147A of the Licensing Act 2003 (persistently selling alcohol to children) in these circumstances?

A No, the alcohol was sold to different individuals.

B Yes, regardless of the fact that alcohol was sold to different individuals.

C No, there is only evidence that alcohol was sold to individuals on two occasions.

D No, this section does not apply to premises authorised to be used for permitted temporary activities.

Question 17.20

GREEN owns an off-licence which is being monitored by the local Neighbourhood Policing Team, because of complaints that alcohol is being sold to young people on a regular basis. During an operation in March, the police caught GREEN selling alcohol to ZENDEN, aged 16. In April, the police again detected GREEN selling alcohol to ZENDEN on one other occasion.

Would GREEN's behaviour amount to an offence under s. 147A of the Licensing Act 2003 (persistently selling alcohol to children under the age of 18)?

A Yes, GREEN has sold alcohol to a person under 18, on two or more occasions, in two consecutive months.

B No, GREEN has not sold alcohol to a person under 18, on three or more occasions, in three consecutive months.

C No, GREEN has not sold alcohol to a person under 18, on two or more occasions in three consecutive months.

D No, GREEN has not sold alcohol to a person under 18, on four or more occasions, in three consecutive months.

Question 17.21

FABIEN, aged 21, was entering an off-licence one evening when a group of young people were standing outside. One of the group asked FABIEN to buy four cans of lager for them. FABIEN suspected that the young people were under age, but agreed to buy the cans. However, the conversation was overheard by the owner of the off-licence, who refused to sell the lager to FABIEN.

Does FABIEN commit an offence under s. 149 of the Licensing Act 2003, in these circumstances?

A No, because the shop owner refused to sell the alcohol to FABIEN.

B No, the alcohol was not intended for consumption on relevant premises.

C No, both because the shop owner refused to sell the alcohol to FABIEN *and* it was not intended for consumption on relevant premises.

D Yes, regardless of whether the shop owner refused to sell the alcohol to FABIEN, or where it was to be consumed.

Question 17.22

GARDINER is 17 years old and works for ASDA as a temporary worker. His supervisor is YANCEY. Whilst on the tills GARDINER checks through a four-pack of Fosters Ice bottles. YANCEY is at the till next to GARDINER but does not notice that the sale of alcohol has happened and she did not tell GARDINER he was not allowed to sell alcohol.

In relation to the sale of alcohol by GARDINER, which of the following statements is correct?

A YANCEY has committed an offence as she failed to supervise the sale of alcohol properly.

B YANCEY has committed an offence as she failed to train GARDINER in the sale of alcohol.

C GARDINER has committed an offence of selling alcohol whilst under 18 years of age.

D Neither has committed an offence in these circumstances.

Question 17.23

Constable PERRY was walking through the Anchor public house one evening. The officer saw FLETCHER sitting at a table with a group of people, drinking a pint of beer. On two occasions in the past six months, Constable PERRY had confiscated alcohol from FLETCHER in a public place, and was aware that the person was under 18 years of age.

Has FLETCHER committed an offence under s. 30(1) of the Policing and Crime Act 2009 (persistently possessing alcohol in a relevant place) in these circumstances?

A No, a public house is not a relevant place for the purposes of this section.

B Yes, FLETCHER has been in possession of alcohol in a relevant place on two or more occasions in six consecutive months.

C Yes, FLETCHER has been in possession of alcohol in a relevant place on three or more occasions in 12 consecutive months.

D Yes, FLETCHER has been in possession of alcohol in a relevant place on three or more occasions in six consecutive months.

Question 17.24

Whilst on patrol in a housing estate, Constable CAMPBELL came across HICKS, who was in possession of four unopened cans of lager. HICKS admitted being aged 13, but stated she was taking the drink home to her father. HICKS did not appear to be drunk at the time; however, the officer took the decision to confiscate the lager.

Did Constable CAMPBELL have an additional power to remove HICKS to a place of safety, or take her home?

A No, because HICKS was not drunk at the time.

B Yes, provided Constable CAMPBELL reasonably suspected HICKS was going to drink from the cans.

C Yes, because HICKS was under 14 years of age.

D Yes, because HICKS was under 16 years of age.

Question 17.25

Constable SINGH was walking through a park when he came across two young people, who were intoxicated. He discovered they were 15 years old and that they had been given drink by HAWKINS. Constable SINGH intercepted HAWKINS, who was walking away from the park, and saw that he was in possession of a can of lager from which he was drinking. HAWKINS is over 18 years old.

What are Constable SINGH's powers to deal with HAWKINS in these circumstances?

A He has the power to confiscate the alcohol from HAWKINS and demand his name and address.

B He has no powers, as HAWKINS did not intend to supply the alcohol to a person under 18.

C He has no powers, as HAWKINS is not under 18.

D He has no powers, as HAWKINS is not in the company of a person under 18 to whom he intends to supply the alcohol.

Question 17.26

The police have conducted a series of test purchase operations over a period of a month at the Railway public house, due to suspected under-age drinking. The officers conducting the exercise have reported that GREEN, the premises licence holder, served alcohol to five under-age drinkers during this period. The duty inspector considers that an offence has been committed under s. 147A of the Licensing Act 2003, and a closure notice should be served on GREEN, to prevent further sales to young people.

Which of the following statements is correct, in relation to such a notice, under s. 169A of the Act?

A The inspector may authorise a closure notice, provided GREEN accepts responsibility for the offence under s. 147A.

B The inspector may authorise a closure notice in these circumstances alone.

C A superintendent may authorise a closure, provided GREEN accepts responsibility for the offence under s. 147A.

D A superintendent may authorise a closure, provided there is a realistic prospect of prosecuting GREEN for an offence under s. 147A.

Question 17.27

Constable PARIS was on patrol in a public park, which the local authority has designated as an area where alcohol may not be consumed. Constable PARIS saw BELL sitting on a park bench with four unopened cans of lager. BELL was intoxicated, but did not consume alcohol from the cans in the officer's presence.

What power was available to Constable PARIS to deal with BELL under the Criminal Justice and Police Act 2001 (alcohol consumption in designated places)?

A Constable PARIS had a power to direct BELL not to drink from the cans.

B None, Constable PARIS did not see BELL drinking from the cans.

C None, as the cans were unopened.

D Constable PARIS had a power to confiscate the cans, but not to dispose of them.

Question 17.28

Over several weekends, young people have been congregating in a local park, where they have been drinking. Residents have experienced anti-social behaviour by the group and minor damage and graffiti has been caused to a play area in the park. Whilst on patrol in the park, Constable THAME, the local neighbourhood police officer has come across a group of ten young people, all of whom are drunk.

What powers, if any, does Constable THAME have to direct the individuals to leave the locality to prevent crime and disorder, under s. 27 of the Violent Crime Reduction Act 2006?

A None, the young people have not been responsible for serious crime or disorder.

B Constable THAME may give written notice, directing the individuals to leave the locality.

C Constable THAME may give oral directions for individuals to leave the locality, which must be confirmed in writing as soon as possible by an inspector.

D Constable THAME may give oral directions for individuals to leave the locality, which must be confirmed in writing as soon as possible by any constable.

Question 17.29

A direction has been given to a large group of individuals to leave a locality, because local residents have been experiencing serious alcohol-related disorder.

To which members of the group would such a direction apply, according to s. 27(1) of the Violent Crime Reduction Act 2006?

A To any individual over the age of 10.

B To any individual over the age of 16.

C To any individual under the age of 16.

D To any individual under the age of 18.

Question 17.30

The police have become increasingly concerned about a park area, where there are ongoing problems with young people causing anti-social behaviour, which is related to the consumption of alcohol. The police and partners have tried several intervention initiatives, but these have not solved the problem. Consideration is being given as to whether the area should be designated as an alcohol disorder zone, under the Violent Crime Reduction Act 2006.

Who would have responsibility for deciding whether such a zone can be designated?

A It may be designated by the local authority, following a period of consultation with the police and other interested parties.

B It may be designated by the chief officer of police for the area.

C It may be designated by a magistrate, following an application by the local authority or the police, who must have consulted beforehand.

D It may be designated by the local authority, with the consent of the police and following a period of consultation with interested parties.

Question 17.31

COURTNEY lives in a local justice area which is trialling drinking banning orders, under the Violent Crime Reduction Act 2006. COURTNEY has been made subject of such an order.

Which of the following statements is correct, in relation to the conditions that can be imposed on COURTNEY under a drinking banning order?

A COURTNEY may be excluded from specified licensed premises in a defined area.

B COURTNEY may only be excluded from the licensed premises connected with an offence.

C COURTNEY must be excluded from all licensed premises in a defined area.

D COURTNEY must be excluded from consuming alcohol in specified licensed premises in a defined area.

Question 17.32

The Albion public house is situated in the middle of a residential estate. The premises has live bands playing on weekend evenings. One Saturday afternoon, Constable TELFORD was called to speak to several residents in the area, who were complaining about the noise that had come from the live band the night before. They all stated that there was another live band booked for that evening, and that the excessive noise was causing a serious disturbance in the area. As a result of speaking to the neighbours, Constable TELFORD contacted her inspector, who attended the scene. The inspector was considering whether or not to type out a closure order to serve on the licensee.

In the circumstances, would the inspector be able to implement a closure order under s. 161(1)(b) of the Licensing Act 2003?

A No, because the disturbance was not ongoing at the time.

B Yes, provided the noise was actually coming from the premises itself.

C No, closure orders are designed for disorder at licensed premises, not noise complaints.

D Yes, provided the noise was coming either from the premises, or from the vicinity of the premises.

Question 17.33

Inspector CARROLL was working a late shift when she received information that several disturbances had taken place in the Admiral public house during the evening.

Inspector CARROLL was aware that the police had dealt with a number of public order situations at the Admiral in the previous week and that the owner, HALL, had a reputation of being unable to control his customers. The inspector typed out a closure order for the premises, which she intended serving on HALL; however, she was called away to deal with a firearms incident in another area before she could serve the notice.

Could Inspector CARROLL delegate the serving of the notice to another officer?

A No, the order must be served by the inspector making it.

B Yes, the order may be served by any other inspector.

C Yes, the order may be served by any other officer.

D Yes, the order may be served by the senior officer on duty in the area.

Question 17.34

Inspector CLINTON was working late shifts on a Sunday. During the weekend, he had dealings with PARKS, the licensee of the Ship public house. The police were called to the premises several times on Friday evening because of fighting and persons were arrested. Intelligence suggested on the Saturday evening that further trouble was likely, and Inspector CLINTON served a closure order on PARKS at 8 pm. There was no court on the Sunday and Inspector CLINTON visited the Ship again at 5 pm that evening. PARKS said that he was going to open the pub again that night, because it was costing him too much money to stay closed.

What powers would be available to Inspector CLINTON, if he reasonably believed there was likely to be further disorder at the premises on the Sunday evening?

A None, the closure order has expired; he must wait until Monday to report the matter to the court.

B He may extend the closure order by serving a notice on PARKS when the existing one expires at 8 pm.

C He may extend the closure order, provided he serves a notice on PARKS before 8 pm.

D He must serve a new closure order on PARKS, and attend court on Monday to report the matter.

ANSWERS

Answer 17.1

Answer **A** — A person 'provides late night refreshment' under the Licensing Act 2003 if he or she supplies hot food or hot drinks to the public at any time between the hours of 11 pm and 5 am. Answers B, C and D are incorrect.

General Police Duties, para. 4.17.2

Answer 17.2

Answer **C** — Under s. 179 of the Licensing Act 2003, where a constable or an authorised person has reason to believe that any premises are being, or are about to be, used for a licensable activity, they may enter the premises with a view to seeing whether the activity is being, or is to be, carried on under and in accordance with an authorisation (s. 179(1)). A person exercising the power conferred by this section may, if necessary, use reasonable force (s. 179(3)). Since the power under this section is not restricted to police officers, answer B is incorrect. Also, there is no requirement for a police officer to be in uniform, therefore answer A is incorrect.

There is a separate power, under s. 180 of the Act, for a constable to enter premises in order to investigate offences. A constable may enter by reasonable force under this section. However, s. 179 above shows that a constable or authorised person may enter premises using reasonable force simply to make sure that licensing activities are being carried out within the law. Answer D is therefore incorrect.

(Note that an authorised person exercising the powers conferred on them must, if so requested, produce evidence of their authority to exercise the power.)

General Police Duties, para. 4.17.2.3

Answer 17.3

Answer **A** — The Secretary of State may impose s. 19(4) mandatory conditions for all relevant premises licences.

These conditions must be for the promotion of the licensing objectives and the conditions must not (when added together) exceed at any time *nine* (s. 19A) (inserted by the Policing and Crime Act 2009, s. 32 and sch. 4).

Answers B, C and D are therefore incorrect.

General Police Duties, para. 4.17.4.2

Answer 17.4

Answer **D** — Members of the relevant licensing authority *may* act as interested parties, allowing them to object to licence applications *or* to call for a licensing review (s. 13(3)(e) of the 2003 Act) (inserted by the Policing and Crime Act 2009, s. 33). Answers A and C are incorrect.

The licensing authority may potentially revoke the premises licence, which can be said to be a power of commercial life or death over the licence holder. Therefore, the authority have a duty to act fairly and the European Convention on Human Rights, Art. 6 (the right to a fair trial) is clearly engaged and needs to be tested rigorously (see *R (Harpers Leisure International Ltd)* v *Chief Constable of Surrey* [2009] EWHC 2160 (Admin)). However, this case does not affect the power under s. 13(3)(e), it merely means that the licensing authority must consider Art. 6 when conducting a review of a licence. Answer B is therefore incorrect.

General Police Duties, para. 4.17.4.3

Answer 17.5

Answer **C** — Section 53A of the Licensing Act 2003 provides for an accelerated review of licensed premises by a licensing authority, and the attaching of temporary conditions to a premises licence pending a full review of the licence.

The procedure provides for a senior police officer (of or above the rank of superintendent) to certify to a licensing authority, that he or she considers licensed premises to be associated with serious crime and/or serious disorder.

On receiving the application the licensing authority will be obliged to consider *within 48 hours* whether it is necessary to take interim steps pending a full review of the licence which must take place within 28 days. Answers A, B and D are therefore incorrect.

General Police Duties, para. 4.17.4.3

Answer 17.6

Answer **B** — There is a general provision under s. 51 of the Licensing Act 2003 for an interested party or responsible authority to apply to a relevant licensing authority for a review of the premises licence. For example, a local resident may consider that the measures taken by the licensee to prevent public nuisance are insufficient and request that they be reviewed. Similarly, the police may consider that the measures put in place to prevent crime and disorder are not being effective and need to be reviewed.

However, s. 53A of the Act provides for an accelerated review of licensed premises by *a licensing authority*, and the attaching of temporary conditions to a premises licence pending a full review of the licence. Answer C is therefore incorrect.

The procedure involves a senior police officer—of or above the rank of superintendent—certifying to a licensing authority that he/she considers licensed premises to be associated with serious crime and/or serious disorder. Answers A and D are therefore incorrect.

General Police Duties, para. 4.17.4.3

Answer 17.7

Answer **C** — Under s. 115 of the Licensing Act 2003, a personal licence is valid for *10 years*, unless revoked or surrendered, therefore answers A, B and D are incorrect.

It should be noted that under s. 26 of the Licensing Act 2003, a *premises licence* lasts until it is either revoked or surrendered. There is no specific time limit attached to this particular licence.

General Police Duties, para. 4.17.4.4

Answer 17.8

Answer **C** — *A constable or an authorised person* may require production of a club premises certificate (or a certified copy of it) (s. 94(7)), and a person who fails, without reasonable excuse, to produce the certificate (or certified copy) commits a summary offence (s. 94(9)). Answers A, B and D are therefore incorrect.

General Police Duties, para. 4.17.5.1

Answer 17.9

Answer **D** — Under s. 97 of the Licensing Act 2003, where a club premises certificate has effect in respect of any premises, a constable may enter and search the premises if he/she has reasonable cause to believe:

(a) that an offence under section 4(3)(a), (b) or (c) of the Misuse of Drugs Act 1971 (supplying or offering to supply, or being concerned in supplying or making an offer to supply, a controlled drug) has been, is being, or is about to be, committed there, or

(b) that there is likely to be a breach of the peace there.

This section does not allow a constable to enter the premises to detect licensing offences; therefore answers A and C are incorrect. Entry is allowed (using reasonable force if necessary) in order to detect offences under the Misuse of Drugs Act 1971, or if a breach of the peace is likely to occur in the premises. Answers A and B are incorrect for this reason.

General Police Duties, para. 4.17.5.2

Answer 17.10

Answer **C** — If a person intends holding a temporary event, under s. 100(4) and (5) of the Licensing Act 2003, he or she must provide a temporary event notice that must be in a form prescribed in regulations by the Secretary of State and set out certain details about the proposed event. Such details include the licensable activities that are to be carried out, the total length of the event, the times the licensable activities are to be carried out and the maximum number of people to be allowed on the premises at any one time.

The number of people attending such an event must be fewer than 500— answers A and D are incorrect, because the number of people *cannot* exceed 500.

Whatever the number of people attending the event, the total length of the event may not exceed 96 hours. Answers A and B are incorrect for this reason.

General Police Duties, para. 4.17.6.1

Answer 17.11

Answer **B** — Under s. 104(1) of the Licensing Act 2003, the premises user must give a copy of any temporary event notice to the relevant chief officer of police no later than ten working days before the day on which the event period specified in the notice begins.

Where the chief officer is satisfied that allowing the premises to be used in accordance with the notice would undermine the crime prevention objective (mentioned in s. 4(2)(a)), he or she must give a notice stating the reasons why he or she is so satisfied (an 'objection notice') to the relevant licensing authority, and the premises user (see s. 104(2)). Answers A and D are incorrect.

Section 100(2) of the Act states that the 'premises user', in relation to a temporary event notice, is the individual who gave the notice. Answer C is therefore incorrect.

General Police Duties, para. 4.17.6.2

Answer 17.12

Answer **B** — The Licensing Act 2003, s. 141 states:

(1) A person to whom subsection (2) applies commits an offence if, on relevant premises, he knowingly—
    (a) sells or attempts to sell alcohol to a person who is drunk, or
    (b) allows alcohol to be sold to such a person.

This subsection applies:

(2) (a) to any person who works at the premises in a capacity, whether paid or unpaid, which gives him authority to sell the alcohol concerned,
    (b) in the case of licensed premises, to—
        (i) the holder of a premises licence in respect of the premises, and
        (ii) the designated premises supervisor (if any) under such a licence.

Under s. 141(2)(a) above, the offence may be committed by any person who works on the premises, whatever their capacity. However, on licensed premises (which is the case in this question) the offence is covered by s. 141(2)(b), which restricts liability to the holder of a premises licence and/or the designated premises supervisor. Answers A and D are therefore incorrect. It is irrelevant that RICHARDS did not consume the drink—the offence is complete when the alcohol is sold to a person who is intoxicated. Answer C is therefore incorrect.

General Police Duties, para. 4.17.8.6

Answer 17.13

Answer **B** — Under s. 143(1)(a) of the Licensing Act 2003, a person who is drunk or disorderly commits an offence if, without reasonable excuse, he or she fails to leave relevant premises when requested to do so by a constable or by a person to whom subs. (2) applies (the holder of a premises licence in respect of the premises, and/or the designated premises supervisor). Since HOULIE left when requested by GREEN, no offence was committed under this subsection; answer D is therefore incorrect.

    Under s. 143(1)(b) of the Act, a further offence is committed if a person enters or attempts (answer A is therefore incorrect) to enter relevant premises after a constable or a person to whom subs. (2) applies has requested him or her not to enter. GREEN was not so requested and therefore would also not commit this offence; answer C is therefore incorrect.

General Police Duties, para. 4.17.8.8

Answer 17.14

Answer **B** — Under s. 91(1) of the Criminal Justice Act 1967, a person commits an offence if, in a public place, he or she is guilty, while drunk, of disorderly conduct. Since the offence may only be committed in a public place, answer D is incorrect.

The offence will not be committed when a person does not commit a disorderly act until after their arrest (*H* v *DPP* (2006) 170 JP 4). However, in *McMillan* v *Crown Prosecution Service* [2008] EWHC 1457 (Admin), it was held that where a police officer took hold of a drunken person by the arm to steady them for their own safety it was not an arrest. The circumstances in this case entailed the officer leading the drunken person from a private garden to a public place. It was then legitimate for the officer to arrest for this offence where the accused then displayed disorderly behaviour. The circumstances in *McMillan* mirror those in this question—it is irrelevant where the original incident commenced, the disorderly behaviour occurred in a public place, *before* the officer decided to make an arrest. Answers A and C are therefore incorrect.

General Police Duties, para. 4.17.8.9

Answer 17.15

Answer **A** — For this offence the drunkenness must be caused by excessive amounts of alcohol; where this is not the case and his state is caused by some other intoxicant, e.g. a drug, the offence is not made out (*Neale* v *RMJE (a minor)* (1985) 80 Cr App R 20) and therefore answer B is incorrect. In *Neale*, Goff LJ held that 'drunkenness' means taking intoxicating liquor to an extent that affects steady self-control. However, where there are several causes of a person's intoxicated state, one of which is alcohol, a court can find the person was in fact drunk even though some other intoxicant had an effect on this 'steady self-control' and therefore answer C is incorrect. Answer D is a defence from the Public Order Act 1986 and has no impact on this offence and is incorrect.

General Police Duties, para. 4.17.8.9

Answer 17.16

Answer **C** — Section 145 of the Licensing Act 2003 states that it is an offence for a person holding roles in public houses that would allow them to take appropriate action to prevent the presence of children in the way prohibited to allow unaccompanied children on those premises. This applies to licensees, staff working in the pub, etc.; the children themselves commit no offence by just being in there. Answer B is therefore incorrect.

No offence is committed if the unaccompanied child is on the premises solely for the purpose of passing to or from some other place to or from which there is no other convenient means of access or egress (s. 145(5)).

However, by virtue of s. 145(2)(a), 'child' means an individual aged under 16, and APPLEBY is 16. No offence is committed as she is not an 'unaccompanied child' as defined by the Act and not because she is passing through; that exception to the legislation applies only to unaccompanied children. Answers A and D are therefore incorrect.

General Police Duties, para. 4.17.9.1

Answer 17.17

Answer **D** — It is an absolute offence to sell alcohol to someone who is under 18, but there are some defences available.

To begin with, the person selling the alcohol must believe the person is aged 18 or over; lack of this belief loses the defence immediately. However this belief must then be supported by either of the following circumstances:

- nobody could reasonably have suspected from the individual's appearance that he was aged under 18; *or*
- all reasonable steps to establish the individual's age had been taken.

JABLONOWSKI's belief is not enough on its own; answer A is therefore incorrect.

In the scenario TINNEY did not look over 18, so JABLONOWSKI would have to follow the reasonable steps route to establish identity.

The Licensing Act 2003 further defines what 'reasonable steps' are in relation to establishing identification. They are:

- the individual was asked for evidence of his age; *and*
- the evidence produced would have convinced a reasonable person.

Producing identification does not negate the offence if such identification is obviously fake (as it was in the scenario). Answers B and C are therefore incorrect.

In summary then, for the defence to succeed, the person selling must believe the individual buying to be 18 or over. If it is not obvious to everyone else that this individual, by appearance, is over 18 then proof of age is required; such proof has to be convincing.

General Police Duties, para. 4.17.9.4

Answer 17.18

Answer **A** — The offences referred to in this question relate to various sections of the Licensing Act 2003:

- s. 147, allowing the sale of alcohol to children;
- s. 149, purchase of alcohol by or on behalf of children;
- s. 150, consumption of alcohol by children.

They all relate to selling and consumption of alcohol by a person aged under 18, and if the person is indeed under 18 then the offences are complete. However, offences under ss. 149 and 150 do not apply where a person is 16 or 17, provided they are accompanied at a table meal by someone aged 18 or over. In these circumstances they can have bought for them and consume beer, wine and cider (although hopefully not all in the same glass!).

In the scenario the buying and consumption of the beer was lawful and in consequence the selling was also lawful and no one commits an offence. Answers B, C and D are therefore incorrect.

General Police Duties, paras 4.17.9.5, 4.17.9.9, 4.17.9.10

Answer 17.19

Answer **B** — Under s. 147A(1) of the Licensing Act 2003, a person is guilty of an offence if:

(a) on 2 or more different occasions within a period of 3 consecutive months alcohol is unlawfully sold on the same premises to an individual aged under 18;

(b) at the time of each sale the premises were either licensed premises or premises authorised to be used for a permitted temporary activity; and

(c) that person was a responsible person in relation to the premises at each such time.

Under s. 147A(5), the individual aged under 18, to whom the sale is made, can be the same person or different people, therefore answer A is incorrect.

The Policing and Crime Act 2009, s. 28, amended s. 147A(1)(a) so that the offence is committed if alcohol is sold on 'two or more different occasions' whereas it was previously 'three or more different occasions'. Answer C is therefore incorrect.

No, this section *does* apply to premises authorised to be used for permitted temporary activities and answer D is incorrect.

General Police Duties, para. 4.17.9.6

Answer 17.20

Answer **C** — Under s. 147A(1) of the Licensing Act 2003, a person is guilty of an offence if:

(a) on 2 or more different occasions within a period of 3 consecutive months alcohol is unlawfully sold on the same premises to an individual aged under 18;

The Policing and Crime Act 2009, s. 28, amended s. 147A(1)(a) so that the offence is committed if alcohol is sold on 'two or more different occasions' whereas it was previously 'three or more different occasions'.

Answers A, B and D are therefore incorrect.

General Police Duties, para. 4.17.9.6

Answer 17.21

Answer **D** — Under s. 149(3)(a) of the Licensing Act 2003, a person commits an offence if he or she buys or attempts to buy alcohol on behalf of an individual aged under 18. The offence is complete when the person attempts to purchase the alcohol; therefore answers A and C are incorrect.

There is a separate offence under s. 149(4) of the Act, of a person buying or attempting to buy alcohol for consumption by a person under 18, for consumption on relevant premises—however, since the offence may be committed in either of the above circumstances, answers B and C are incorrect.

General Police Duties, para. 4.17.9.9

Answer 17.22

Answer **D** — Clearly selling alcohol in premises like ASDA has to be controlled and there is an offence under s. 153(4) of the Licensing Act 2003 of unsupervised sales by children (those under 18). The offence is committed by 'a responsible person' allowing an individual aged under 18 to make on the premises any sale of alcohol, a responsible person being defined as:

- the holder of a premises licence in respect of the premises;
- the designated premises supervisor (if any) under such a licence; or
- any individual aged 18 or over who is authorised for the purposes of this section by such a holder or supervisor.

(s. 153(4) of the Licensing Act 2003).

Only the responsible person commits this offence not the person under 18; answer C is therefore incorrect. The offence, however, is perpetrated 'knowingly' and as such there has to be such conscious awareness of what was happening. Answer A is incorrect because YANCEY has no such knowledge.

It is not committed by omission or error in training; answer B is therefore incorrect.

General Police Duties, para. 4.17.9.13

Answer 17.23

Answer **A** — Under s. 30(1) of the Policing and Crime Act 2009, a person under the age of 18 is guilty of an offence if, without reasonable excuse, the person is in possession of alcohol in any relevant place on three or more occasions within a period of 12 consecutive months.

Section 30(2) defines a 'relevant place' as:

(a) any public place, other than excluded premises, or

(b) any place, other than a public place, to which the person has unlawfully gained access.

In relation to subs. (2)(a), 'excluded premises' means premises with a premises licence or permitted temporary activity used for the supply of alcohol, and premises with a club premises certificate used for the supply of alcohol to members or guests.

Therefore, while FLETCHER has previously been in possession of alcohol in a relevant place on two occasions in 12 consecutive months, a public house is an 'excluded premises' and the provisions of this section do not apply there. Answers B, C and D are incorrect for this reason.

Answers B and D would also have been incorrect, had FLETCHER been in possession of alcohol in a relevant place, as the time period which triggers this offence is three or more occasions in 12 consecutive months.

General Police Duties, para. 4.17.9.14

Answer 17.24

Answer **D** — Under s. 1(1)(a) of the Confiscation of Alcohol (Young Persons) Act 1997, a constable who reasonably suspects that a person who is in a relevant place is in possession of alcohol, may confiscate the alcohol if the person is under 18.

Under subs. (1AB), a constable who imposes a requirement on a person under subs. (1) above may, if the constable reasonably suspects that the person is under the age of 16, remove the person to the person's place of residence or a place of safety. Answer C is therefore incorrect.

Subsection (1AB) has been inserted by s. 29 of the Policing and Crime Act 2009 and does not specifically define a 'place of safety', although this may be with a relative or friend, or where necessary, a police station or social services accommodation. There is no requirement for the officer to reasonably suspect that the person was going to drink from the cans if they are unopened, or that they were drunk at the time. Answers A and B are incorrect.

General Police Duties, para. 4.17.9.15

Answer 17.25

Answer **A** — Under s. 1(1) of the Confiscation of Alcohol (Young Persons) Act 1997, a constable who reasonably suspects that a person who is in a relevant place (public place, etc.) is in possession of alcohol, may confiscate the alcohol if:

(a) the person is under 18; *or*

(b) the person intends that any of the alcohol shall be consumed by a person under 18 in a relevant place; *or*

(c) the person is with *or* has recently been with a person under 18 and that person has recently consumed alcohol in the relevant place.

Under para. (c) above, as HAWKINS has recently been with a person under 18 who has consumed alcohol, regardless of whether he intends to supply more alcohol to the children, the officer will have the power to confiscate the alcohol he is in possession of. Answers B and D are therefore incorrect.

Also, alcohol may be confiscated from a person who is over 18 if he or she has committed an act mentioned under paras (b) and (c) above—the power is designed to prevent alcohol either being consumed by, or supplied to, people under 18. Answer C is therefore incorrect.

Note that under subs. (1AA) of the Act (inserted by s. 29 of the Policing and Crime Act 2009), a constable exercising the power under s. 1 above *shall* require the person to state their name and address. The previous subsection (now omitted) stated that a constable *may* require the person to give their name and address.

General Police Duties, para. 4.17.9.15

Answer 17.26

Answer **D** — Section 169A of the Licensing Act 2003 provides that a senior police officer (of the rank of superintendent or higher), or an inspector of weights and measures, may give a closure notice where there is evidence that a person has committed the offence of persistently selling alcohol to children at the premises in question. Answers A and B are therefore incorrect.

A further condition exists under s. 169A—the superintendent must consider that the evidence is such that there would be a realistic prospect of conviction if the offender was prosecuted for it. Answer C is incorrect.

General Police Duties, para. 4.17.9.17

Answer 17.27

Answer **A** — Under s. 13 of the Criminal Justice and Police Act 2001, local authorities may identify and designate public places within their areas as 'alcohol free zones', provided they are satisfied that nuisance, annoyance or disorder has occurred as a result of consumption of intoxicating liquor in those areas. Section 12 of the Act provides a constable with powers to deal with people who contravene orders, if he or she reasonably believes that a person is or has been consuming, or intends to consume alcohol in that place. Answer B is therefore incorrect.

A constable is provided with three distinct powers:

- to require the person not to consume alcohol;
- to require the person to surrender the alcohol;
- to dispose of anything surrendered in a manner he or she considers appropriate.

Answer D is incorrect, because the officer may exercise any of the above powers and dispose of anything surrendered in such a manner as he or she considers appropriate. The fact that the cans were unopened is not relevant and they may be confiscated utilising the powers described above. Answer C is therefore incorrect.

General Police Duties, para. 4.17.10.2

Answer 17.28

Answer **B** — Section 27(1) of the Violent Crime Reduction Act 2006 states that where an individual aged 10 or over is in a public place, a constable in uniform may give a direction to that individual requiring him or her to leave the locality of that place and prohibiting the individual from returning to that locality for such period (not exceeding 48 hours) from the giving of the direction as the constable may specify.

Under s. 27(2), such a direction may only be given if:

(a) the presence of the individual in that locality is likely, in all the circumstances, to cause or to contribute to the occurrence of alcohol-related crime or disorder in that locality, or to cause or to contribute to a repetition or continuance there of such crime or disorder; and

(b) the giving of a direction under this section to that individual is necessary for the purpose of removing or reducing the likelihood of there being such crime or disorder in that locality during the period for which the direction has effect or of there being a repetition or continuance in that locality during that period of such crime or disorder.

Since there is no mention of *serious* crime or disorder, answer A is incorrect.

A direction under this section must be given in writing (see s. 27(3)). Answers C and D are therefore incorrect.

Note that the Policing and Crime Act 2009, s. 31, amended subs. (1) from 'an individual aged 16 or over' to 'an individual aged 10 or over'.

General Police Duties, para. 4.17.10.4

Answer 17.29

Answer **A** — Section 27(1) of the Violent Crime Reduction Act 2006 states that where *an individual aged 10 or over* is in a public place, a constable in uniform may give a direction to that individual requiring him/her to leave the locality of that place and prohibiting the individual from returning to that locality for such period (not exceeding 48 hours) from the giving of the direction as the constable may specify.

The Policing and Crime Act 2009, s. 31, amended subs. (1) from 'an individual aged 16 or over' to 'an individual aged 10 or over'.

Answers B, C and D are therefore incorrect.

General Police Duties, para. 4.17.10.4

Answer 17.30

Answer **D** — Sections 15 to 20 of the Violent Crime Reduction Act 2006 provide a local authority with the power to designate, *with the consent of the police*, a locality as an alcohol disorder zone where there is a problem with alcohol-related nuisance and disorder. Answer A is incorrect as the local chief officer of police must give consent before an alcohol disorder zone is designated by the local authority (s. 18(4)).

The police may also make application to the local authority (not a magistrate) for a locality to be so designated, but it is the local authority that makes the designation. Answers B and C are incorrect.

Local authorities are required to give notice of their intention to designate a particular zone following which there is a period of 28 days' consultation where all interested parties can make representations about the proposal.

General Police Duties, para. 4.17.10.5

Answer 17.31

Answer **A** — Section 1 of the Violent Crime Reduction Act 2006 provides for a civil order, a drinking banning order, which is designed to protect persons and their property from criminal or disorderly conduct by an individual while he/she is under the influence of alcohol.

Orders may be made on the application (by way of complaint) of the police or local authority to a magistrates' court that an individual, aged 16 or over, has engaged in criminal or disorderly conduct while under the influence of alcohol, and that such an order is necessary to protect other persons from further conduct by him/her of that kind while he/she is under the influence of alcohol (s. 3(2)). Such orders must be for not less than two months and not more than two years in duration.

Under s. 1(2), such an order may impose any prohibition on the subject which is necessary for the purpose of protecting other persons from criminal or disorderly conduct by the subject while he/she is under the influence of alcohol. Under s. 1(3)(a), the order *must* include such prohibition as the court making it considers necessary, on the subject's entering premises in respect of which there is a premises licence authorising the use of the premises for the sale of alcohol by retail; however, the section is not prescriptive as to what those conditions are (answers C and D are incorrect).

On the other hand, the wording of s. 1 means that the court can be flexible in other respects regarding the conditions it sets, such as being able to exclude the person from specified licensed premises in a defined geographic area, depending on what it considers necessary. The power is not restricted to excluding the person from the licensed premises connected with a particular offence committed by an individual and answer B is incorrect.

General Police Duties, para. 4.17.10.6

Answer 17.32

Answer **A** — There are two general powers to serve closure orders under s. 161 of the Licensing Act 2003. First, when a senior police officer (an officer of at least the rank of inspector) has reason to believe that there is disorder on, or in the vicinity of and related to the premises, or there is likely to be disorder on, or in the vicinity of and related to the premises, and in either case he or she reasonably believes that the order is necessary in the interests of public safety (s. 161(1)(a)).

Secondly, a closure notice may be served when it is reasonably believed that a disturbance is being caused to the public by excessive noise emitted from the premises and a closure order is necessary to prevent the disturbance. Since a closure order may be served in relation to noise only (s. 161(1)(b)) answer C is incorrect.

However, this power is restricted to ongoing incidents and may be used only where a disturbance is occurring, which means that answers B and D are incorrect. Lastly, the senior police officer must be satisfied that the excessive noise is actually being emitted from the premises (unlike the power to deal with disorder, which may occur in the vicinity of the premises). Answer D is also incorrect for this reason.

General Police Duties, para. 4.17.11.2

Answer 17.33

Answer **C** — Under s. 161 of the Licensing Act 2003, a senior police officer (an inspector) may make an order requiring the relevant licensed premises to be closed if it is necessary in the interests of public safety, where disorder is occurring or where it is likely to occur, either on the premises or in the vicinity. Past conduct of the licensee may be taken into consideration.

The closure order must be a written notice and comes into effect when a constable serves notice on the holder of the premises licence or the designated premises supervisor in respect of licensed premises (s. 161(5)). Because another police officer of any rank may actually serve the written notice on the relevant person, the senior police officer making the order need not be present on the premises when the order is served. Answers A, B and D are therefore incorrect. Note that the power to order the closure cannot be delegated to a person below the rank of inspector.

General Police Duties, para. 4.17.11.2

Answer 17.34

Answer **C** — Under s. 164(1) of the Licensing Act 2003, where a closure order has been made, the responsible officer must apply to the relevant justices for them to consider the order as soon as reasonably practicable after the order was made, so that the court may consider the order and any extension to it. The responsible officer must also notify the relevant licensing authority.

However, a closure order will expire 24 hours after the notice was served on the relevant person. The legislators have allowed for the fact that most areas do not have a court sitting on a Sunday by allowing the senior police officer to extend the existing closure order by serving a new written notice on the relevant person (s. 162). This extension will last for another 24 hours, allowing the responsible officer to attend court on the Monday. Answers A and D are therefore incorrect.

The original closure order in the question expired at 8 pm on the Sunday. The further extended period of 24 hours commences when the previous order expires; however, the written notice must be served on the relevant person before the existing closure order expires (see s. 162(3) and (4)). Answer B is incorrect.

Note that in order to extend a closure order the senior police officer would still reasonably have to believe that it is necessary in the interests of public safety or to prevent excessive noise. Therefore, if the inspector in the question had no reason to suspect that there would have been further problems on the Sunday, he could not have closed the premises down. He would still have to attend court on the Monday to report on the facts of the closure order served on the Saturday.

General Police Duties, paras 4.17.11.3, 4.17.11.4

18 Offences and Powers Relating to Information

STUDY PREPARATION

The management—and mismanagement—of information is an area of increasing importance to the police generally and therefore to its supervisors, managers, trainers and examiners.

The key issues here are the statutory restrictions on who can access what type of information and for what purpose. Much accessing of information involves the use of computers and it is necessary therefore to understand the relevant aspects of the Computer Misuse Act 1990.

Also covered are the control measures, which are required to be in place to protect data held on individuals, under the Data Protection Act 1998, and the powers given to the Information Commissioner to regulate the storage of such data.

A large part of this chapter contains the provisions of the Regulation of Investigatory Powers Act 2000 (RIPA), which covers the covert acquisition of information about people, through the use of covert human intelligence sources (CHIS), surveillance and the interception of communications.

QUESTIONS

Question 18.1

Section 1 of the Computer Misuse Act 1990 makes provision in relation to unauthorised access to computer material.

Where a person is not authorised and they have the required intent and knowledge, at which point would an offence under this section first be committed?

A When the computer is switched on.

B When the 'log on screen' is filled out.

C When they are successfully logged onto the system.

D When the actual program is accessed.

Question 18.2

BIGNELL worked for a large bank and was dating BRADY who, unknown to her, had ties with an organised crime gang. BRADY persuaded BIGNELL to access information from customers' accounts and pass the details to him. BIGNELL was afraid to ask BRADY why he wanted the information and was unaware that he was selling on the data to credit card forgers.

What would have to be proved, in order to convict BIGNELL of an offence contrary to s. 1 of the Computer Misuse Act 1990?

A That she was not authorised to access the data and that she knew this was the case.

B That she was not authorised to access the data and that she knew this was the case, or was reckless as to whether or not this was the case.

C Only that she was not authorised to access the data.

D That she was not authorised to access the data and that she knew what the information was being used for.

Question 18.3

DAVIDSON is a computer programmer who has been asked by JELLIS to assist in a crime. JELLIS wants him to access the computer records of a Ferrari dealership's new customers' accounts and add JELLIS' details as a bona fide customer. This will, he believes, enable him to test drive a Ferrari. He intends not to return the car but take it for a 'joy-ride', amounting to an offence under s. 12(1) of the Theft Act 1968 (taking a motor vehicle or other conveyance without authority, etc.). DAVIDSON 'hacks' into the company's computer and makes the changes. However, in reality, JELLIS will not be able to carry out his plan as the company always sends a representative on the test drive.

Has DAVIDSON committed an offence under s. 2 of the Computer Misuse Act 1990 (unauthorised access with intent to commit or facilitate commission of further offences)?

A Yes, even though the commission of the offence intended was impossible.

B Yes, even though he was merely facilitating the crime.

C No, as the intention to commit the crime lay with JELLIS.

D No, as the offence intended is not covered by s. 2.

Question 18.4

LENNON was a computer software engineer who worked for a company which distributed electronic equipment bought by customers online. LENNON was sacked by the company for allegedly stealing. Seeking revenge, LENNON devised a program which sent three million emails to the company's inbox in one day. LENNON hoped that the volume of emails would cause the company's online computer package to crash. However, another software engineer working for the company realised what was happening and implemented a program which intercepted the emails. In the end, no damage was done to the company.

If LENNON were to be prosecuted for an offence under s. 3 of the Computer Misuse Act 1990, which of the following statements would be correct in respect of the 'intent' required for this offence?

A The prosecution would have to show that LENNON intended causing an economic loss to the company.

B The prosecution must show that LENNON intended to impair the operation of the company's software program.

C The prosecution would have to show that LENNON intended to impair the operation of the company's software program, or was reckless as to whether it would be impaired.

D The prosecution would have to show that LENNON intended causing permanent damage to the company's computer program.

Question 18.5

Westshire Constabulary had been subject to a number of complaints from people who had been arrested because of faulty data on the Police National Computer (PNC), which should have been deleted by the force. The Information Commissioner undertook a review of the force's data systems to establish the extent of the problem. The review revealed serious contraventions relating to data storage, which the Information Commissioner felt were likely to cause substantial damage or substantial distress.

Could the Information Commissioner serve the data controller for the force with a monetary penalty notice, in these circumstances?

A Yes, if the Information Commissioner was satisfied the data controller knew the extent of the problem.

B Yes, if the Information Commissioner was satisfied that the contravention was deliberate, or that the data controller knew or ought to have known the extent of the problem.

C No, the chief officer of police bears the liability for such serious breaches of the Act.

D Yes, if the Information Commissioner was satisfied that the contravention was deliberate.

Question 18.6

PREEDY is a security guard in a hospital and suspects a colleague, WALL, of stealing from patients' lockers. PREEDY approached Constable HARPER with his concerns. There was insufficient evidence to act on at this stage. Constable HARPER asked PREEDY to keep an eye on WALL and to report any unusual activity. PREEDY decided to take matters a step further and undertook some covert questioning of WALL, trying to get information on the thefts. WALL inadvertently let slip where some of the stolen property was hidden and PREEDY contacted Constable HARPER to pass on the information.

In relation to PREEDY, could he be described as having acted as a covert human intelligence source (CHIS), in these circumstances?

A Yes, when Constable HARPER asked PREEDY to keep an eye on WALL, they established a relationship.

B Yes, when PREEDY undertook covert questioning of WALL, he established a relationship.

C Yes, but only when PREEDY passed on the information to Constable HARPER.

D No, Constable HARPER did not task PREEDY or direct his activities.

Question 18.7

The use and conduct of a CHIS must be authorised by a designated officer.

In relation to the prevention of crime, what must the designated officer believe to authorise a CHIS?

A It is reasonable to prevent a crime.

B It is suspected that it will prevent a crime.

C It is reasonable in the circumstances to prevent a crime.

D It is necessary to prevent a crime.

Question 18.8

Officers from the Dedicated Source Unit are seeking to recruit CURTIS, aged 17, as a CHIS. CURTIS is known to circulate with local drug dealers and will be in a position to provide valuable source information.

If the authorising officer agrees to CURTIS' recruitment, what restrictions, if any, would there be in relation to authorisation?

A Because CURTIS is under 18, the initial authorisation may only last for 72 hours.

B Because CURTIS is under 18, the initial authorisation may only last for one month.

C Because CURTIS is over 17, the initial authorisation may last for 12 months.

D If the authorisation is non-urgent, it will last for 12 months, regardless of CURTIS' age.

Question 18.9

The police have received information relating to corruption in a local authority. Officers from a dedicated source unit have recruited O'CALLAGHAN, who is able to pass on confidential information about a multimillion pound contract to redevelop a landfill site, which is subject to a tender application by several building companies. O'CALLAGHAN has intimated that officers from the legal and planning departments of the local authority and some councillors have taken 'bungs' from a certain building company, in order to secure the contract. The officers would like to recruit O'CALLAGHAN as a CHIS and have spoken to their detective inspector.

Which of the following statements is correct in relation to the authorisation for the recruitment of O'CALLAGHAN as a CHIS?

A O'CALLAGHAN's recruitment as a CHIS may be authorised by the detective inspector.

B O'CALLAGHAN's recruitment as a CHIS must be authorised by a superintendent.

C O'CALLAGHAN's recruitment as a CHIS must be authorised by an assistant chief constable.

D O'CALLAGHAN's recruitment as a CHIS must be authorised by a chief constable.

Question 18.10

Detective Constable WONG has conducted an intelligence interview with FRATTON, aged 21, who is in the cells, due to be bailed shortly. FRATTON gave information about a large quantity of Class A drugs due to be delivered to a local drug dealer imminently. FRATTON said she knows the dealer well enough to make a direct approach to find out the delivery time. Detective Constable WONG has asked Detective Inspector YOUNG for an urgent authorisation to recruit FRATTON as a CHIS to discover the delivery time.

Does Detective Inspector YOUNG have the authority to authorise CHIS activity in such circumstances?

A Yes, the inspector may give urgent written authorisation for CHIS activity; the authorisation will last for 72 hours unless renewed.

B Yes, the inspector may give urgent oral authorisation, but the authorisation must be confirmed in writing by a superintendent after 24 hours.

C Yes, the inspector may give urgent oral authorisation for CHIS activity; the authorisation will last for 72 hours unless renewed.

D No, only a superintendent may give an urgent authorisation for CHIS activity.

Question 18.11

Officers received information that JOHNSON was dealing drugs while sitting in his car in a car park on the outskirts of town. After some research, the officers discovered that a new closed circuit television (CCTV) camera had been installed in the area, overlooking the car park, which was powerful enough to see inside parked cars. The officers considered using the CCTV office as an observation point, in an operation to catch JOHNSON handing over the drugs and collecting his money inside his vehicle.

Would the use of the CCTV camera to look inside JOHNSON's vehicle amount to intrusive surveillance?

A No, intrusive surveillance applies to residential premises only.
B Yes, this would amount to intrusive surveillance and would require the appropriate authorisation.
C No, this would amount to directed surveillance and would require the appropriate authorisation.
D No, it would be intrusive surveillance only if the vehicle was on residential property.

Question 18.12

DAWSON was arrested for a series of frauds against elderly people, involving the theft of £250,000. The police believed that SHELLEY, a solicitor, had been passing information to DAWSON about clients and their bank accounts in a conspiracy to commit fraud. DAWSON asked for SHELLEY to represent him while he was in custody. The officer in charge, DCI PATTERSON, considered making an application to place covert listening devices in the police station interview room, to listen in on their consultation.

Which of the following statements is correct, in relation to the police being allowed to use such surveillance methods?
A This is not permissible, as it amounts to directed surveillance.
B This is permissible, as it only amounts to directed and not intrusive surveillance.
C This is permissible, even though it amounts to intrusive surveillance.
D This is not permissible; all communications between lawyers and their clients are subject to legal privilege.

Question 18.13

Police officers wish to use surveillance on a newspaper office, with a view to obtaining material of a journalistic nature, which will be used in the investigation of an offence of murder.

Who can grant authorisation for such surveillance?
A An officer of at least the rank of superintendent only.
B An officer of at least the rank of superintendent, or an inspector in cases of urgency.
C The chief officer only.
D Any Association of Chief Police Officers (ACPO)-ranking police officer.

Question 18.14

Section 5(3) of the Regulation of Investigatory Powers Act 2000 allows for the application for a warrant to intercept communications, for the purpose of safeguarding the economic well-being of the United Kingdom, where the relevant acts or intentions relate to people outside the United Kingdom.

For how long is such a warrant valid?

A One month.
B Two months.
C Three months.
D Six months.

Question 18.15

Undercover police officers have infiltrated a large gang which is organising armed robberies in banks and building societies throughout the country. It is estimated that the gang is responsible for 30 crimes which have so far yielded over £500,000. The investigating officers believe that the investigation would be assisted by obtaining a warrant to intercept communications between the various members of the gang.

Would the authorising officer be able to agree to such a warrant under s. 5 of the Regulation of Investigatory Powers Act 2000?

A Yes, provided the information would prove valuable to the investigation.
B No, the case is not one which affects the interests of national security.
C No, the case is not one which affects the interests of national security or which would affect the economic well-being of the United Kingdom.
D Yes, provided the information would prove necessary to the investigation.

Question 18.16

PRIESTLEY is employed by the police as an analyst in a police staff role, in a force intelligence bureau. He goes home one evening and, as a matter of conversation, he tells his wife, a serving police officer, that he saw an interception warrant issued in relation to a local company, but does not mention which company it is.

In relation to unauthorised disclosures, contrary to s. 19 of the Regulation of Investigatory Powers Act 2000, which of the following is true?

A   PRIESTLEY cannot commit the offence as he is a member of the support staff.

B   PRIESTLEY does not commit the offence as he does not name the company.

C   PRIESTLEY commits the offence simply by mentioning it to his wife.

D   PRIESTLEY commits the offence, but has a defence that he did not disclose it outside the police service.

ANSWERS

Answer 18.1

Answer **A** — An offence under s. 1 of the Computer Misuse Act 1990 is committed by causing a computer to perform a function, and all the above answers would amount to 'functions'. As you were asked at which point an offence would first be committed, answer A is the correct answer. Although answers B, C and D all may fall under the section, they are incorrect, as switching the computer on is the first function that would amount to the offence.

General Police Duties, para. 4.18.2.1

Answer 18.2

Answer **A** — Under s. 1(1) of the Computer Misuse Act 1990, a person is guilty of an offence if—

(a) he causes a computer to perform any function with intent to secure access to any program or data held in any computer;
(b) the access he intends to secure is unauthorised; and
(c) he knows at the time when he causes the computer to perform the function that that is the case.

In order to prove the offence under s. 1, you must also show that the defendant knew the access was unauthorised and that he/she intended to secure access to the program or data. More proof is required than simply showing the defendant was not authorised to access the data and answer C is incorrect.

This is an offence of 'specific intent', therefore lesser forms of *mens rea* such as recklessness will not be sufficient to convict a person. Answer B is incorrect.

The offence is complete when the person knowingly accesses unauthorised data. There is no requirement to show that he/she knew what the information was being used for (albeit if BIGNELL *did* know what the data was being used for, she could commit an offence under s. 2 of the Act). Answer D is incorrect.

General Police Duties, para. 4.18.2.1

Answer 18.3

Answer **D** — Section 2 of the Computer Misuse Act 1990 requires intent on the part of the defendant; and this is either intention to commit an offence to which s. 2 applies, or the intention to facilitate the commission of such an offence. DAVIDSON has this intention, as he knows the purpose of his actions and is aware that it will facilitate the taking and driving away (TADA), and therefore answer C is incorrect. Section 2 applies to the particular classes of offences set out in s. 2(2) of the 1990 Act. Section 12(1) of the Theft Act 1968 (taking a motor vehicle or other conveyance without authority, etc.) is such a summary offence and therefore does not fall within offences outlined in s. 2(2), and therefore answer B is incorrect. As to impossibility, s. 2(4) of the 1990 Act makes clear that a person may be guilty of an offence even though the facts are such that the commission of the further offence is impossible; but as the offence intended is not covered by s. 2 of the 1990 Act this is immaterial. Therefore answer A is incorrect.

General Police Duties, para. 4.18.2.3

Answer 18.4

Answer **C** — Under s. 3(1) of the Computer Misuse Act 1990, a person is guilty of an offence if he/she does any unauthorised act in relation to a computer and at the time he/she does the act he/she knows that it is unauthorised; and either subs. (2) or subs. (3) applies.

Under subs. (2), the person must *intend* by doing the act:

(a) to impair the operation of any computer;
(b) to prevent or hinder access to any program or data held in any computer; or
(c) to impair the operation of any such program or the reliability of any such data.

Section 3(3) of the Act states that this subsection also applies if the person is *reckless* as to whether the act will do any of the things mentioned in paras (a) to (c) of subs. (2) above. Therefore, the offence can be committed by a person who intends or is reckless as to whether the program is impaired and answer B is incorrect.

There is no requirement to prove an intent to cause an economic loss to the company and answer A is incorrect.

An 'unauthorised act' can include a series of acts and a reference to impairing, preventing or hindering something includes a reference to doing so temporarily (s. 3(5)) and answer D is incorrect.

General Police Duties, para. 4.18.2.4

Answer 18.5

Answer **B** — A crucial element in the Data Protection Act 1998 is the data protection principles set out at sch. 1. As well as introducing the principles, s. 4(4) makes it clear that it is the duty of the relevant 'data controller' to comply with those principles wherever they apply. Answers C and D are incorrect.

Section 55A(1) provides that the Information Commissioner may serve the data controller with a monetary penalty notice if satisfied there has been serious contravention of s. 4(4), and the contravention was of a kind likely to cause substantial damage or substantial distress.

This subsection only applies if the contravention was deliberate (subs. (2)), or the data controller knew or ought to have known there was a risk that the contravention would occur and would be of a kind likely to cause substantial damage or substantial distress (subs. (3)).

Answers A, C and D are therefore incorrect.

General Police Duties, paras 4.18.3.2, 4.18.3.3

Answer 18.6

Answer **B** — A covert human intelligence source is someone who establishes or maintains a relationship with another person for the *covert* purpose of:

- obtaining information
- providing access to information

or who *covertly* discloses information obtained by the use of such a relationship.

The main purpose of the Regulation of Investigatory Powers Act 2000 is to control the use of surveillance and Covert Human Intelligence Sources (CHIS) operations by public authorities and to ensure that any infringement of a person's human rights is lawful.

The definition would not usually apply to members of the public generally supplying information to the police. Similarly, people who have come across information in the ordinary course of their jobs who suspect criminal activity (such as bank staff, local authority employees, etc.) do not have a covert relationship with the police simply by passing on information. However, if the person supplying the information is asked by the police to do something further in order to develop or enhance it, any form of direction or tasking by the police in this way could make the person a CHIS and thereby attract all the statutory provisions and safeguards.

In the circumstances in this question, the officer has simply asked PREEDY to keep an eye on things and this would not actually amount to 'tasking' or 'directing' a person's activities and Constable HARPER has certainly not asked him to develop a relationship with WALL. Answer A is incorrect, as PREEDY was not acting as a CHIS as a result of his conversation with the officer.

Nevertheless, PREEDY went on to act as a CHIS, according to the above definition, when he covertly questioned WALL for information (and thus formed a 'relationship' with him) and later when he covertly disclosed the information to the officer. Answer D is incorrect. The first point that this happened was during the questioning, therefore, answer C is incorrect.

General Police Duties, para. 4.18.4.4

Answer 18.7

Answer **D** — A designated person must not authorise any activity by a CHIS unless he or she believes it is necessary, and that to do so is proportionate to what is being sought. It is not enough to believe it was reasonable to prevent a crime (answer A is incorrect), nor that it is reasonable in the circumstances to prevent a crime (answer C is incorrect), nor that it was suspected that it would prevent a crime (answer B is incorrect). It can be authorised only if the designated officer believes that it is both necessary and proportionate to the legitimate objective of the operation.

General Police Duties, para. 4.18.4.4

Answer 18.8

Answer **B** — Generally, the authorisation for use and conduct of a CHIS will last for 12 months (unless an urgent authorisation has been made, when it will last for 72 hours unless renewed).

However, stricter controls are in place in respect of a juvenile CHIS (see Regulation of Investigatory Powers (Juveniles) Order 2000). Under the Order, an authorisation for a juvenile CHIS will last for 1 month, even if it is a non-urgent authorisation (answers A and D are incorrect).

A juvenile CHIS is a person under the age of 18, therefore, answer C is incorrect.

General Police Duties, para. 4.18.4.4

Answer 18.9

Answer **D** — Authorisations for CHIS activity under the Regulation of Investigatory Powers Act 2000 must normally be given by officers of the rank of at least superintendent. In cases where an urgent authority is required, it may be given by an inspector, when it is not reasonably practicable to have the application considered by a superintendent.

However, stricter controls are in place in respect of a juvenile CHIS or a situation where a CHIS may obtain confidential information. In the case of a juvenile CHIS, authorisation must be given by an officer of at least the rank of assistant chief constable. In the case of a CHIS who may obtain confidential information, authorisation must be given by an officer of at least the rank of chief constable.

Answers A, B and C are therefore incorrect.

General Police Duties, para. 4.18.4.4

Answer 18.10

Answer **A** — Authorisations for CHIS activity under the Regulation of Investigatory Powers Act 2000 must normally be given by officers of the rank of at least superintendent. However, urgent authorisations *may* be given by an inspector, when it is not reasonably practicable to have the application considered by a superintendent. Answer D is therefore incorrect. However, s. 43 of the Regulation of Investigatory Powers Act 2000 sets out general rules about grant, renewal and duration of authorisations surrounding CHIS activity. This section states:

(1) An authorisation under this Part—
  (a) may be granted or renewed orally in any urgent case in which the entitlement to act of the person granting or renewing it is not confined to urgent cases; and
  (b) in any other case, must be in writing.

This is a rather long-winded way of saying that because inspectors are restricted to granting urgent authorities, they may only give such authorities in writing. Only a person of the rank of superintendent and above may give an urgent, oral authority for CHIS-related activities. Answer C is incorrect for this reason.

The authorisation will cease to have effect 72 hours later, unless it is renewed. Answer B is incorrect.

General Police Duties, para. 4.18.4.4

Answer 18.11

Answer **B** — Normally, the use of CCTV to prevent and detect crime will not amount to covert surveillance. However, if CCTV is used for a planned operation, it may amount to covert surveillance, which will require authorisation. Under s. 26(3) of the Regulation of Investigatory Powers Act 2000, if surveillance is covert and is carried out in relation to anything taking place on any residential premises, or in any private vehicle, and it involves the presence of an individual on the premises or in the vehicle, or is carried out by means of a surveillance device, it will generally be intrusive surveillance. Since the officers in the scenario were seeking to monitor activities inside a private vehicle, the operation would amount to intrusive surveillance, and answers A and D are incorrect. Note that the use of a surveillance device will be 'intrusive' if that device consistently provides information of the same quality and detail as might be expected from a device that was actually present on the premises or in the vehicle (s. 26(5)). Surveillance will be either 'directed' or 'intrusive', it cannot be both; therefore answer C is incorrect.

General Police Duties, para. 4.18.4.5

Answer 18.12

Answer **C** — In relation to 'legal privilege' the House of Lords held that the Regulation of Investigatory Powers Act 2000 permits covert surveillance of communications between lawyers and their clients even though these may be covered by legal professional privilege (*Re McE (Northern Ireland)* [2009] UKHL 15). Answers A and D are incorrect.

The Regulation of Investigatory Powers (Extension of Authorisation Provisions: Legal Consultations) Order 2010 (SI 2010/461) provides that directed surveillance carried out in relation to anything taking place on any premises that are being used for the purpose of legal consultations shall be treated as 'intrusive surveillance'. The consultation may be between a professional legal adviser and their client or person representing their client, or with a medical practitioner, where legal proceedings are contemplated and for the purposes of such proceedings.

'Any premises' include prisons, police stations, legal advisers' business premises and courts. Since the proposal amounts to intrusive surveillance, answers A and B are incorrect.

General Police Duties, para. 4.18.4.5

Answer 18.13

Answer **C** — In general, directed surveillance can be authorised by an officer of at least the rank of superintendent, or an inspector in cases of urgency, making answer A incorrect. However, the Codes of Practice again restrict this practice. For instance, where the material sought by the surveillance is subject to legal privilege, or is confidential personal information or journalistic material, the only person who can authorise it is the chief officer; therefore, answers B and D are incorrect.

General Police Duties, para. 4.18.4.5

Answer 18.14

Answer **D** — An interception warrant is normally valid for three months. However, where such a warrant is applied for as being necessary under s. 5(3) of the Regulation of Investigatory Powers Act 2000 (safeguarding the economic well-being of the United Kingdom) the warrant is valid for six months from the date of issue. Answers A, B and C are incorrect.

General Police Duties, para. 4.18.4.8

Answer 18.15

Answer **D** — Section 5 of the Regulation of Investigatory Powers Act 2000 allows the Secretary of State to issue interception warrants under certain, very stringent, conditions. Section 5(2) says that the Secretary of State must not issue an interception warrant unless he or she believes that the warrant is necessary:

- in the interests of national security;
- for the purpose of preventing or detecting 'serious crime', e.g. offences for which a person aged 18 or over could reasonably expect to be sentenced to at least three years' imprisonment on his or her first offence, or offences resulting in substantial financial gain, involving the use of violence or a large number of people pursuing a common purpose;
- for the purpose of safeguarding the economic well-being of the United Kingdom (where the relevant acts or intentions relate to people outside the United Kingdom);
- for the purpose of 'international mutual assistance'.

Therefore, although a warrant may be issued when it is necessary in the interests of national security or for the purpose of safeguarding the economic well-being of the

United Kingdom, one may also be issued where the offence is one in which people commit offences resulting in substantial financial gain and which involve the use of violence or a large number of people pursuing a common purpose. Answers B and C are incorrect.

It is not enough that the Secretary of State 'suspects' that these threats or needs exist, nor that he or she considers that an interception warrant might be useful, valuable or effective. The Secretary of State must believe that the warrant is necessary for one of the purposes set out. Answer A is therefore incorrect.

General Police Duties, para. 4.18.4.8

Answer 18.16

Answer **C** — This offence applies to police officers and police staff alike, and would apply to anyone involved in an investigation (answer A is incorrect). It deals with interception warrants, and requires those to whom it applies to keep secret any knowledge they have in relation to that warrant. The offence would be committed by simply mentioning the warrant's existence, irrespective of whether any individual or company was named (answer B is incorrect). Although there is a defence, it relates to the accused taking steps to prevent the disclosure; in the circumstances of the question this is clearly not the case and PRIESTLEY has no defence (answer D is incorrect). Note that there are other defences available to s. 19, but they relate to communication with legal advisers and the Interception of Communications Commissioner.

General Police Duties, para. 4.18.4.9

19 | Equality

STUDY PREPARATION

At last, the final chapter!

Although it would be easy to dismiss this area as merely a bit of political correctness, this chapter contains some of the most relevant and important legislation for supervisors and managers.

This area of legislation has undergone a complete overhaul with the Equality Act 2010 pulling together all strands of diversity and discriminatory behaviour under one umbrella.

It is essential that all employers understand their legal obligations in relation to the equal and/or fair treatment of others. You will need to know what will amount to discrimination, how to distinguish between direct and indirect discrimination, and familiarise yourself with the protected characteristics covered in the Act.

It is also as important to understand the concept of victimisation and to recognise when and where it can arise.

When dealing with this area, it is worth remembering that in some circumstances you have to treat everyone in the same way, while in others treating everyone in the same way is discriminatory—and if you don't understand this point, you need to revise this chapter!

QUESTIONS

Question 19.1

PORTER is 65 years of age and has applied for a job in a large retail store; however, his application has been rejected because of his age.

Could PORTER claim discrimination under the Equality Act 2010 in these circumstances, because of his age?

A Yes, age is a protected characteristic and PORTER has been discriminated against.

B Yes, because PORTER is 65, he has been discriminated against; anyone older than PORTER would not be protected.

C Yes, people aged 65 and over are protected in relation to employment, but they do not benefit from the protections in relation to goods, services and public functions.

D No, people aged 65 and over do not benefit from the protections in relation to employment.

Question 19.2

Westshire Constabulary is the respondent in a case of discrimination brought by Chief Inspector ASHTON, who claims that he has been passed over several times for promotion to superintendent because of his sexual orientation.

Which of the following statements is correct in relation to the burden of proof that the court would have to consider?

A Chief Inspector ASHTON must establish facts that point to a presumption of discrimination; the burden of proof then shifts to Westshire Constabulary to prove that he was not treated unfairly.

B Westshire Constabulary must establish the facts in their entirety that Chief Inspector ASHTON was not treated unfairly.

C Chief Inspector ASHTON must establish the facts in their entirety that he was treated unfairly by Westshire Constabulary.

D Westshire Constabulary must establish that Chief Inspector ASHTON was not treated unfairly; the burden then rests with him to rebut the facts.

Question 19.3

MORTON was a probationer constable who joined a response team. The team had a tradition of giving its new officers 'nicknames' and MORTON became known as the 'only gay in the village' because of his similarity in appearance to a well-known television character. MORTON was unhappy with the nickname and asked the officers to stop. The officers were aware that MORTON was not gay, but did not stop calling him by the nickname, because they felt it was good for team bonding.

Which of the following statements is correct, in respect of whether the officers' behaviour amounts to harassment, under the Equality Act 2010, in these circumstances?

A The name-calling could amount to sexual harassment, if it can be demonstrated that the officers intended to offend MORTON.

B The name-calling is inappropriate, but does not amount to harassment, because MORTON is not gay.

C The name-calling does not amount to harassment because MORTON is not gay; however, the behaviour may amount to indirect discrimination.

D The name-calling amounts to harassment, regardless of MORTON's sexuality.

Question 19.4

Constable JOHN is a response officer and is the sole carer of his elderly parent, who is 94 years of age. Constable JOHN has submitted a flexible working request to the senior management team, which would mean working fewer night shifts, but would assist the officer financially due to the cost of carers. The senior management team has rejected the application for operational reasons. Constable JOHN is considering taking action against the force for discrimination, citing that the decision of the senior management team is unreasonable.

Which of the following statements would be correct, in relation to Constable JOHN's potential claim of discrimination?

A Constable JOHN would only have to demonstrate that the senior management team's decision was unreasonable, in order to succeed with the claim.

B Constable JOHN could succeed with the claim, by showing that some other hypothetical person would have been treated more favourably.

C Constable JOHN would have to demonstrate that some other person was treated more favourably, in order to succeed with the claim.

D Constable JOHN would have to demonstrate that there would be a tangible or material loss as a result of the decision.

Question 19.5

GOODE worked in the post room in the offices of a large company. He had slight learning difficulties but was perfectly able to carry out his work, which consisted of sorting and distributing internal mail. GOODE applied for a job in another part of the company, which involved filing paperwork. The pay was the same, but it would have meant working in a larger office, with more people for company. GOODE's application was turned down, on the grounds that his learning difficulties would mean that he could not sort the files as quickly as his co-workers. GOODE subsequently made a claim of discrimination against the company.

Would his employer's actions be justified in these circumstances?

A No, they would not be able to justify their actions and have acted unlawfully.

B Yes, they would be able to show that their reasons were proportionate.

C Yes, they would be able to show that the decision was made in the best interests of the company.

D No, employers will never be able to justify discrimination in the workplace.

Question 19.6

A force motor cycle section has advertised a vacancy. One selection criterion is that police officers must be able to pick up a large, heavy motor cycle from being on its side, and put it on its stand.

Would the selection criterion amount to indirect discrimination?

A Yes, this is not a fair condition and could disadvantage a person with a protected characteristic.

B No, it is a legitimate expectation of the job and must be able to be performed by all successful applicants.

C Yes, any condition other than one related to performance of duties is unlawful.

D No, provided the condition is the same for all applicants.

Question 19.7

Constable MELROSE has just started work on a response team in a new area. Officers are aware that before moving to the team, Constable MELROSE had made a complaint of racial discrimination against colleagues on another team and that the complaint had been unsubstantiated. Some officers on Constable MELROSE's new team decided to record problems they encountered with the officer, in fear that they may be the subject of a race discrimination claim at some future date.

Would the officers' behaviour amount to victimisation, because of Constable MELROSE's previous complaint?

A Yes, even though the previous complaint was unsubstantiated, this amounts to victimisation.

B No, if a complaint is unsubstantiated, any future complaint of similar actions cannot amount to victimisation.

C No, however the officers' behaviour could amount to direct discrimination.

D No, the behaviour of the officers concerned would not amount to victimisation in these circumstances.

Question 19.8

Constable THORNE resigned from the service 14 months ago due to her dissatisfaction at the way her sexual harassment complaint was dealt with. Since leaving, she has applied for, and been offered, a job as a police staff member with her old force. However, prior to starting, the job offer was withdrawn. THORNE has found out that this was because Superintendent CHANG had spoken to the recruitment department and told them that THORNE was a rebellious person who could not be trusted.

Could Constable THORNE take action against the police service for discrimination by way of victimisation?

A Yes, but only because her new job is in the same service.

B Yes, as her former employer had deliberately set out to spoil her subsequent employment.

C No, victimisation cannot extend post-employment.

D No, as more than one year has passed since she resigned.

Question 19.9

Westshire Constabulary is being sued by Constable AMIR. The claim relates to a failure by the force to allow Constable AMIR time off to attend a number of religious festivals throughout the year. Constable AMIR's line managers have not been cited, as the officer understands the pressures of delivering operational policing; however, the claim is made against the force for failing to have policies and procedures in place to account for the religious beliefs of its staff.

Which of the following statements is correct, in relation to Westshire Constabulary's liability under s. 42 of the Equality Act 2010?

A Constable AMIR's line managers and the Chief Constable may be liable; the Police Authority is only liable for discrimination by members of staff towards people outside the force.

B The Chief Constable alone may be liable in these circumstances; the Police Authority has no liability under this Act.

C The Chief Constable and the Police Authority may be liable in these circumstances.

D Constable AMIR's line managers may be liable; the Chief Constable and the Police Authority are only liable for discrimination by members of staff towards people outside the force.

Question 19.10

Detective Inspector FRENCH is in charge of the Public Protection Unit and has a vacancy. The officer is of the opinion that children of female victims seem to respond more positively to female officers, and would like the replacement to be a female officer. Detective Inspector FRENCH wishes to place the following words in the advertisement of the post: 'On this occasion only female officers can apply for this post.'

In relation to these words, which of the following is true?

A This is direct discrimination and is unlawful.

B This is positive action and is lawful.

C This is a case of a genuine occupational requirement and is not unlawful.

D This is indirect discrimination and is unlawful.

Question 19.11

The Armed Response Unit has advertised a 'familiarisation day for female officers only'. This is with the intention of recruiting female officers for a forthcoming firearms course, as they are under-represented in the department and below the Home Office target for minority officers. The selection process will remain the same as usual, and is open to all staff. Constable BRYAN, a male officer, is keen to join the unit and claims that he is being discriminated against, and that being able to attend this day advantages female officers.

Is the officer the victim of discrimination in these circumstances?

A No, employers are allowed to use direct discrimination where people having the protected characteristic are at a disadvantage or are under-represented.

B Yes, female officers would be disproportionately advantaged by this day and this is positive discrimination.

C Yes, male officers are disadvantaged by this day and this is direct discrimination.

D No, employers are allowed to use positive action where people having the protected characteristic are at a disadvantage or are under-represented.

Question 19.12

Constable STUBBS is currently suing her employers for discrimination in the workplace. She has cited several instances of inappropriate sexual behaviour towards her by her line managers in work. Constable STUBBS has also included evidence in her statement of inappropriate sexual behaviour towards her by work colleagues while they were at a social Christmas function in a nearby public house.

Would Constable STUBBS be able to rely on *all* of this evidence in her claim of discrimination against her employers?

A Yes, she may be able to rely on this evidence because the function was an extension of the workplace.

B No, but she would have been able to if the behaviour had taken place at an off-duty function at her actual workplace

C Yes, she may rely on evidence of any inappropriate behaviour, inside or outside the workplace.

D No, her employers cannot be held liable for the behaviour of her colleagues outside the workplace.

ANSWERS

Answer 19.1

Answer **D** — Age is one of the protected characteristics covered by the Equality Act 2010 and it would generally be unlawful to discriminate against a person due to their age. Section 5 of the Act states:

(1) In relation to the protected characteristic of age—
   (a) a reference to a person who has a particular protected characteristic is a reference to a person of a particular age group;
   (b) a reference to persons who share a protected characteristic is a reference to persons of the same age group.

(2) A reference to an age group is a reference to a group of persons defined by reference to age, whether by reference to a particular age or to a range of ages.

However, two specific age groups are *not* protected by the Act: people aged 18 and under do not benefit from the protections in relation to goods, services and public functions; and people aged 65 and over do not benefit from the protections in regard to employment.

Because PORTER is 65, unfortunately he receives no protection from the Act in relation to employment, and answers A, B and C are incorrect.

General Police Duties, paras 4.19.2, 4.19.2.1

Answer 19.2

Answer **A** — Sexual orientation is one of the protected characteristics covered by the Equality Act 2010 and it is unlawful to discriminate against a person due to their sexual orientation.

In proceedings relating to contraventions of the Act the burden of proof initially rests with the complainant. Answers B and D are therefore incorrect.

Once the complainant establishes facts from which it might be presumed that there had been discrimination the burden of proof shifts to the respondent to prove no breach of the principle of equal treatment (s. 136). Answer C is therefore incorrect.

General Police Duties, para. 4.19.3

Answer 19.3

Answer **D** — Harassment is one of the seven different forms of discrimination listed in the Equality Act 2010 and is defined as *behaviour deemed offensive by the recipient*. Discrimination by perception is another form and is described as *direct discrimination against someone because others think they have a protected characteristic*.

Section 13 of the Equality Act 2010 states:

> (1) A person (A) discriminates against another (B) if, because of a protected characteristic, A treats B less favourably than A treats or would treat others.

Therefore, a claim for discrimination may be brought where the less favourable treatment is based on a person's *perceived* protected characteristics, i.e. where others think a person has a characteristic even if they don't. In *English* v *Thomas Sanderson Ltd* [2008] EWCA Civ 1421, the Court of Appeal has held that homophobic banter amounts to unlawful harassment, even when the victim's tormentors knew he was not gay. Therefore, the circumstances in the question will amount to harassment, regardless of MORTON's sexuality and answer B is incorrect.

Indirect discrimination is an entirely different matter to harassment, and generally involves employers not applying the same working conditions to all relevant people (e.g. job applicants and employees). It is out of context in this scenario, and answer C is incorrect.

Although the state of mind of the people exhibiting discriminatory behaviour may be a contributing factor, there would be no requirement to show an 'intent to offend' in these circumstances. The behaviour amounts to harassment regardless of the officers' intent. Answer A is incorrect.

General Police Duties, paras 4.19.3, 4.19.3.1

Answer 19.4

Answer **B** — Section 13(1) of the Equality Act 2010 states:

> A person (A) discriminates against another (B) if, because of a protected characteristic, A treats B less favourably than A treats or would treat others.

Less favourable treatment of a person because that person is associated with a protected characteristic, for example, because the person has a friend or partner with a particular protected characteristic, or carries out work related to a protected characteristic, is within the scope of this section. This might include carers of disabled people and elderly relatives, who can claim they were treated unfairly because of duties that they had to carry out at home relating to their care work. For example, the non-disabled mother of a disabled child can be discriminated against because of the child's disability (*Coleman* v *Attridge Law* (Case C-303/06) [2008] IRLR 722). This is known as 'associative discrimination'.

To constitute direct discrimination the treatment experienced by B must be different from that of another person. This difference is often referred to as a 'comparator'. The treatment of B must be less favourable than the treatment afforded a comparator. The comparator can be hypothetical where B can establish direct discrimination by showing that if there was another person in similar circumstances, but without B's protected characteristic, that person would be treated more favourably (for an explanation of hypothetical comparators see *Shamoon* v *Chief Constable of the Royal Ulster Constabulary* [2003] UKHL 11). This is why answer B is correct, and answer C is incorrect.

Less favourable treatment is a broad concept and any disadvantage to which B has been subject will constitute such treatment. B need not have suffered a tangible or material loss (*Chief Constable of West Yorkshire Police* v *Khan* [2001] UKHL 48) and answer D is incorrect.

However, it is not enough merely to show unreasonable treatment (*Bahl* v *The Law Society* [2004] IRLR 799). Answer A is incorrect.

General Police Duties, para. 4.19.3.1

Answer 19.5

Answer **A** — Section 15 of the Equality Act 2010 states:

(1) A person (A) discriminates against a disabled person (B) if—
   (a) A treats B unfavourably because of something arising in consequence of B's disability, and
   (b) A cannot show that the treatment is a proportionate means of achieving a legitimate aim.

(2) Subsection (1) does not apply if A shows that A did not know, and could not reasonably have been expected to know, that B had the disability.

It is discrimination to treat a disabled person unfavourably not because of the person's disability itself but because of something arising from, or in consequence of, their disability, such as the need to take a period of disability-related absence. It is, however, possible to justify such treatment if it can be shown to be a proportionate means of achieving a legitimate aim. Answer D is therefore incorrect.

In this case, it would be difficult for the company to argue that their decision was proportionate because the employee in question was already working in their company in a similar capacity to the vacant role. It would be different, for example, if the person had severe learning difficulties and was applying for a role operating heavy machinery, and the employer had concerns about their safety. However, in the case in this question, not allowing the person to even apply for the role is a disproportionate response without justification and answers B and C are incorrect.

Note that for this type of discrimination to occur, the employer or other person must know, or reasonably be expected to know, that the disabled person has a disability.

General Police Duties, para. 4.19.3.3

Answer 19.6

Answer **A** — Indirect discrimination is one of the seven different forms of discrimination listed in the Equality Act 2010 and is defined as *a rule or policy that applies to everyone but disadvantages a person with a protected characteristic.*

Indirect discrimination occurs when a policy which applies in the same way for everybody has an effect which particularly disadvantages people with a protected characteristic. Where a particular group is disadvantaged in this way, a person in that group is indirectly discriminated against if he or she is put at a disadvantage, unless the person applying the policy can justify it.

When a policy would put a person at a disadvantage if it were applied, for example, where a person is deterred from applying for a job or taking up an offer of service, because a policy which would have applied would result in his or her disadvantage, this may also amount to indirect discrimination. Examples of indirect discrimination include: requiring all employees to work within 'normal office hours' (*Bhudi v IMI Refiners* [1994] IRLR 204); requiring all workers to have short hair thereby making it difficult for some groups such as Sikhs to comply (*Mandla v Dowell Lee* [1983] 2 AC 548); where 100 per cent of males could comply with a policy relating to rostering duties, but only 95.2 per cent of women were able to do so, the policy discriminated indirectly against females (*London Underground Ltd v Edwards* (No. 2) [1998] IRLR 364).

Given the size and weight of the machine in the question, it is likely that fewer women than men could comply with the condition, and it is this that potentially makes the requirement discriminatory and unlawful. Even if only one female officer could not comply with a condition of employment, it could still be indirect discrimination.

There is nothing inherently unlawful about setting legitimate conditions for a job vacancy (e.g. 'must have two A levels'), and therefore answer C is incorrect as it is too broad. However, any criteria must not disadvantage a significant proportion of people from a protected group. Simply setting the same condition for all does not make it lawful (e.g. 'applicants must be able to climb stairs' is the same for all, but would disadvantage wheelchair users) and therefore answer D is incorrect.

As far as answer B is concerned, is it a legitimate requirement of the job? Imposing this requirement on all applicants appears to be far too broad, wholly unreasonable and, in relation to the differences in relative strength of male and female applicants, appears disproportionately to disadvantage the latter, and therefore answer B is incorrect.

General Police Duties, para. 4.19.3.7

Answer 19.7

Answer **D** — Victimisation is one of the seven different forms of discrimination listed in the Equality Act 2010 and is defined as *discrimination against someone because they made or supported a complaint under Equality Act legislation.*

Section 27 of the 2010 Act states:

(1) A person (A) victimises another person (B) if A subjects B to a detriment because—
   (a) B does a protected act, or
   (b) A believes that B has done, or may do, a protected act.

(2) Each of the following is a protected act—
   (a) bringing proceedings under this Act;
   (b) giving evidence or information in connection with proceedings under this Act;
   (c) doing any other thing for the purposes of or in connection with this Act;
   (d) making an allegation (whether or not express) that A or another person has contravened this Act.

This would mean that generally, if a person makes a claim, he or she could still be the subject of victimisation at some time in the future, regardless of whether the claim was substantiated. Answer B is incorrect.

However, in *Bayode* v *Chief Constable of Derbyshire* [2008] UKEAT 0499 07 2205, the tribunal held that the complainant, a police constable who was a black African and Nigerian by national origin, had *not* been victimised where his colleagues recorded any problems they encountered with him in their PNBs for fear that he might make a race discrimination claim at some future date. Previous unsubstantiated discrimination claims had been made by the complainant. Answer A is therefore incorrect.

Direct discrimination is an entirely different matter to victimisation, and generally involves employers treating one group of people less favourably than others based on protected grounds, such as their racial origin, marital status, sex, religion or belief or sexual orientation. It is out of context in this scenario, and answer C is incorrect.

General Police Duties, para. 4.19.3.10

Answer 19.8

Answer **B** — Victimisation is one of the seven different forms of discrimination listed in the Equality Act 2010 and is defined as *discrimination against someone because they made or supported a complaint under Equality Act legislation.*
   Section 27 of the 2010 Act states:

(1)   A person (A) victimises another person (B) if A subjects B to a detriment because—
   (a)   B does a protected act, or
   (b)   A believes that B has done, or may do, a protected act.

(2)   Each of the following is a protected act—
   (a)   bringing proceedings under this Act;
   (b)   giving evidence or information in connection with proceedings under this Act;
   (c)   doing any other thing for the purposes of or in connection with this Act;
   (d)   making an allegation (whether or not express) that A or another person has contravened this Act.

The test to be applied in assessing whether or not victimisation has taken place is, 'was the real reason for the victim's treatment the fact that he/she had carried out a protected act?' (See the House of Lords' decision in *Chief Constable of West Yorkshire Police* v *Khan* [2001] 1 WLR 1947.) Victimisation takes place where one person treats another badly because he or she in good faith has done a 'protected act', for example, taken or supported any action taken for the purpose of the Act, including in relation to any alleged breach of its provisions.
   It also provides that victimisation takes place where one person treats another badly because he or she is suspected of having done this or of intending to do this.
   This section is not restricted to victimisation of a person applying for a job with his or her previous employer. Provided a former employer had deliberately set out to spoil an employee's subsequent employment, or so acted knowing of the likely consequences of its actions, there would be sufficient proximity and a sufficiently close connection with the employment to establish *prima facie* liability. Answer A is therefore incorrect.
   A claim of discrimination by reason of victimisation could still be laid notwithstanding that a person was no longer employed by another (see *Metropolitan Police Service* v *Shoebridge* [2004] ICR 1690), however long after the previous employment had ceased. Answers C and D are therefore incorrect.

General Police Duties, para. 4.19.3.10

Answer 19.9

Answer **C** — Section 42 of the Equality Act 2010 states:

(1) For the purposes of this Part, holding the office of constable is to be treated as employment—

    (a) by the chief officer, in respect of any act done by the chief officer in relation to a constable or appointment to the office of constable;

    (b) by the responsible authority, in respect of any act done by the authority in relation to a constable or appointment to the office of constable.

The Equality Act 2010 makes provisions for chief officers *and* police authorities to be liable for acts done by them towards their staff. Answer B is incorrect.

This liability is not limited to discrimination by members of staff towards people outside the force; it can include discrimination by members of staff towards people within the force and answers A and D are incorrect.

The chief officer of police is also vicariously liable for acts of race discrimination by staff under his or her direction and control. The statutory defence that an employer took all reasonable steps to prevent the acts of discrimination complained of is also available to chief officers (s. 109(4)).

General Police Duties, paras 4.19.4, 4.19.6

Answer 19.10

Answer **A** — An attempt to recruit female officers into a specialist department by excluding male applicants has been held to be unlawful (*Jones* v *Chief Constable of Northamptonshire Police*, The Times, 1 November 1999). Answer C is incorrect as a genuine occupational requirement is where there is a legitimate reason (such as grounds of decency) to state that only certain groups may apply and not just a hunch by the Detective Inspector!

Answer B is incorrect because positive action refers to measures to alleviate disadvantage experienced by people who share a protected characteristic, reduce their under-representation in relation to particular activities, and meet their particular needs (see s. 158 of the Equality Act 2010). Here the officer's actions go way beyond simple encouragement.

It is direct discrimination because it is treating one group of people less favourably than others based on their sex. Answer D is incorrect because indirect discrimination involves setting the same criteria for a job, but the criteria are such that a significant proportion of people from a protected group are less likely to be able to achieve the criteria because of their membership of that group (e.g. a height restriction, which would affect female and some minority ethnic groups).

General Police Duties, para. 4.19.5

Answer 19.11

Answer **D** — 'Positive action' refers to measures to alleviate disadvantage experienced by people who share a protected characteristic, reduce their under-representation in relation to particular activities, and meet their particular needs (see s. 158 of the Equality Act 2010). It allows for measures to be targeted to particular groups, including training to enable them to gain employment, but any such measures must be a proportionate way of achieving the relevant aim.

An employer may also take a protected characteristic into consideration when deciding whom to recruit or promote, where people having the protected characteristic are at a disadvantage or are under-represented (see s. 159). This can be done only where the candidates are as qualified as each other. The aim is to help employers achieve a more diverse workforce by giving them the option, when faced with candidates of equal merit, to choose a candidate from an under-represented group.

Since the actions referred to in the questions are allowed in law, answers A, B and C are incorrect.

General Police Duties, para. 4.19.5

Answer 19.12

Answer **A** — Section 109 of the Equality Act 2010 states:

(1) Anything done by a person (A) in the course of A's employment must be treated as also done by the employer.

(2) ...

(3) It does not matter whether that thing is done with the employer's or principal's knowledge or approval.

Where acts amounting to discrimination take place outside the workplace, the employer and employees may still be caught within the framework of the legislation. So, for instance, where police officers engage in inappropriate sexual behaviour towards a colleague at a work-related social function, a tribunal may be entitled to hold that the function was an extension of the workplace and so hold the chief officer liable for the acts of his/her officers at that function (see *Chief Constable of Lincolnshire* v *Stubbs* [1999] IRLR 81). Answer D is therefore incorrect.

This case deals with a specific example of behaviour where the officers were at a work-related function, which was an 'extension of the workplace'. The decision therefore does not mean that any behaviour can be included in such a claim (although it is worth noting that discrimination and victimisation are included in the Code of Conduct for police officers, which may include the conduct of an off-duty officer). Answer C is therefore incorrect. Lastly, the above case did not specify that the location of the function was important, merely that it was an off-duty function and an extension of the workplace. Answer B is therefore incorrect.

General Police Duties, para. 4.19.6

Question Checklist

The checklist below is designed to help you keep track of your progress when answering the multiple-choice questions. If you fill this in after one attempt at each question, you will be able to check how many you have got right and which questions you need to revisit a second time. Also available online, to download visit www.blackstonespolicemanuals.com.

	First attempt Correct (✓)	Second attempt Correct (✓)
1 Police		
1.1		
1.2		
1.3		
1.4		
1.5		
1.6		
1.7		
2 Complaints and Misconduct		
2.1		
2.2		
2.3		
2.4		
2.5		
2.6		
2.7		
2.8		
2.9		
2.10		

	First attempt Correct (✓)	Second attempt Correct (✓)
3 Unsatisfactory Performance and Attendance		
3.1		
3.2		
3.3		
3.4		
3.5		
3.6		
3.7		
3.8		
3.9		
3.10		
3.11		
4 Extending the Policing Family		
4.1		
4.2		
4.3		
4.4		
4.5		

	First attempt Correct (✓)	Second attempt Correct (✓)
4.6		
4.7		
4.8		
4.9		
4.10		

5 Human Rights

5.1		
5.2		
5.3		
5.4		
5.5		
5.6		
5.7		
5.8		
5.9		
5.10		
5.11		
5.12		
5.13		
5.14		

6 Powers of Arrest (including Code G Codes of Practice) and Other Policing Powers

6.1		
6.2		
6.3		
6.4		
6.5		
6.6		
6.7		
6.8		
6.9		
6.10		
6.11		
6.12		
6.13		
6.14		
6.15		

	First attempt Correct (✓)	Second attempt Correct (✓)

7 Stop and Search

7.1		
7.2		
7.3		
7.4		
7.5		
7.6		
7.7		
7.8		
7.9		
7.10		
7.11		

8 Entry, Search and Seizure

8.1		
8.2		
8.3		
8.4		
8.5		
8.6		
8.7		
8.8		
8.9		
8.10		

9 Harassment, Hostility and Anti-social Behaviour

9.1		
9.2		
9.3		
9.4		
9.5		
9.6		
9.7		
9.8		
9.9		
9.10		
9.11		
9.12		

	First attempt Correct (✓)	Second attempt Correct (✓)
9.13		
9.14		
9.15		
9.16		
9.17		
9.18		
9.19		
9.20		
9.21		
9.22		
9.23		

10 Offences Involving Communications

	First attempt Correct (✓)	Second attempt Correct (✓)
10.1		
10.2		
10.3		
10.4		
10.5		
10.6		
10.7		

11 Terrorism and Associated Offences

	First attempt Correct (✓)	Second attempt Correct (✓)
11.1		
11.2		
11.3		
11.4		
11.5		
11.6		
11.7		
11.8		
11.9		
11.10		
11.11		

12 Public Disorder

	First attempt Correct (✓)	Second attempt Correct (✓)
12.1		
12.2		
12.3		
12.4		
12.5		

	First attempt Correct (✓)	Second attempt Correct (✓)
12.6		
12.7		
12.8		
12.9		
12.10		
12.11		
12.12		
12.13		
12.14		
12.15		
12.16		
12.17		
12.18		
12.19		
12.20		
12.21		

13 Sporting Events

	First attempt Correct (✓)	Second attempt Correct (✓)
13.1		
13.2		
13.3		
13.4		
13.5		
13.6		
13.7		
13.8		

14 Weapons

	First attempt Correct (✓)	Second attempt Correct (✓)
14.1		
14.2		
14.3		
14.4		
14.5		
14.6		
14.7		
14.8		
14.9		
14.10		
14.11		
14.12		

	First attempt Correct (✓)	Second attempt Correct (✓)
14.13		
14.14		
14.15		
14.16		
14.17		
14.18		
14.19		
15 Civil Disputes		
15.1		
15.2		
15.3		
15.4		
15.5		
15.6		
15.7		
15.8		
16 Offences Relating to Land and Premises		
16.1		
16.2		
16.3		
16.4		
16.5		
16.6		
16.7		
16.8		
16.9		
16.10		
16.11		
16.12		
16.13		
17 Licensing and Offences Relating to Alcohol		
17.1		
17.2		
17.3		
17.4		
17.5		

	First attempt Correct (✓)	Second attempt Correct (✓)
17.6		
17.7		
17.8		
17.9		
17.10		
17.11		
17.12		
17.13		
17.14		
17.15		
17.16		
17.17		
17.18		
17.19		
17.20		
17.21		
17.22		
17.23		
17.24		
17.25		
17.26		
17.27		
17.28		
17.29		
17.30		
17.31		
17.32		
17.33		
17.34		
18 Offences and Powers Relating to Information		
18.1		
18.2		
18.3		
18.4		
18.5		
18.6		
18.7		
18.8		
18.9		

	First attempt Correct (✓)	Second attempt Correct (✓)
18.10		
18.11		
18.12		
18.13		
18.14		
18.15		
18.16		
19 Equality		
19.1		
19.2		

	First attempt Correct (✓)	Second attempt Correct (✓)
19.3		
19.4		
19.5		
19.6		
19.7		
19.8		
19.9		
19.10		
19.11		
19.12